SOULS OF
LONELY PLACES

SOULS OF LONELY PLACES

Some Sequestered Spots in Cumbria

JAMES DEBOO

HAYLOFT PUBLISHING LTD
CUMBRIA

First published by Hayloft 2014

Hayloft Publishing Ltd, South Stainmore,
Kirkby Stephen, Cumbria, CA17 4DJ

tel: 017683 41568
email: books@hayloft.eu
web: www.hayloft.eu

ISBN 978 1 910237 00 7

A CIP catalogue record for this book is available
from the British Library

Papers used by Hayloft are natural, recyclable products made from
wood grown in sustainable forests. The manufacturing processes
conform to the environmental regulations of the country of origin.

Designed, printed and bound in the EU

Frontispiece: *The author on High Street*
Jacket: *Watson Dodd and Thornthwaite Beacon*

For Thirza Deboo

Acknowledgements

Many of the walks, locales and viewpoints mentioned in this book were 'tried out' on a stream of visitors over the four years we lived in Oxenholme. Thanks, in no particular order, to Doug and Emma Satterford; Emily, Jonny and Ally Craze; Helen and Bryn Jones; Jo and Tom Thorp; Phil and Ali Smith; Muriel and Alan Deboo; Helen Simmons; Matthew Phillips and Andrew Dawson, Geoffrey Shaw, and last but definitely not least Melanie, Kevin, Dan and Charlie.

Ye presences of Nature, in the sky
And on the earth! Ye visions of the hills!
And souls of lonely places!

Wordworth, *The Prelude*
1805, I, 493-5

Nor greater pleasure could Columbus feel,
When first beyond the Trans-Atlantic deep
His wandering eye beheld another world,
Than I, when in my wand'rings I have found
Some sweet sequestered spot unknown before.

Isabella Lickbarrow, *The Naiad's Complaint*,
from *Isabella Lickbarrow: Collected Poems*,
ed. Constance Parrish (Wordsworth Trust, 2004)

"We've come out of the Lake District where all the beau-
ties are so obvious, you can't avoid them.   Here we're
going to have look a little bit harder.   But will we find
beautiful things still?"
"Oh yes. [Pause...] Many."

Eric Robson, in conversation with Alfred Wainwright, at
Oddendale Stone Circle, from *Wainwright's Coast to Coast Walk*,
Striding Edge Presentations DVD 2003,
© BBC Worldwide 2007

Contents

Overview map key

Fell

1.	The Helm
2.	The Howgills
3.	Black Combe
4.	Hallin Fell
5.	Nine Standards to Wild Boar Fell
6.	Lowick High Common
7.	Castle Crag
8.	Back O'Skiddaw
9.	Askham Fell
10.	Holme Fell
11.	Scout Scar and Whitbarrow

Dale

12.	Mallerstang
13.	Bretherdale
14.	Eden Valley
15.	Lyth Valley
16.	Little Langdale
17.	Lowther Valley
18.	Kentmere and Longsleddale
19.	Martindale
20.	Wasdale
21.	Smardale Gill

Woodland

22.	Whinlatter and Grizedale
23.	Brigsteer Park
24.	Crag Wood
25.	Fairy Steps

Coast

26.	Walney Island 1
27.	Roa, Piel and Foulney Islands
28.	Eskmeals
29.	Cartmel Peninsula
30.	North Coast
31.	Walney Island 2

OVERVIEW MAP

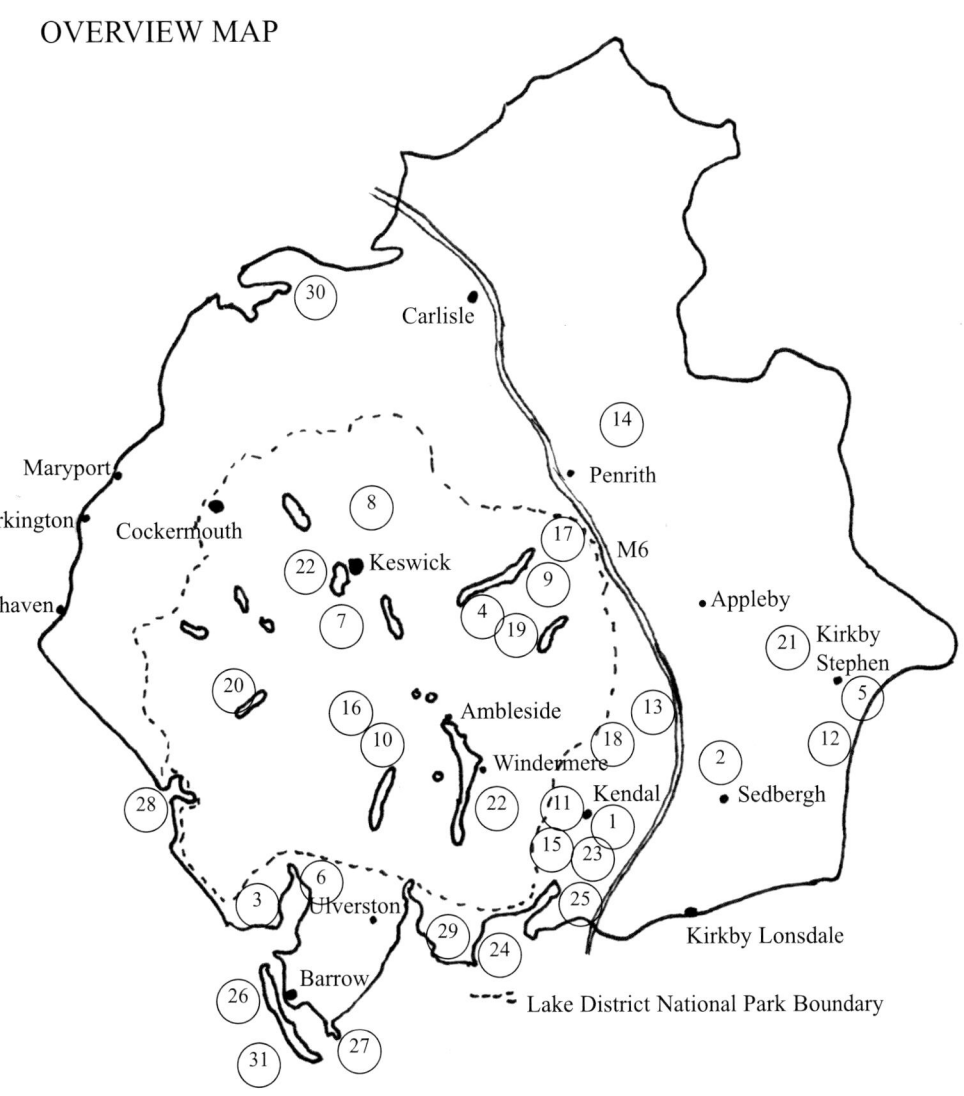

Lake District National Park Boundary

Introduction

THE LAKE DISTRICT: awarded National Park status some three weeks after the Peak District, making it, just, our second National Park; the biggest National Park in Britain; the most distinctive, most varied, most beautiful National Park in Britain. It's no surprise, therefore, that it's also the most visited National Park in the country, by a margin of about 50 per cent.

Take Striding Edge. Here is the greatest mountain ridge route in England – if, that is, you discount Crinkle Crags, or Sharp Edge on Blencathra, which I'd be loath to do. But anyway, Striding Edge is a fine, if much easier third to Scotland's Aonach Eagach and Snowdonia's Crib Goch. It's fineness is such that, once you've negotiated the Ambleside traffic, finally found a parking space in Patterdale, walked up to Hole-in-the-Wall, queued patiently while all those on the ridge ahead of you who hadn't realised how exposed it was going to be shriek, yell and, clinging on, white-knuckled, inch towards Helvellyn, you'll find you're a lot later on the summit, and have said a lot more hellos, than you might have bargained for.

This is A Good Thing. If I'm going to "do" Striding Edge I'll generally choose a sunny bank holiday weekend in the summer holidays, actually, as I find the most fun thing about it is the camaraderie involved in helping teenagers coax their grandmothers along the top of the ridge. People say the sheer number of walkers up here is responsible for the considerable wear and tear of the paths on popular routes. They are: but on the other hand visitors pay, directly or indirectly, for the upkeep of paths which, without the revenue they generate, would be worn anyway, albeit more slowly, and probably not repaired tot he same extent. The Lake District's tourist economy has grown substantially in recent years, especially since the area recovered from the 2001 Foot and Mouth outbreak, which left Cumbrian farmers feeling cut off from and unsupported by Westminster – I remember signs by the M6 reading "Blair fiddles while Cumbria burns." This sense of isolation made businesses in many cases realise that by adopting a policy of producing high-quality, local produce for local consumption, taking advantage of a network of other, like-minded, local suppliers and of the tourists' ready cash, everyone was a winner – and this has only increased the area's attractiveness to visitors. There is a link between the quality of the local food and accommodation and the standard of the footpaths.

Striding Edge isn't the only way up Helvellyn, though. One wet, windy

---

Crinkle Crags from the shoulder of Pike o'Stickle.

Tuesday in February 2006 I left my ancient Vauxhall Nova by what's reputed to be the tomb of the last king of Cumbria at the top of Dunmail Raise, climbed up Raise Beck, quickly reaching the snow line and frozen waterfalls just beneath Grizedale Tarn. Grizedale Tarn (from the Norse for 'lake in the valley of the pigs', the same derivation as Grasmere below) was still and silent, and I could feel the cold pouring off the surface, which was studded with miniature ice floes. A few hundred yards across the moor, then up foot-print-snow to Dollywagon Pike and along the ridge, in brilliant sunshine and the kind of clear, sharp, endless views you only get in midwinter, brought me to the shelter and the summit, just as the sun neared the horizon. Despite the weather, and it being midweek, there were still half a dozen people on the summit, cramponed and with ice axes in hand, who'd just done Striding Edge, the first people I'd seen since leaving the car.

Let's go back to Patterdale. Leave your car there, or at the car park on the main road by Hartsop. Walk through the lovely hamlet of Hartsop, and then either up to Boredale Hause and Angle Tarn (or scramble straight up Dubhow Crag, if you don't mind dangling from tree roots); or go up to Hayeswater and The Knott. Skirt or summit Rest Dodd, and make your way onto The Nab. You're looking down into Martindale, as empty as Patterdale is busy. I won't say much about Martindale now as it's explored in detail in its own chapter in the Dale section, but for now: you're looking at a deer forest whose recorded history goes back to 1247, but which holds evidence of at least 2000 years of human history, and probably a lot more. You're almost guaranteed, unless it's misty, to be able to see the largest red deer herd in England, the only herd not to have cross-bred with non-native sika deer introduced from East Asia. You're also looking at a stunning view, one which is just as good seen from the other end of the valley, looking up to where you are now. And the chances that there's anyone else out walking in the landscape you can see are pretty slim.

You'll also be able to see, if you know where you're looking, the old chapel in Martindale, in whose churchyard is a 1300-year-old yew I recorded for the Woodland Trust's Ancient Tree Hunt project. With reference to this, one of my fellow Ancient Tree Hunt volunteers said: "Lovely to see this tree up at last. I'd like to see it sometime but Martindale isn't one of those places you just drop in on!" People just don't 'drop in' there, but I've really not much idea why (well, I do, but more on that in due course). Martindale (which Wordsworth described as a "sequestered spot") sums this book up perfectly. It has rewards different from, but no less rewarding than, those of the infinitely more popular Patterdale next door: and one of these rewards is the knowledge that you're poking around corners of the Lake District National Park quite out of the radar of most visitors. Your sense of understanding of the landscape will be correspondingly higher, and more rewarding.

Writers from Thomas West, who published an early and influential *Guide to the Lakes* in 1778, to the present, have continually emphasized that the extraordinary variety to be found in the wider landscapes and smaller nooks of the Lake District is the region's strongest point, and it seems to me that by concentrating on the more obvious, most-visited areas the majority of visitors miss out. And spend a lot of time in traffic jams or searching for parking spaces.

William Wordsworth's *Guide to the Lakes* says: "I do not indeed know of any tract of country in which, within so narrow a compass, may be found an equal variety in the influences of light and shadow upon the sublime or beautiful features of the landscape." So here we'll be exploring, and celebrating, not just mountain ridges and summits, though there'll be a share of those, but less-celebrated environments, like hidden valleys, conifer plantations and deserted slate quarries.

Similarly, around the edges of the Lake District proper, spread across the remainder of Cumbria is a host of places with features and atmospheres all of their own, beautiful places steeped in history, rich in natural history, blessed by views of the Lakes, or of the Pennines, southern Scotland or the North Sea, which are way off the usual tourist trails and all the more rewarding for it. This book explores some of these places in and around the Lakes. It is a necessarily selective survey, and there are any number of places which could have been included but weren't: it's a personal selection of the places that mean the most to me.

This book had a working title, which is now the subtitle: Some Sequestered Spots in Cumbria. I knew "sequestered spots" was a phrase of Wordsworth's: I thought it was a description of Grasmere in Wordsworth's long poem *The Excursion*, but on looking I found that what I was remembering was "sequestered dell' (in Book V). I found "sequestered spot" in his poem *The Waterfall and the Eglantine*, and he describes Martindale as a "sequestered spot indeed" in his prose *Guide to the Lakes*. The phrase also appears in a poem by John Edwards, a shoemaker's son born in 1772, whose first published poem, on *All Saint's Church, Derby* of 1805, was quoted by Wordsworth in his prose work *Essay upon Epitaphs*. "Sequestered nook", "sequestered spot", "sequestered dell", "sequestered region", "sequestered steep" all appear at least once in Wordsworth's poems; the word "sequestered" is used nineteen times in total. In the end I settled on another phrase of Wordsworth's, "Souls of lonely places", from his long poem *The Prelude*, as best expressing what I wanted to say. Besides, the publishers rightly felt that "Sequestered" was perhaps too obscure a word to print on the spine of a book. I'll come to my reasons for the choice of title in the first chapter.

Anyway, while I was casting around for titles I unexpectedly found "sequestered spot" in a poem by another, far less well known Lake Poet, or Poetess, Isabella Lickbarrow. Born in 1784, when Wordsworth was fourteen, Isabella, the daughter of a Kendal, Quaker schoolmaster, lived all her life in

Kendal, publishing poetry in local newspapers to help support her two sisters, who were in and out of Lancaster Lunatic Asylum. Isabella uses "sequestered spots" in *The Naiad's Complaint*:

> *My native vale! with heightened pleasure still*
> *I trace thy simple scenes, my partial eye*
> *Surveys new beauties each returning spring,*
> *Each summer gives delight unfelt before!*
> *Thy fertile vales, thy green knolls gentle rise,*
> *Thy rocky hills with blossom'd furze adorn'd,*
> *Thy wood-fring'd rivers and thy heathy moors,*
> *And the brown mountains which encircle thee,*
> *(O'er which the passing clouds for ever cast*
> *Their varying shadows) all are dear to me!*
> *Nor greater pleasure could Columbus feel,*
> *When first beyond the Trans-Atlantic deep*
> *His wandering eye beheld another world,*
> *Than I, when in my wand'rings I have found*
> *Some sweet sequestered spot unknown before. –*
> *Dear native vale! and must thou still remain*
> *To future times unnoticed, and unsung?*

Langdale Pikes in winter.

It's good poetry, if hardly original. I won't go into its similarities to passages in Wordsworth's *Excursion*, *Prelude* and *Home at Grasmere*; the poem also contain another obvious influence, that of Keats's 1816 sonnet *On first looking into Chapman's Homer*. Keats, who couldn't read Greek, records that he had been reading Homer in Chapman's English translation for the first time:

> *Then felt I like some watcher of the skies*
> *When a new planet swims into his ken;*
> *Or like stout Cortez, when with eagle eyes*
> *He star'd at the Pacific – and all his men*
> *Look'd at each other with a wild surmise –*
> *Silent, upon a peak in Darien.*

Substitute Isabella's Columbus for Keats's Cortez, and you can see that what Isabella has done is take a number of very similar passages from Wordsworth, an apparently unrelated but strangely appropriate passage from Keats, and combined them into a new whole about a valley a few miles south of the one Wordsworth was writing about.

Except she hasn't. Wordsworth's *Excursion* was published in 1814. The *Prelude* wasn't published until after his death in 1850, *Home at Grasmere* in 1888. Keats's poem was first published in 1818. The poems in Isabella Lickbarrow's only published collection, *Poetical Effusions*, were written before this and published the same year as *The Excursion*, 1814, thanks to the contributions of a number of subscribers who had enjoyed her poems in *The Westmorland Gazette* over the previous three years. These subscribers included Wordsworth, De Quincey, Southey, Wordsworth's landlady Lady le Fleming, and many other notable names. So Wordsworth knew her poetry, it's just about possible Keats did, and it seems the poetical influence, if any, went the other way round. It's easy to make false assumptions.

She is not as well-known as Keats or Wordsworth – in fact, she's barely known at all. Yet, by finding out about her, I found out something I never knew, a new influence over Wordsworth's poetry, perhaps. And as I'd spent four years writing a PhD thesis on Wordsworth, and teaching his poetry, I thought I knew most of what there was to know already. Inspiration, and new things to discover, are found in the unlikeliest places, and in Isabella Lickbarrow I discovered a poetess who deserves to be far better known than she is, and who wrote beautifully about many of the little-known places in the Lake District which I have enjoyed exploring. How many poets have written about the Howgills? That question will be answered in the Howgills chapter below, but suffice to say no one has given them the attention they deserve, save Lickbarrow. Scout Scar, too.

As with Lickbarrow, so with the places she wrote about. They are obscure, out-of-the-way, tucked between and around the greatest giants the English landscape has to offer, but that doesn't necessarily mean they're devoid of a beauty, or an interest, of their own. If Martindale or the Howgills were anywhere else in England, they'd without doubt be full of pubs, hotels and shops selling shortbread and boxes of assorted Kendal Mint Cake with Alfred Wainwright's name puzzlingly printed on them; but, thanks to Martindale's proximity to Patterdale, and to the Howgills' proximity to the Lake District itself, these places are virtually empty.

As these places are generally fairly obscure they often don't appear much in recorded history, and often this obscurity means that what few mentions there are, hidden away in libraries and archives, are difficult to find. As they've perhaps not been looked at before, these references often shed interesting light on the lives of the people who've lived in or used these landscapes. For example, an obscure mention in the Public Records Office archive reveals an interesting custom to do with the return of sheep which have strayed from one shepherd's flock to another's, as we'll see at Martindale.

Isabella Lickbarrow is to William Wordsworth as the Howgills are to the Lake District, as Martindale is to Patterdale, as Black Combe is to Skiddaw. But that doesn't mean she, or they, are any the less rewarding. As Gareth Hayes says at the beginning of his *Odd Corners around the Howgills*, "I like the Howgills. It may be no coincidence that they usually sit behind the Lakes, Pennines and Dales in terms of popularity and my fondness derives from that lesser distinction. Perhaps I prefer to champion the underdog..."

Often the knowledge that you are treading ground, either literally, historically,

Moonrise, Kentmere.

or imaginatively, that few others have brings with it rewards of its own. When you take it on yourself to get to know that ground well, as only a handful of people before you have, that piece of ground becomes special in a very personal way. And as you will have had no problem parking your car in the morning, you won't have lost a second of excited anticipation of things waiting to be found.

ABOUT THIS BOOK

The book is divided into four sections: Fell, Dale, Wood, Coast. There are inevitably crossovers, especially between dales and associated fells and also between woodlands and pretty much everywhere: cross-references are given where appropriate.

I'm a southern boy, born in Lincolnshire but a Wiltshire boy from the ages of 18 months to 18 years, when, after school, fresh from studying Wordsworth for A level English, I found myself on my way to Lancaster University to read English. After eight years and three degrees – BA, MA, PhD, the latter on Wordsworth – my wife to be, a doctor (the medical sort, that is), who'd finished her training at the Royal Lancaster Infirmary, got a job at Westmorland General on the southern edge of Kendal, and we moved to Oxenholme. For all my reading of Wordsworth and for all the years spent in Lancaster I had not explored Cumbria much. I knew the woods and the open spaces of Bowland Forest well, and the view across the Bay, and that seemed to be enough. It wasn't that I planned some Wordsworthian move to the Lakes. It just happened.

This book is the, sometimes unexpectedly connected, story of some of the more out-of-the-way places I explored in the four years we lived there, before relocating with our nine-month-old daughter back to Wiltshire in the summer of 2010. It's a story which begins on the Helm, a little hill with a superlative view, in sight of which most of this book was written. So it's a story of a place, but also of one particular journey through a place, a journey whose itinerary was suggested by many different things: somewhere glimpsed from a fell top which I knew I'd have to go and visit: somewhere mentioned in passing in an old record book at the library. It is, therefore, necessarily a personal and patchwork selection, and an incomplete one. I sometimes think that if we hadn't moved I'd never have finished writing it, and would have watched it stretch into volumes. Perhaps it still will.

It also shows a geographical bias to the south east of what's now Cumbria, specifically to the south of old Westmorland and the east of Lancashire-North-of-the-Sands, simply because that's where I was living when I set out on the journeys here recorded.

This book was mostly written on the edge of Kendal, but was finished after our move south. Those passages which make reference to home as being in

Cumbria I've left as I think they feel more immediate written as they were. I hope this doesn't cause much confusion.

A word about the title, which, as I've said, is from Wordsworth, and which I return to in the first chapter. To me, the most moving object in Cumbria is the tiny font in the old church of St Martin in Martindale. The church itself is ancient; the churchyard yew, growing over the church's north east shoulder, and whose branch-breadth nearly matches the church itself for size, is doubtless more ancient still. It's a long-held belief of mine that many old churches were built on sites of pre-Christian worship, particularly sites where the spirit-denizens of individual trees, or even the trees themselves, were worshipped long ago. We often read that such and such a church was built in such and such a year, on the site of an earlier church: in many of England's big old graveyard yews, the first churches on the site, are still standing, and still growing. Accounts are agreed that this yew is at least 1,300 years old (there's a certificate on the wall of the new church which gives this dating). The most recent guess I've read is 2,000 years old. I do know a bit about old trees and could well believe the latter figure. One yew recently inspected on Whitbarrow Scar had 215 growth rings in a 1.5cm radius section of the trunk. These things grow slowly.

Old Martindale church's now Christian font is another relic of the old worship of the spirits of places. It was placed by Romans as an altar, presumably to the spirits of the mountains to ensure safe passage through the hills. The Romans left but the stone remained, and found itself a new use as a sharpening

Jet from Walla Crag.

Font, Martindale Old Church.

stone for the knives of passing shepherds. The deep, slowly worn out slashes of those days still adorn the sides of the stone, and I think of meetings between otherwise lonely shepherds, lingering over their task, enjoying a rare bit of company and, between the slow scratches of blade on stone, telling the oft-repeated tale of the stone's first use, embezelled probably with bloody tales of sacrifice.

There's a tremendous evocation of space and silence and the long trajectory of human time to be found in a few silent minutes sitting in some of Cumbria's loneliest churches, but only in Martindale, the loneliest of all, is some of the vastness of the hills, and their history, brought inside. But the vastness of the hills are never the same: the evocation of each lonely chapel and church is different. No two valleys are anything like the same. The county's coasts are wildly diverse. Many of Cumbria's less-visited corners really do feel as if they have souls of their own. In this book I've tried to capture some of them.

James Deboo
Wiltshire

Fell

I OFTEN WONDER if the Lake District would be called the Peak District if there wasn't already a Peak District further south, as in north-south relationships in the British Isles south generally comes first. Although the Peak District is in fact named after a 6th century Anglo-Saxon group, the Pecsætan, so in reality the Peaks' name is a lot older than that of the Lakes, which seems to be an invention of the age of the Picturesque. In fact there's only one lake in the Lakes, Bassenthwaite, the others all being meres, tarns or waters, as those in the know like to point out. But there's no doubt what brings most visitors to the Lakes: mountains.

There are five kinds of hill in the Lakes. There are the big, classic hillwalker's hills, the ones the more occasional visitors head for: Helvellyn, Skiddaw, Blencathra, the Old Man, Gable, and obviously Scafell and Scafell Pike. There's the little ones, some of them in Wainwright's list, that have brown tourist signs pointing up them: Orrest Head, Gummer's Howe, Loughrigg, even Cat Bells and Helm Crag. Then there are those of the 214 Wainwrights that fall between these two categories, to pick a random selection let's say Haystacks, Fairfield, Wetherlam for the better-known; Pike o'Blisco, Tarn Crag, Armboth Fell for the less well-known. Then there are the 325 out of 541 Birketts that aren't Wainwrights (541 minus 214 = 327: if you're wondering

Blencathra from near Pooley Bridge in winter.

how the maths works, there are two Wainwrights that aren't Birketts, Mungrisdale Common and Castle Crag; a Birkett is simply an eminence above 1,000 feet.) Finally there are the less well known little ones, like the Helm above Oxenholme. Many of the less frequented hills are lonely just because they're not on the usual routes or not close to populated centres; the same is true for the odd group of hills, like the Caldbecks north of Skiddaw. Why climb here when you can climb Skiddaw or Blencathra? Why stop at junction 36 of the M6 to climb Farleton Fell when Kirkstone Pass is so close? You'll never know until you try.

Then there are groups of hills, the Howgills, for example, or the limestone hills of the south of the county or the Cumbrian Pennines, which are well worth getting to know.

The Helm

VISIONS OF THE HILLS

There was a poster on the wall of the classroom in which I studied A level English, advertising the annual Wordsworth Trust summer conference at Grasmere, which featured the lines from Wordsworth's long autobiographical poem *The Prelude* which give this book its title:

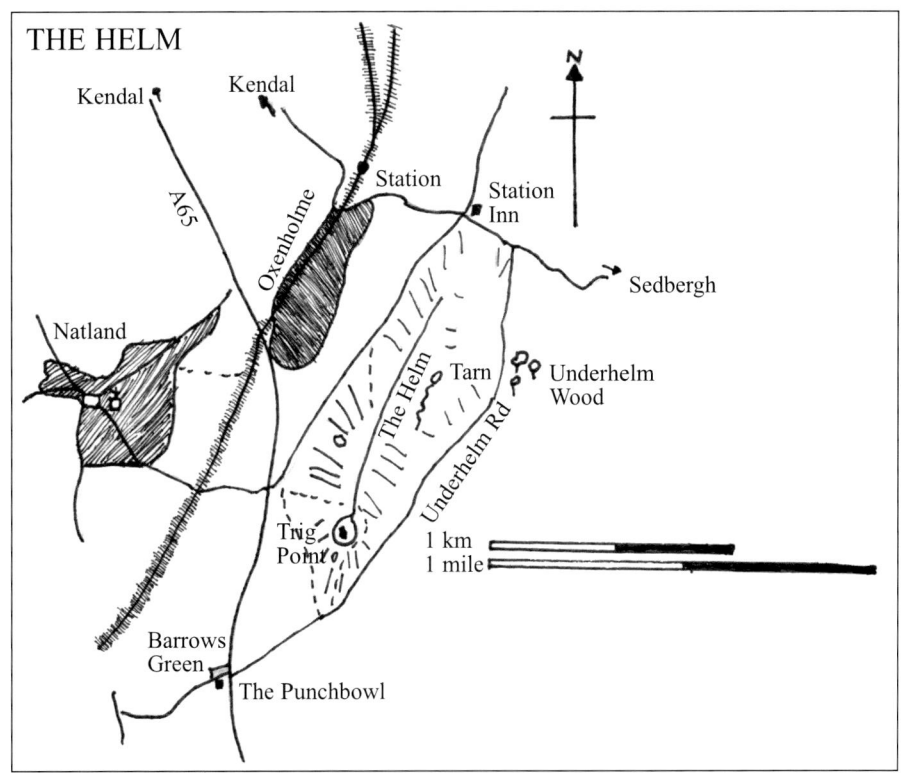

> *Ye Presences of Nature, in the sky*
> *Or on the earth, ye Visions of the hills!*
> *And Souls of lonely places.*
>> (Wordsworth, *Prelude* (1805), I: 464-6)

Floods at Sedgwick, the Helm in the distance.

It was this poster which first got me interested in the man to whom I'd eventually devote nearly four years of my life writing a PhD.

Alfred Wainwright, another writer central to the written history of the Lakes, moved from Blackburn to Kendal to take up the post of town treasurer (and taking a twelve per cent pay cut along with it) in November 1941. He was 34 – my age as this book goes to press – and it would be a good decade before he would embark on the seven-book series of *Pictorial Guides* which would make his name.

In February 1942 he wrote to his old Blackburn friend Lawrence Wolstenholme:

> On Saturday afternoon I climbed the Helm, a strange isolated hill two miles out of the town, which sticks up above the countryside like a stranded ship with keel upturned. Snow-covered and detached, it looked as if terrific winds had piled up a mammoth drift, for the gorse and bracken on its steep sides were deeply covered beneath the glittering whiteness.
>
> I made my way slowly to the top, ploughing through snow [...] The panorama was indescribably beautiful. Morecambe Bay, Arnside, Grange, the great wall of the Lake mountains, Shap Fells, the Sedbergh Hills, the Pennines: these were the boundaries of my vision [...].

It was, in a way, a lesser version of the day in 1930 when Wainwright had climbed up to Orrest Head from a Windermere bus stop with a cousin, and had seen the Lakeland fells for the first time: now, he was seeing them as a resident.

In August 2006 my soon to be fiancée, at the time three years out of medical school, finished a training post at the Royal Lancaster Infirmary and began one at Westmorland General Hospital, nestled under the Helm to the south of Kendal. I was in a bad way: I'd recently completed my PhD, and like many (I suspect most) humanities PhD students, was exhausted and depressed, worried whether or not my academic career was going to come together or whether I'd simply wasted the last four gruelling years making myself over-qualified and unemployable outside Academia, a world I wasn't entirely certain I belonged in anyway.

Then, not long before, had come the final blow: I'd not, as I'd been promised, had my teaching contract at Lancaster renewed. I was going to have to find something else to make some money, to fill the gap until the next round of research posts came round: I'd recently very narrowly missed getting one. But this news made it a lot less likely I'd be successful applying for more in the future.

Except, to cap everything, I couldn't even go in search of a way to make some money, to fill in the empty days. My wife-to-be was going to be commuting from Lancaster to Kendal, and not just regular, do-on-the-train-able hours, but all the early shifts, late shifts, nights and days that being a junior slave to the NHS entails. And she didn't yet have a driving licence. It meant, in short, that until I'd managed to sell our house in Lancaster and move to Kendal (which at least would keep me busy) I was doomed to be a full-time taxi-driver-on-demand.

In truth, it wasn't so bad. In between house buying and selling, my father had very generously bought me a correspondence course in proofreading and editing, with the idea that that might be something I could do to earn money and make use of the skills and experience gained doing the PhD, and hopefully edge myself closer to being a published author into the bargain. I spent less and less time bothering to drive back down the M6 and more and more in Kendal coffee shops and estate agents, and exploring the place that would soon be home.

It seems odd, with hindsight, that during all the time I'd spent studying Wordsworth at Lancaster I hadn't got to know the Lake District better. But then, not so long before, I hadn't even been able to bring myself to go walking out in the Forest of Bowland, because the fact that not even the great outdoors seemed able to lift my mood just made me more miserable. "Nature never did betray the heart that loved her," Wordsworth wrote in 'Tintern Abbey', and I had had occasion to disagree with him.

Then, one hot, clear, grapefruit-yellow late summer day, one of those days

that makes the horizon look at arm's length, I wandered up onto the Helm, discovering for the first but not the last time that the smaller hills can inexplicably seem the toughest, and saw that astonishingly varied view: south, over Arnside and Warton Crag to Clougha Pike and Heysham and Blackpool Tower, the places I was leaving behind: north and east to Whinfell and the Howgills and the Pennines, new places to me: but above all, west to the overwhelmingly tangled mass of mountains I was barely acquainted with. "Visions of the hills" indeed. I wondered how long it would be before I could name them all (about four months, as it turned out). I felt, for the first time in a long while, that everything would be all right. Soon afterwards we moved, and I finished my correspondence course.

Two more climbs I did in the autumn/winter of 2006 stick in my mind. One day in October (the 11th, according to my accounts book) I went into Kendal, to Stramongate Press on Aynam Mills, and collected the printed business stationery I'd ordered, then set off in the car to go for a walk and to think up a strategy to market my new editing, proofreading and indexing skills. From the Helm I'd been intrigued by an elegant-looking limestone hill, glaringly white like a newly-arrived holidaymaker on a tourist beach, just left of shot as you look westwards. The map told me it was called Whitbarrow. I drove over there, parked for the first time ever at Mill Side, amazed at the numbers of by then well past it damsons scattered everywhere, and set off eastwards, intending to make my way round the foot of the cliff to Rawsons and then head up the track there.

I didn't get very far thinking about marketing. Just past Raven's Lodge, I glanced up at the cliff above me and, buoyed with a new self-confidence at the thought of the 500 business cards sitting on my passenger seat proudly declaring: "Dr James Deboo, Editing, Proofreading and Indexing," I thought to myself, "You could make it up there." Then I thought, "Don't be an idiot." Then "No, you could..." (I should here point out that there's in fact a ban on climbing these cliffs which I was unaware of at the time: see the beginning of the Whitbarrow section of the Scout Scar and Whitbarrow chapter below).

Anyway, before I knew it, I was scrambling up the limestone strata, moving forward millions of years each time I edged further up. I remember stopping half-way up, hanging from a stunted yew, and being astonished to see that the vast majority of Foulshaw Moss had been deforested, then looking down – briefly – then up. I couldn't see how I was going to get any higher, and it suddenly occurred to me that, especially given the vagaries of soft, water-soluble limestone, what from the bottom I'd taken for the top (if you see what I mean) wasn't necessarily the top of the cliff. I had a clear vision of reaching what I thought to be the top, only to find myself on a narrow ledge backed by an

Opposite: The Helm in winter.

unclimbable slope, with no option but to head back the way I'd come. I looked down again, and regretted it. I didn't fancy the descent, even from here.

Then a little of my earlier gung-ho-ness returned. I thought again of the optimistic, as-yet-unrealised statement made over and over again on all those business cards and letters boxed up in the car. I decided there and then that the cliff and the business were linked: scale the first, and I'd achieve the second. Up I went.

Before long, a heart-stopping slip or two and a vertigo-inducing incident with a crow later, I pulled myself onto the grassy clifftop and lay, panting, among scrubby bushes heaving with sloes and juniper. Breath slightly returned, I heaved myself to my feet and trotted over to a small cairn on the highest point around, disturbing a roe deer on my way. I folded myself onto the grass next to the cairn and watched the tide ebb out of the Kent estuary, adrenaline coursing pleasurably. I pictured myself coming back here the next summer, after a long, hard week of editing or proofreading something, a few hundred more quid in the bank, being my own boss. For the first time I genuinely thought to myself, "it might just work."

Then Christmas Day – my wife was working a 12½ hour shift (for the second Christmas running) and, once I'd packed her lunch and packed her off, I headed off to Grasmere to have a go at climbing my first ever proper Lake District mountain. I'd chosen Grasmere as a tribute to Wordsworth, and

Wind-wizened tree on the Helm.

Fairfield partly because I liked the name and partly because I'd have a chance to hunt out the sheepfold central to Wordsworth's poem *Michael* on the way up.

Grasmere is, nowadays, hardly a sequestered spot – but it is early on Christmas morning. I panted my way up to Stone Arthur, just short of which I disappeared into thick, frozen cloud. It was eerily still, and weird, long ice crystals bowed the blades of grass to the ground. I rested a few minutes, ate some Kendal Mint Cake (as one does) and then plodded on for what seemed like forever towards Great Rigg.

Where, miraculously, the

Seat Sandal from Grasmere in winter.

cloud cleared and I stepped into blazing sunshine. There, improbably close and looking almost indecently easy to reach, was the summit of Fairfield, and studded all around me were the summits of all the highest fells, islands in the unmoving waves of cloud. I could hear voices from the top of Helvellyn: they sounded like voices in the next room. I bleeped my wife at work and did my best to describe the view and how I was feeling, then ran up to Fairfield, all tiredness forgotten. By six that evening I was back home putting a guinea fowl in the oven, aware that something seismic had changed.

By Easter I'd done 30-odd Wainwrights, had a list of half a dozen clients, including one called Hayloft (look on the spine of this book) and as much free-lance work as I wanted (usually more).

THE DARK SIDE OF THE HELM
Anyway, we've come a long way from the Helm. Not, as you might expect, limestone like Scout Scar and Whitbarrow, or Coniston Grit like Benson Knott and the Howgills, the Helm is in fact made of the same 450-million year old Silurian rocks as the central Lake District: it's a proper mini-fell in its own right. On the summit you can clearly see the remains of Castlesteads, a pre-Roman Bronze or Iron Age fort. Before the Romans arrived this area formed part of the border of lands occupied by two tribes, the Setantii to the south (who occupied most of historical Lancashire) and the Carvetti to the north,

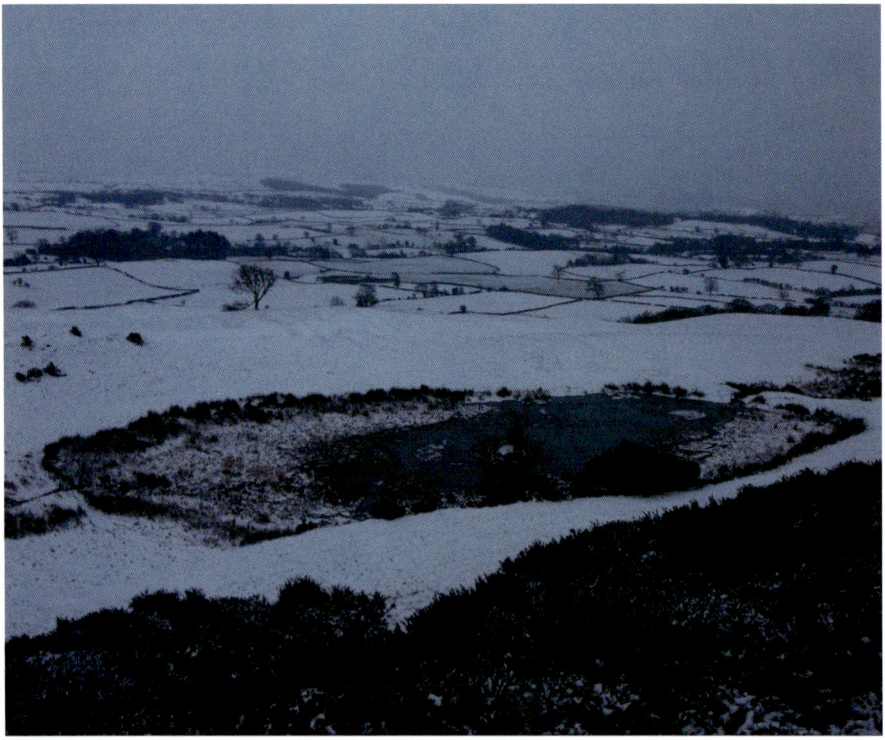

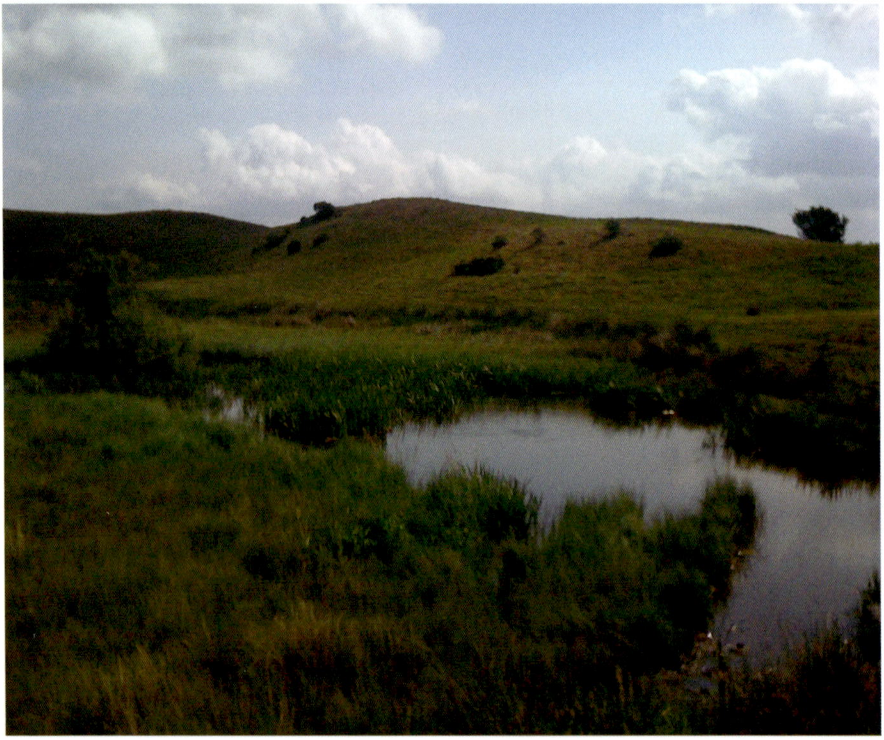

both of whom were under pressure from a bigger and more peaceable people, the Brigantes, who got on better with the Romans, and who would become the people of the dark age kingdom of Rheged. I like to think, given that the Helm is easy to approach from the north, much less so from the south, that it was a Carvetti outpost, the edge of their mountain fastness, and I've often sat on the top of the trig point on the Helm and imagined an Iron Age soldier up there, looking out south for signs of Setantii activity, being the first of his people to see a vast, alien Roman force come rumbling into view.

For all of its recent history the Helm has been Natland's common (it's still part of Natland parish), and it was never enclosed, the scarcity of sheep on it today explaining why, especially in the autumn, its conspicuousness from a distance belies its small size, as the heather and bracken which cover its slopes glow in evening sun. It's especially fine viewed from Whitbarrow. Apparently in the 1840s it was occupied by a group of travelling potters who tried to deny commoners access. There's a small disused quarry on the west side of the hill due north of the summit, from where building stone was mined – the cottages near Helm Mount Farm on Helm Lane are of a strikingly similar colour to the rock in the quarry. Perhaps the most significant change to have happened to the Helm since the old fort was abandoned and it became common grazing occurred in 2007, when the eastern side of the hill was bought by Friends of the Lake District. Over the next two Christmas/New Years, new gates were installed in the wall that runs along the top of the hill and the eastern side, 'The Dark Side of the Helm', became open access land.

Opposite: The dark side of the Helm and above, looking along the wall to the summit in snow.

The great thing, is, though, that, humans being humans, few people are so far using the 'new' land on the other side. It's a beautiful, sheltered area, with some stunted trees, masses of gorse (or is it broom?) and an enchanting little tarn – keep an eye out for herons – but mostly it's deserted. Good thing, as I don't know what the majority of local dog walkers would make of my tree climbing antics. The new access land also means it's much easier to get from the Helm to Underhelm Wood on Helm Lane, where there are picnic tables where I've spent many a happy day proofreading. Thanks to mobile broadband I'm able to work there even when I need to be computer-based. There's nothing quite like sitting in a wood, watching the cows wandering to and fro out in the fields and the buzzards overhead and the wrens and the robins (and, once, a weasel) gradually becoming less and less concerned that you're there, all the while doing a day's work.

On the subject of birds of prey, it's not just the ubiquitous buzzards either. When I am desk-bound, half the time I can look out of my home office window and be sure of seeing a kestrel or two hunting along the summit ridge: if I can't see them I know it's because they're hovering out of sight over the tarn. I've seen a marsh harrier and a little owl, as well as two tawny owls (perhaps the same one twice) in the marshy area around Helmside Farm. Then, a few weeks ago, I was standing at my kitchen window, watching the kestrels up on the ridge and waiting for the kettle to boil, when there was the most almighty commotion at the bird table. The sparrows scarpered, the normally super-plucky robin shot into my neighbour's yard and, so quickly I didn't really know what was happening, a starling shot across the yard, straight into my

The Helm from the author's office window.

Looking east from the Helm to the Howgills in winter.

kitchen window, leaving a Jackson Pollock trail of bird shit on the glass, and the next thing I know it's on the concrete under the window with a sparrowhawk sitting on it, its rising Mars of an eye fixed on me, evaluatively. It was still there when I rushed back with the camera, and allowed me one shot of it before it casually flapped away, starling still clasped in its talons. I don't know where it lives but I'm keeping my eyes out.

SAP, CISTERNS AND PROSPECTING FOR TREACLE

The week I wrote the above I had other, more prosaic business on the Helm. It was March, and the birch sap was rising. I'd a couple of birches near the crab apple that contributed to my batch of cider two autumns ago in mind (I can see them, red with evening sun, out of the window as I type); it's good to use the commons, somehow, as they're supposed to be used – I sometimes gather firewood there, too – and who knows, I thought maybe I might spot that sparrowhawk.

Anyway, one evening I sat, watching first birch sap trickling down a piece of wine maker's siphon tubing into a demijohn and then one of the kestrels hovering high above the overhead branches, and as I glanced around looking for another likely birch I saw something I'd never noticed before. It was a low, roughly mortared wall of local stone which, on closer inspection, turned out to be an old stone-walled, concrete-topped cistern hidden among the bracken and brambles (mostly brambles) 150 metres or so from the summit of the Helm, and about forty vertical metres below it. There were a couple of openings on

33

the top covered in broken concrete slabs, through whose holes I dropped small stones. After a second's pause there came a deep, echoey, satisfying 'plop'. Intrigued, I started rummaging around in the undergrowth and down the hill towards my favourite old beech tree trying to figure out what on earth the cistern was for.

And I drew a blank. Down the hill, following the line of the ridge of the Helm southwards, there were a couple of brick structures like overflow outlets, and at the bottom of the hill near the beech two leaf – and mulch – filled brick edged holes leading down to who knows what. Thereafter no sign.

Presumably it was situated on the site of a spring, and it's no surprise to find a spring near an ancient hill fort like Castlesteads. But what could this cistern be collecting water for? Filling water troughs in the fields below seemed the most likely explanation, although I did wonder for a moment whether it was something to do with topping up the nearby reaches of the Lancaster Canal. If you look at the map you'll see that, oddly, there are no streams that flow from the Helm down to the Kent, and speculating about the cistern reminded me of this odd fact, and of a story which, tongue in cheek, I'd been told in St. Mark's Church in Natland.

If you drive out of Kendal on the A65 past Westmorland General Hospital and turn right into Natland you'll notice in a front garden a small miner's cart and a bicycle proudly bearing the livery of the Natland Treacle Mines Limited Westmorland (its product: Hand Hewn Quality Treacle, one of the company directors a Mo Lasses...). This is a reflection of an old shaggy dog story the locals have told for longer than anyone can remember, which goes something like this.

In the suspiciously precisely remembered year of 1211 a man searching for buried Roman treasure in a cave near Natland found a pot filled with what looked like gold, being guarded by a snake. Overcome with greed he grabbed the pot, whereupon the snake struck at him and bit him. He fainted from the effects of poison, and, coming round, found that he had put his hand into a seam of naturally occurring treacle, which miraculously cured him. The source of this curative treacle has been a closely guarded secret ever since, and has brought health and happiness to the Natlanders.

The story is not unique to Natland: other treacle mines are located as far apart as Pudsey, Maidstone, Bisham, Chobham, Tadley and Thurham, to give a random selection. In *Alice's Adventures in Wonderland*, at the Mad Hatter's tea party the Dormouse tells a story:

> 'Once upon a time there were three little sisters,' the Dormouse began in a great hurry; 'and their names were Elsie, Lacie, and Tillie; and they lived at the bottom of a well—'
> 'What did they live on?' said Alice, who always took a great interest in questions of eating and drinking.

'They lived on treacle,' said the Dormouse, after thinking a minute or two.

'They couldn't have done that, you know,' Alice gently remarked; 'they'd have been ill.'

'So they were,' said the Dormouse; 'very ill.'

Alice tried to fancy to herself what such an extraordinary way of living would be like, but it puzzled her too much, so she went on: 'But why did they live at the bottom of a well?'

It's a relation of stories about wild Highland haggis or spaghetti trees in Italy. One origin of the story may be etymological: treacle, originally meaning any kind of thick, sticky paste, came into English from the Old French *triacle*, itself derived from Latin *theriaca*, meaning 'antidote to poison'. Robert Gambles in an article in *Cumbria* magazine has pointed out that 1211 in Roman Numerals is MCC XI – just right for an English tall story. There are various stories about the idea of treacle coming from the brownish colour of the local stone, as quarried on the Helm, or from a thick layer of tar supposed to lie under Natland Green.

But while the idea of there being treacle in caves under the village is far-fetched, the caves themselves certainly do exist. This story begins in January 1855, when the *Westmorland Gazette* published a story about a man from Barrow's Green, the hamlet under the cistern end of the Helm, who had gone out into his garden one morning to find that a large part of it had subsided into a cave which had appeared twenty feet below. Said the *Gazette* (20 January),

> This remarkable phenomenon, had sufficiently roused the curiosity and won-der of the neighbours, a tramp who was passing that way was induced to allow himself to be let down into the hole by a rope, with a lantern to assist his inves-tigations. The man came up again with a magnificent tale about an extensive and beautiful cave, and it has been since imagined that the roof of the cave was hung with beautiful stalactites.

John Ruthven, a local geologist, later explored the cave, which was about seven feet high: how long or wide doesn't seem to have been recorded. The cave seems subsequently to have been filled in, and now the site – on the left hand side of the road immediately behind the Punchbowl Inn – is overgrown with nettles.

Next, in 1982 contractors for North West Water were digging in the area, assessing the route of a proposed water pipeline which was to run under the railway near the junction of Oxenholme's main through road, Helmside Road, and the A65. They discovered a large cave under a field on the edge of Natland which, being contractors, they concreted over and told no one about. The site is in the field through which passes the public footpath from the A65 railway bridge into Natland, at the far (southern) end of the long, curving spoil mound

Winter skyscape.

left over from the construction of the railway cutting.

When the pipeline was being built the cave entrance opened up again in the same manner as at Barrow's Green, and this time two cavers from Dentdale were assigned to explore it before it was properly sealed up with tonnes of concrete. Their report was published in *Descent* magazine, November 1983. I've managed to obtain a copy of this issue, and they report that the cave, of which they explored a total of 2,000 feet, runs very close under the railway line.

In fact if you stand on the A65 railway bridge and look Natland-wards you'll see that sections of the cutting wall have been bricked over, suggesting they may once have contained openings. I wonder whether whoever built the West Coast Mail Line was aware that the area may not be entirely geologically stable. Latterly excavations have been done in a small cave whose entrance is in the small wooded area known as Little Helm, immediately west of the A65 opposite the dog walker's car park by the gate which leads onto the commons opposite the end of Helm Lane. The entrance is small enough to have put me off wriggling myself into it, but apparently it leads to a small cavern with no obvious way forwards.

This at any rate explains where rainwater running off the west side of the Helm goes: it goes underground. Over the wall from the above-mentioned dog walker's car park is a marshy area which contains an obvious water sink: there are several more in the area, including one next to Oxenholme Station. And there is a line of springs discharging water into the Kent from its limestone river banks. There's a very amusing article describing an attempt to trace the links between these various sinks and springs using coloured dyes on Natland's website, which proved only that none of the known sinks seem to connect with any of the known springs.

Disappearing water; a mysterious cistern; legends and hidden caves. It's nice to think that under Natland are some very sequestered spots indeed. That nearly concludes the Helm chapter, but I will briefly mention two other small hills nearby which are worth a visit.

HAY FELL

There's only one thing that blocks the 360° panorama from the top of the Helm, and that's Benson Knott, the distinctive, notched summit of the hill called Hay Fell, 127m taller than the Helm, with its trig point placed, surprisingly, on the lower of the two tops, to the north. It stands to reason, therefore, that the views from Hay Fell should be impressive, and they do not disappoint: a continual ring of hills of all shapes and sizes, from the elegant Howgills, round past flat Middleton and stony-topped Farleton fells to Warton Crag and Arnside Knott, then the huge sweep of the Lakeland Fells all the way from Black Combe to the hills east of Longsleddale, then, finally, closer at hand, the gently undulating Whinfell Ridge. Not dissimilar to the Helm, but bigger, higher, boggier underfoot and with no quarry, but with the beautiful Fisher Tarn nestled in its southern shoulder, Hay Fell is well worth an ascent, and the pleasant, partly wooded south-east of the area is a nice place to wander, if boggy.

Then there's Fisher Tarn. Something of a folly of a reservoir, work on Fisher Tarn started in 1894 and was completed five years later. Built to provide water for a growing Kendal, and disused since the advent of the much bigger Thirlmere and then Haweswater reservoirs (the former actually the same age as Fisher Tarn), it's nowadays owned by United Utilities and used by a local angling club, who stock it artificially. I don't know what, if any, formal public access arrangements there are, but in United Utilities' recent *Conservation, Access and Recreation Reports* the map of their sites in north-west England has an 'environmental trail' symbol next to Fisher Tarn as well as an angling one. Certainly no one's ever questioned my presence there: but I've never known more than two anglers there at any one time. It's particularly worth visiting when migrating birds are coming through, and in the spring: in one half hour walk round the tarn (which is about 500 metres north-south and 400 east-west), I saw roe deer, swans, coots, moorhens, a family of three buzzards, frogs, toads and masses of frogspawn (most of it all over the path, so I carefully scooped it into the reeds), and got dive-bombed by nesting black-headed gulls. There's no access from the United Utilities land onto the Hay Fell access land, although, shall we say, the more agile walker might manage it.

FARLETON FELL

Although hardly a giant, at 265m, Farleton Fell is still 80m higher than the Helm and does have a couple of claims to fame. While lower than neighbouring Hutton Roof Crags, of which I suppose Farleton is technically a subsidiary summit, it's far more a separate fell, a hill in its own right, than Hutton Roof; the loose limestone of the northern slopes make for an amusing, if slippery, scramble; and the slab of inclined limestone that forms its upper surface is fascinating, both from a distance – Farleton dominates the near horizon from the

Looking south to Farleton Fell.

area, between Heversham and Warton, that stretches along the far north-east coast of Morecambe Bay, as well as playing a more significant part than its size suggests in views from the south-east of Westmorland – and close up: the pockmarked surface of Farleton's limestone pavement is home, like that of Whitbarrow, to many rare grasses and flowers, and from the lush miniature flower and lichen rainforest gullies of its grykes (one of English's finer words, and so, unsurprisingly, from Old Norse) I once rescued a stuck lamb, to whose presence its distressed mother had, I'm convinced, deliberately alerted me.

Farleton Fell is a signpost. Towering over the M6 at junction 36, unmissable from the West Coast Main Line, and appearing far more impressive than its modest height should allow, it marks the true beginning of Cumbria for the traveller from the south. It welcomed us home for many years, and before that, before Cumbria was home, passing it was like a covenant, promising greater – in height, though not necessarily in interest close at hand – hills ahead. It also says goodbye, as we've driven past, so many times, in the half light of early dawns on trips 'home' to the south. I guess, one day soon, it will wave good-bye one last time, as we follow a removals van south.

The Howgills

England's Mountains Green?

STRANDED BETWEEN THE tourist hotspots of the Lake District – whose mountains feed the Howgills with a generous supply of mist, hill fog and torrential downpours – and the Yorkshire Dales, the Howgills are remarkable for being almost entirely fenceless – and almost entirely unremarked. They get a brief mention in written history in 1844, when the shepherds who looked after sheep on the Howgills petitioned to have the hills enclosed after the 'Select Committee on Parliamentary Inclosure' heard the case of Edmond Bannister of Dentdale, whose sheep had been driven off the commons by another farmer: Bannister's sheep were eventually found scattered around Mallerstang, Kirkby Stephen and Ravenstonedale Common. But the fells were never enclosed.

The lack of fences up there is a defining feature: in fact, the lack of features is a defining feature, and it's always odd when you reach the edge of the Howgills after miles of wilderness and find yourself having to open and close gates or (as no one's looking) scale a wall. The fence to the right of the path leading from Arant Haw up to the summit of Calders, as well-trodden a route

The Howgills from Lambrigg.

as there is in the
Howgills, is an odd
exception. But generally,
if wilderness in the sense
of lonely, empty land-
scape is your thing, the
Howgills are by no
means a poor second to
the Lakes.

Howgills hillside.

Wainwright, AW to his
friends, took to walking
here later in life, partly to
escape the crowds of
summer tourists out on
the Lakeland fells, many
of whom were out deliberately to catch a glimpse of the great guidebook
writer, and he wrote of the Howgills that: "the meeting of Stanley and Dr.
Livingstone could hardly have been more poignant than the confrontation of
one walker by another in the northern sector – it simply does not happen." But,
clipped at their eastern edge by the west coast main line and the M6, AW, writing in 1972 (in *Walks on the Howgill Fells*) was worried that the Howgills' isolation and loneliness would not last.

You could argue (but this is a complex idea, and will be returned to later)
that if what drew Wainwright to the Howgills was their loneliness, then should
he not have been more reticent about publishing a guidebook to them? But 35
years later the Howgills are still fairly empty. My wife and I have found
English elms growing in valleys within an earshot of the motorway and the
Virgin trains making their way to and from Scotland, in valleys nevertheless
so remote not even the elm bark beetles seem to have found them. You might
expect that countless users of the M6 and the railway would be inspired by
views of the Howgills to venture out and visit them, but this hasn't happened.

That gap through the Lune gorge has been used as a thoroughfare for thousands of years. Some of Cumbria's earliest stone age settlers passed this way.
Two thousand years ago the Romans considered the route so important that
they built a fort, including a bath house, at Low Borrow Bridge, where Borrow
Beck meets the Lune, right under the modern-day road and rail viaducts
(Borrowdale is from *Borgherdal*, 'the valley of the fort'): but how many of
them ever braved the bears and wolves up in the fells?

I have met walkers – and mountain bikers, or 'nutters', as my wife calls
them – on the Calf, the Howgill's highest summit, and Sedbergh boys and girls
may be regularly seen running up and down Winder, a hill which, says
Wainwright, is to Sedbergh as the Matterhorn is to Zermatt. A few visitors can

generally be found peering approvingly at Cautley Spout, England's highest waterfall, at the hills' eastern edge. But, these comparative tourist traps aside, it's rare to encounter a shepherd, let alone a walker. Walking from Sedbergh to Tebay one August, I was crossing the gap called Wyndscarth Wyke, only a mile or so on from the Calf. The fog had just come down as if from nowhere, as it often does up there – I sometimes think that England's Atlantic fogs hide in the Howgills when they're off duty, as they know they'll never be seen there – when out of the monochrome came two bright red Gore-Tex jackets, one of them being dragged along by a wet, excited Lakeland Terrier. The 'hello' with

Above Lune Gorge from Uldale Head and below Lunesdale from Winder.

which I was greeted from under the red hoods was definitely more one of surprise than greeting.

I should point out that there are plans being drawn up to extend the Dales National Park to include the northern Howgills, along with more of the empty Pennines which lie between the Lakes and the Dales: for more on this read the Mallerstang chapter in the Dales section later in the book.

Uldale in the northern Howgills.

These hills are wilfully obscure. They take their name from a settlement which today is little more than a farm and an outlying cottage or two not far from where the M6 swoops, kestrel-like, into the Lune Gorge, joining the railway in making use of the long but steady climb over Shap Summit and the Lune-Eden watershed.

It's often said they should be called the Sedbergh Fells: in a rare literary reference to the Howgills, Wordsworth calls them "Sedbergh's naked heights" in the poem known as 'Home at Grasmere'. But if they were perhaps they'd be more visited. There's a modern signpost at the end of my road which reads 'Howgill 10', and I often wonder if anyone has ever found any use for this piece of information. To compound this sense of identity crisis further,

Opposite, Cautley Spout and above looking down Bowderdale from Yarlside.

Above, view from Howgill Lane and Howgills signpost.

Sedbergh and the southern Howgills are somehow simulta-neously both in Cumbria and in the Yorkshire Dales National Park. The context of Wordsworth's mention of the Howgills is:

> *how fast that length of way was left behind,*
> *Wensley's long dale and Sedbergh's naked heights*

Wordsworth is describing his and Dorothy's journey to their new home, the house we call Dove Cottage, in 1800. To Wordsworth the Howgills were mere-ly somewhere to be passed by, and it's virtually absent from the annals of his-tory. Isabella Lickbarrow, who spent a lot of her childhood staying with her grandparents at Cautley, wrote of the Howgills that:

> *To Crossdale's wildly-winding stream,*
> *its hanging woods and hollow dell,*
> *(Where wand'ring bards might love to dream)*
> *Reluctantly I bid farewell.*

"Might" is the key word in this stanza. The Lake District is often prized for being wild, untouched even, but of course it couldn't be less untouched: it bears the marks of millennia of human activity, and is all the richer for that. But if untouched, a-historical wilderness is your thing, get out into the Howgills. This is a true working landscape, fastness of the Rough Fell sheep, with no legacy of tourism past or concession to tourism present. And if it's foggy (which it often is) then the sense of wild loneliness, only increases.

But, despite this, I've long thought that the Howgills are in fact one of the best-known landscapes in England, at least when seen from a distance; and the reason for this surprising theory is a much better-known line from another Romantic poet, William Blake.

There is a small indirect link. On the road about a mile east of Cautley Spout is the Cross Keys, which became a Temperance Inn in 1902 in unusual circum-stances. In the summer of 1902 after, presumably, a fairly intemperate evening, the landlord was helping a man find the path to Ravenstonedale. Both men fell into the River Rawthey and drowned. The inn was acquired by an Edith Adelaide Burney, a nonconformist (like the Lickbarrows) and a member of the Temperance movement, who had the alcohol licence removed. Above a door is a couplet from Blake, a longtime favourite of nonconformist groups:

> *Great things are done where men and mountains meet*
> *That are not done by jostling in the street*

The Cross Keys at Cautley.

It's a good pair of lines, but it's not Blake's best-known comment on mountains, which is of course:

And did those feet in ancient time
Walk upon England's mountains green?

Which mountains does Blake mean? As a Londoner who, aside from a year in West Sussex in 1800, Blake was not especially familiar with the hill country of the north. For years, first as a schoolboy and then as a student at Lancaster University, before I moved to Cumbria, I'd head up to the north Lakes or to Scotland on the M6 or on the train, and, seeing the elegant, grassy, uninterrupted panorama of what were to me then nameless hills fill the windscreen or train window, those lines of Blake's jumped unbidden into my mind. And conversely, I see an image of the Howgills whenever I hear the well-known hymn setting of Blake's words. I wonder how many others share the same thought?

THINGS TO DO IN THE HOWGILLS

- Climb the Calf via Winder and Arant Haw. This is, of course, what everyone does; why not, having got the bus to Sedbergh from Oxenholme station, climb the Calf then carry on to Tebay, Newbiggin or Ravenstonedale and then get the bus back?
- Set out to climb a fell other than the Calf. The only tops in the Howgills that are regularly climbed are Winder, Arant Haw and the Calf; the others are generally summited in descent from the Calf. I'd suggest Yarlside at Cautley, which I honestly think as beautiful as any hill anywhere, or Green Bell or Harter Fell above Ravenstonedale. Most tops in the Howgills are closely connected to others: these are exceptions. The source of the Lune is at the springs between Green Bell and Knoutberry.
- Explore the valleys of the north and north east: Uldale, Langdale, Borrowdale, Bowderdale.
- Scramble up Black Force, the Howgill's second waterfall after Cautley, which drops into Carlingill Beck only a mile and a half from the M6, but whose isolation is extraordinary. It's a difficult climb preceded by a difficult approach up the bed of Carlingill Beck (take your boots off), and may prove impossible if it's been raining recently, in which case traverse to the left onto the steep grass and make your way up onto a superb grass ridge between Black Force and its northerly sister waterfall. Thence head up onto Fell Head. Black Force is best viewed from Hand Lake to the north, and can also be glimpsed from the M6. The

Opposite: Cautley Crags, Cautley Spout and fell ponies.

westernmost shoulder of the hills south of Carlingill Beck is called Gibbet Hill on the maps, which Dawn Robertson, in *Secrets and Legends of Old Westmorland*, gives as Hanging Hill: certainly the site of a gallows, it's said the last man hanged here was a local convicted of sheep stealing.

Above, looking to Baugh Fell from the ruins of Mountain View farm, Backside Beck, east of Yarlside and below, sunset after-glow from Green Bell.

One of the most beautiful views of the Howgills from the chapel at Firbank.

- Explore the extent of Ravenstonedale Common east of the Sedbergh to Kirkby Stephen road. For example, cross Bluecaster from the Cross Keys at Cautley then drop down into the Rawthey Valley and follow the Dales National Park boundary up the beautiful Uldale Gill – pastoral beech woods giving way gradually to wild moor – and then left up to Wild Boar Fell and thence to Mallerstang and/or Kirkby Stephen. Uldale Gill is a struggle in places but it's worth it. If you find either of the caves the 1:25,000 OS map shows then do let me know as I don't believe they exist, but the openings to these things can be tiny.
- Visit Fox's Pulpit near Firbank, the opposite side of the Lune from the straggling hamlet of Howgill, the place where George Fox delivered the sermon which began the Quaker movement; aside from its historical interest (the most important bits of which are recorded on a plaque there), the view of the Howgills is about the best there is – certainly the definitive view – and the beautiful little chapel at Firbank, on the road east of the access land on which Fox's Pulpit stands, is also well worth a visit.

I spent a night on Green Bell recently, having climbed straight up the flank of Yarlside from Cautley, then down and up over Kensgriff, down then up to Stockless and Spengill Head. There's a small tarn between Randygill Top and

Above, looking over Kensgriff to Green Bell from Yarlside, and below a dragonfly emerging from a tarn on Green Bell.

Green Bell, where I stopped to fill up my water bottles and noticed a dozen dragonfly larvae clinging to the water-weed: I was surprised to see them so high up, so far from any substantial vegetation. There was an amazingly slow sunset that night, scarlet clouds scudding over the Eden valley while the sun itself went down underneath them into its own furnace onto Shap Fells. In the morning, about five, I went to fill my water bottles at the tarn again and found dozens of dragonfly clinging to the grassblades at the water's edge, clambering out of their larval skin and drying their sticky wings in the sun. They stared at me, knowing that flight was not an option until their wings had cured properly.

Black Combe

"NOWT O' GOOD IVVER comes round Black Combe" is a saying local to Millom, supposedly dating from Robert the Bruce's 'Great Raid' of 1322, Black Combe having been where he turned inland having rounded the bottom of the Cumbrian coast. It's an oddity of a hill; a petulant teenager, cloud pouring gloomily off its summit like a visible bad mood, standing sulkily aloof from the rest of the Lake District.

Black Combe is a unique mountain with a unique view: nowhere else commands the panorama of Lakeland from south to south-west – the Coniston Fells, Scafells and Bowfell in particular – with anything like the altitude of Black Combe. Geologically it's also an odd one out, being a single, massive outlier of the Skiddaw Slates, the rocks laid down at the bottom of an ancient ocean, known as the Iapetus Ocean, off the coast of the continent of Gondwana, modern north-west Africa, roughly in the position of the Antarctic Peninsula today, about 510 million years ago. They are some 60 million years older than the central Lake District, whose rocks were formed when the Iapetus Ocean began to shrink. It lacks the last 300m or so of Skiddaw's stony eminence, being more in character with Skiddaw's little sister Lonscale Fell, but Black Combe dominates the northern skyline of Barrow, Millom and Walney Island just as Skiddaw looms over Keswick. In fact, it dominates the whole south-west of the Lakes in a way that only Skiddaw dominates a significant chunk of the landscape elsewhere.

Black Combe, cloud brushing the summit.

Underfoot Black Combe is like a cross between the Howgills and the Caldbeck Fells, its slopes not as abrupt as those of the Caldbecks, nor as smoothly symmetrical as the Howgills – seen from the side it bulges south-wards considerably – but its top is as smooth as the tops of both. I've already enthused about the view from here but in truth you won't get to appreciate it very often: the top seems to be in cloud most of the time, with a wisp of white trailing from it on even the calmest, clearest balmiest days of summer, making it resemble a miniature, smooth-sided Everest with the jet stream pouring off it. But, to me, cloud is an essential part of Black Combe's fascination.

Mountain summits are magical places, and to reach one in clear weather is to enter a magical world: slogging uphill, panting, becomes breathless exhilaration; when all your attention has been focused on what's immediately above you, suddenly everything is below you, and far away. Your sense of space, of time, of what's important and what's not, your internal as well as your external perspective: everything changes in an instant. When the summit is wrapped in thick cloud, most of these things don't happen, and, generally speaking, this is a disappointment, especially if you've been hoping for that very special treat, a summit above the clouds. But when you reach a summit that you've seen a hundred times, from a hundred different places, and which has been cloud-topped virtually every time, it's like being granted entry to a different kind of magic world from the clear summit: a forbidden kingdom, a hidden abode of the gods. Black Combe, aloof and shrouded in cloud, as tantalisingly history-free as the Howgills, is the Olympus of the Lakes.

Black Combe from Lowick High Common.

Looking south-west from Black Combe with Walney Island left of centre.

It looks very Olympus-esque, somehow, when seen across Lancaster Sands, from Bowland Forest, or from anywhere along the seafront between Heysham and Hest Bank, its solitude, its vast north-south spread and above all its comparative closeness making it look every bit as tall as the Coniston fells, the Langdales and Helvellyn and, though less mountainous, more massive. The Lake District proper seems to be spread out as if playing at mother Black Combe's feet. All the years I was at Lancaster University I used to watch the sunset from Williamson Park, gazing across the Bay to Black Combe guarding the western horizon. It also dominates mile after mile of the road or rail journey around the Cumbrian coast, so that you almost get the impression there's Black Combe, then the Scafell range, then the hills north of Keswick, and that somehow they're all about the same size.

As I've said Black Combe is, like the Howgills, almost entirely a-historical; it's not walled or fenced and, with the exception of a copper mine above Whitecombe Beck, about which little is recorded: the only mention I've found is a brief entry in John Adams' *Mines of the Lake District Fells* (Dalesman Books, 1988) which says the main level is 300 feet long and 'contains no stopes or other features of interest.' It gives no date for the mining.

The mole catcher's been busy near Silecroft.

The tantalysingly-named Leadmine Breast is a little to the north-east, of which I've not found a single mention anywhere, and besides these two cairns and a 'field system' on Bootle Fell on the seaward side, there's little to show that anyone has ever taken much interest in, or made much use of, Black Combe's bulk; no one but the nameless generations of cattle herders and, more latterly, shepherds have taken the time to head up into Black Combe's deep valleys or onto the cloudy top. It's a lone, blank canvas for the imagination, one of those places that retains a hold on your memory which is powerful but hard to account for. It's more intimately connected with the sea than any other Lake District fell, too. Perhaps there really are gods in the clouds on the summit.

Hallin Fell

BLOCKING THE ENTRANCE to Martindale, explored in the 'Dales' section, is Hallin Fell. On your way into Martindale I'd heartily recommend parking at the 'new' church not far from the top of the small pass which blocks the valley and climbing it.

At 388 metres this is the 12th lowest of the 214 Wainwrights and, with the exception of Latrigg and maybe Hardknott, probably the easiest of all to climb: you start at about 220 metres, so there's only 168 to go to the summit at 388 (Wainwright also says it's possible to climb the southern slopes barefoot). There are fantastic views of Martindale, as well as of Ullswater, the most

The summit of Hallin Fell.

Kailpot Crag.

beautiful stretch of water in the Lakes, I think, from here: just the place to spend a few hours, especially on a changeable day in spring or autumn, and watch the changing light on the hills and the water and the islands. The descent to the corner of Hallinhag Wood and back round via the shore of Ullswater is a lovely walk, full of bats in the evenings, and you can pause at Kailpot Crag, a *Swallows and Amazons*-y spot where local legend has it the fairies came to boil kale for their tea in the little depressions in the west-facing rocks under the low, wooded cliffs. In truth there's something fairy about Hallin Fell itself; it's like a miniature, fairy-sized version of Place Fell.

If you like, and if you have a way of retrieving your car or have used the Ullswater steamer, you could carry on and walk from Sandwick back along the shore to Patterdale, a walk described by Wainwright as "the most beautiful and rewarding walk in Lakeland."

Nine Standards to Wild Boar Fell

THIS SECTION DESCRIBES a circular hill route that takes in the best of the Cumbrian Pennines, in a circular route beginning and ending at Kirkby Stephen. Besides being a fine walk, and presenting an interesting aspect of

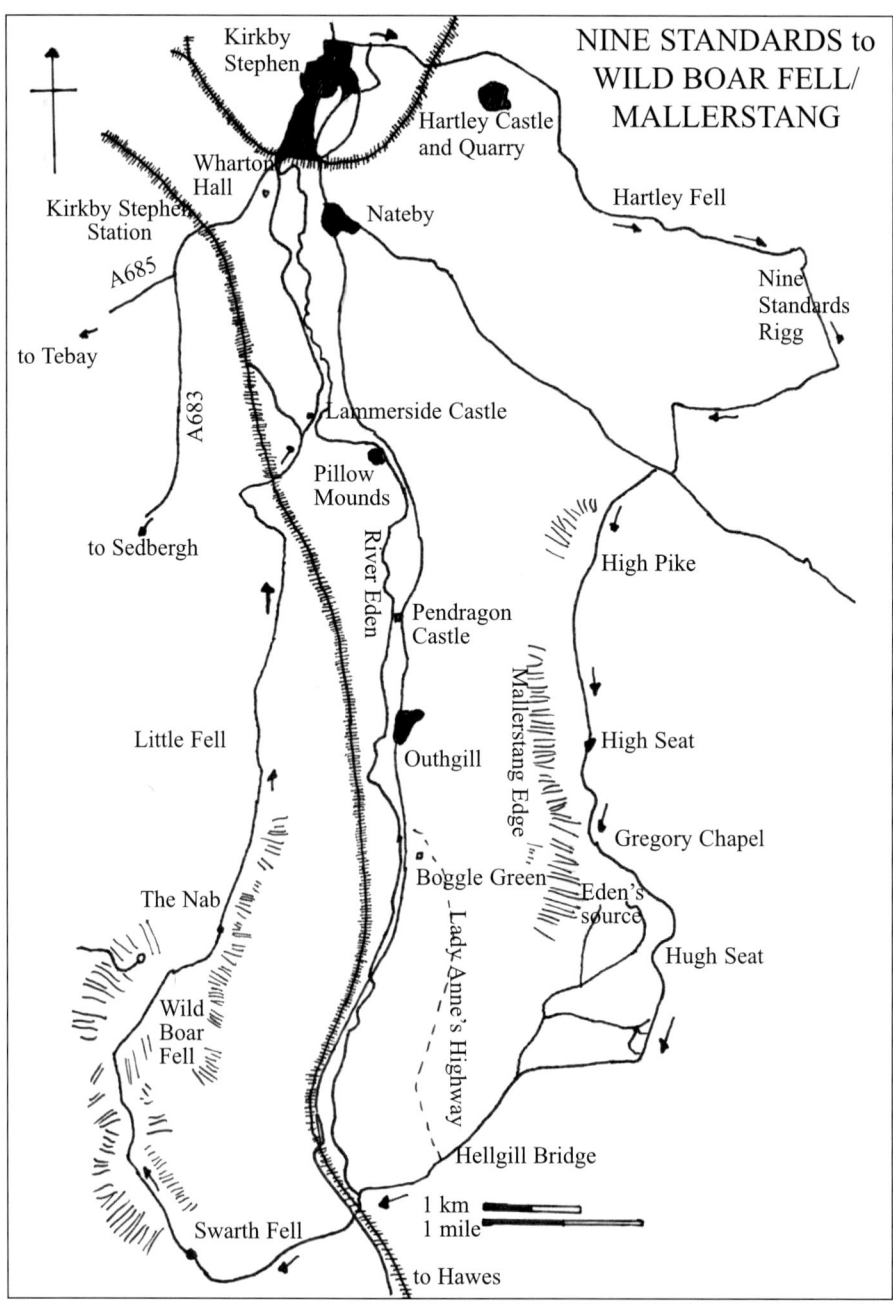

NINE STANDARDS to WILD BOAR FELL/ MALLERSTANG

Kirkby Stephen

Hartley Castle and Quarry

Hartley Fell

Wharton Hall

Kirkby Stephen Station

A685

Nateby

Nine Standards Rigg

to Tebay

A683

Lammerside Castle

Pillow Mounds

to Sedbergh

River Eden

High Pike

Pendragon Castle

Little Fell

Mallerstang Edge

Outhgill

High Seat

Gregory Chapel

Boggle Green

Eden's source

The Nab

Lady Anne's Highway

Hugh Seat

Wild Boar Fell

Hellgill Bridge

1 km
1 mile

Swarth Fell

to Hawes

Cumbria from high on its eastern border (six miles/ten kilometres of it along the Yorkshire Dales National Park and county boundaries), it takes in a number of enigmatic and (probably) ancient cairns, of which the Nine Standards are the best known and by far the most impressive. It also crosses Mallerstang, discussed in its own chapter in the Dale below. Be warned, though: the walk here described is about 20 miles (32km) long, involves a total climb of about 1080 metres (3500 feet) and is, although never hugely steep or difficult, not for the faint-hearted.

Nine Standards Rigg from Kirkby Stephen.

I can't take all the credit for thinking up the route: it's a modified version of the Yomp Mountain Challenge, formerly known as the Mallerstang Horseshoe and Nine Standards Yomp, an annual 23-mile running and walking event organised by the Rotary Club of Upper Eden and first run in 1983 to commemorate the achievements of the British Forces in the Falklands. My route goes clockwise rather than anti-, however, as I feel you get more of the climbing done earlier in the day this way round. Be aware that early on, due to the popularity of AW's Coast to Coast walk, which passes this way, the area around Nine Standards can become very boggy underfoot, and the route is often diverted around last year's morasses.

It's possible to do the route in two legs, via a diversion from the Mallerstang road to Garsdale Station by the Moorcock Inn, taking a train to Kirkby Stephen Station and then a bus back to Kirkby Stephen; the public transport link can then be reversed the next day and the route continued. You can also do a variation on the second half of the walk starting at Cautley (it's the fifth option in the 'Things to do in the Howgills' list in the Howgills chapter).

The first section of the route follows the beginning of stage six of Wainwright's walk, from Kirkby Stephen to Nine Standards Rigg. From Kirkby Stephen, cross Frank's Bridge over the Eden – from where Nine Standards is clearly visible – and make your way through Hartley, past Hartley Castle and up the quarry road, passing the impressively huge and still very much alive Hartley limestone quarry, now managed by Cemex Aggregates. I recommend making a detour of a few yards onto the Merrygill Viaduct, which was acquired by the Northern Viaduct Trust from Cemex in 2005 for £1, after the viaduct was condemned and nearly demolished before being listed, which guaranteed its salvation.

A couple of miles out from Kirkby Stephen the road ends and a very well-trodden path leads up across the moors to Nine Standards Rigg.

The Nine Standards.

Straddling England's watershed, Nine Standards is, to my mind, though lower in order of complexity, as enigmatic and compelling a place as the Stonehenge ritual landscape near which I was brought up. The Standards are a (nearly straight) line of round-topped drystone cairns 2.5 to 3.5m in height, aligned approximately south-southwest to north-northeast. The two most widely heard accounts of their origin states either that they were built by the Romans, who wanted to give the residents of the Eden Valley the impression that there were always troops garrisoned up on the ridge looking down on them; or that the things are an eighteenth or nineteenth century folly. The former is possible I suppose; the latter has been disproved by Stephen Walker, whose definitive *Nine Standards: Ancient Cairns or Modern Folly?* includes accounts of perambulations of the bounds of Kirkby Stephen from the middle of the seventeenth century which mention the 'Nine Standers.' But Stephen Walker argues convincingly that the cairns are much older than that, probably, he says, Bronze Age, which doesn't seem at all far-fetched to me given that many of Cumbria's stone circles are probably of a similar age. Quite what they were meant to signify is, until such time as the site is properly archaeologically examined, anyone's guess: burial cairns, perhaps, or boundary markers. Something ritual, I'd wager: there's a considered solemnity to their layout, a brooding, patient presence. Old? They feel like they've been there longer than the hill on which they sit.

From the cairns, head a little east of south to the summit trig point at 622m, then head to, and follow, the Coast to Coast route a short distance south to the (spectacularly unmarked) county boundary. At this point you should turn south-west and follow the county (and National Park) boundary down, via Dukerdale Head and Lamps Moss, to the B6270 near a shake hole called Jingling Cove: if route finding proves difficult follow the vague path to Lady Dike Head into Yorkshire and then down Lady Dike to join the B6270 half a mile or so south-east of the county boundary signs. Either way, once you're at the county boundary admire the myriad signs (Cumbria, Westmorland, County of North Yorkshire, Yorkshire Dales National Park and Richmondshire all jostle for position, along with an elegant and, at a guess, 17th-18th century milestone proclaiming 'Hamlet of Birkdale County of York.') At nesting time there are also signs asking you not to stray from obvious paths and not to let your dog off the lead: please heed these.

Signs, B6270

Cross the road take the path (past silent, sombre depths, water dripping echoingly into them, revealed by shake holes) up to High Pike, and then along the peaty plateau to High Seat, at 709 metres a metre higher than Wild Boar Fell and the fourth highest point in the Dales (after Whernside, Ingleborough and Great Shunner Fell).

High Seat is one of England's significant watersheds: unlike the higher points in the Dales water falling on the Mallerstang side of High Seat drains into the Eden, and thence into the Irish Sea, while water falling the other side ends up in the Swale, ending up flowing into the North Sea in the Humber. There's a superb view westwards, across Mallerstang to Wild Boar Fell with the Howgills and the distant Lake District: there's an almost tangible sense of being on the very edge of Cumbria. It would feel much more Yorkshire were there a great view eastwards: but there isn't.

Proceed along the top to Gregory Chapel, the next eminence just a couple of contour lines above the main ridge. Here is a curious pile of stones next to a tall, thin cairn: it's unclear whether the stones are the supposed 'chapel', or if the name has something to do with the cairn, which could be said to resemble a chapel tower from a distance: there's no indication of who Gregory was, either. A short distance south of you, at the head of Red Gill, is the source of the Eden; Red Gill soon becomes Hell Gill before becoming the Eden, a pleasing juxtaposition of names, although 'Hell' in this case is simply an old Norse word meaning 'spouting'. The connotations of the name have not, however,

Shake hole under High Pike, guarded by a rabbit.

Looking south along Mallerstang from near High Seat.

been lost on the locals, who named the bridge over the gorge the Devil's Bridge, like the one at Kirkby Stephen.

There's a sad story relating to the source of the Eden in a rare old book, *History and Traditions of Mallerstang Forest and Pendragon Castle* (1883), by the Revd. W. Nicholls, a former vicar of Ravenstonedale. In 1850 a William Mounsey of Carlisle returned home from travels in Egypt and the East and made a homecoming pilgrimage to the source of the Eden, having, as he did so, a stone with a Greek inscription on it set at the river's ultimate source. Nicholls continues:

> the omission [of a translation] led to its destruction, for during the construction of the Midland Railway through this dale, some navvies were spending one Sunday afternoon near the source of the river; discovering the stone, they endeavoured to read it; failing in this, and finding that it was locked up in languages which comparatively few could read, they in a fit of vexation broke it into three pieces.

Next along is the third and final little summit of the ridge, Hugh Seat. The Hugh in question was Hugh de Morville, Earl of Cumberland, Lord of the Manor of Mallerstang and one of the knights responsible for murdering Thomas Beckett in Canterbury Cathedral in 1170. Nearby is Lady's Pillar, erected by Lady Anne Clifford, whose married name was Pembroke: the inscription 'AP1644' can still be seen inscribed into one of the pillar's stones. We'll hear more of the Earl and the Countess in the Mallerstang chapter.

There's a tale relating to Hell Gill, concerning the notorious highwayman Dick Turpin, who supposedly jumped the gorge on his trusty Black Bess, making good his escape into Yorkshire, where the warrant which had been issued for his arrest in Westmorland was useless. It's almost certainly a myth, like most of the stories which attach to Dick Turpin, who so far as is known never came this far north. There is the story that he rode from London to York in eleven hours, an impossible feat: it's likely that this story originated in a feat performed by an earlier highwayman, John 'Swift Nick' Nevison, who rode from Kent to York, using several horses, in fifteen hours in order to establish an alibi for himself, and the story later stuck itself to Dick Turpin: it's possible the same happened in the case of the Mallerstang legend.

From here, either carry on along the Dales park boundary to Scarth of Scaithes and then down to Hell Gill Beck, or just drop down to the beck by whatever route takes your fancy. A little way above Hell Gill Bridge you'll have to detour round the trees which line the ravine above Hell Gill Bridge – from where the view of the river far below you is impressive – then follow the track down to Hellgill Force, the first, and the highest, waterfall on the course of the Eden. I was once absent mindedly filling an empty plastic bottle with water here when I realised the bottle had originally contained Asda's own brand mineral water, which is named Eden Falls.

Once down at the road the climbing begins, via shake holes and small caves up to Swarth Fell then Wild Boar Fell. Legend has it that the last wild boar in England was killed here: there are conflicting stories as to who performed this deed but all the stories agree that whoever did the killing knew he (and it was certainly a he) was killing England's last wild boar, an act which seems a crime to us, like the killing of the last dodo: but, as Dawn Robertson says, in *Secrets and Legends of Old Westmorland:*

Looking up to the Nab, Wild Boar Fell.

Today the poor lonely wild boar would have been a target for sympathy, media attention and conservation. Six hundred years ago the boar was seen simply as a prize – a tusked and savage animal deserving of death. The boar was a symbol of the beast which in race memory haunted man with fear. Times when people huddled round a fire whilst animals lurked and howled in the darkness were not long gone [...] to kill the last wild boar was to lighten the darkness.

Cloud on Wild Boar Fell, from the Kirkby Stephen to Tebay road.

David Bellamy has called the North Pennines 'England's Last Wilderness', and certainly it's a fitting place in which to have found England's last wild boar. The most likely assassin was Sir Richard de Musgrave, who died in 1464. When his tomb was opened in 1847 tusks of a wild boar were found, which are still in Kirkby Stephen church, a circumstance which adds a very rare piece of evidence to such an early legend.

Like most of the north-western Pennines, Wild Boar Fell is limestone topped with Millstone Grit (millstones were in fact made here: you can see roughed out millstones abandoned on the eastern flank around Yoadcomb Scar). There's an ancient tumulus on the summit of the Nab, I guess Bronze Age, the likely age of the Nine Standards, although it's known the Celts frequented here, so really its history is anyone's guess, and on Yoadcomb Scar is a group of cairns suspiciously like miniature versions of those on Nine Standards Rigg. There are more, similar cairns on Little Fell to the north. There have been murmured plans on and off over the last few years about building a wind farm on Wild Boar Fell: for more on this, see the Mallerstang chapter below.

From the Nab make your way down the edge to High Dolphinsty, where you've two choices: either make your way down the bridleway into Mallerstang and back to Kirkby Stephen that way, or simply proceed (or more likely limp) over Little Fell and down to Nateby and Kirkby Stephen. Or, if you're in an armchair, rather than on foot, again, turn to the Mallerstang chapter in the Dales section below.

Golden plovers on Wild Boar Fell (top) and at Jingling Cove (bottom).

Lowick High Common

LATER IN THIS BOOK we'll be exploring quarries in Kentmere, Longsleddale and, especially, Little Langdale, and we passed Hartley gravel quarry in the last chapter. But as quarries, whose aesthetics and historical importance will be explored fully in the Little Langdale chapter, feature significantly in this book, it makes sense to begin with a brief exploration of Lowick High Common, better known as Kirkby Moor: which is, properly speaking, the land the far side of the main Barrow road, where the landscape is dominated not just by quarries old and new but by that much maligned bringer of green energy and local protest, the wind turbine.

It is not, by any stretch of the imagination, a great climb. Not can I much recommend the views: save those up Dunnerdale, if you're set on viewing the Lakes from the south you're miles better off going up Black Combe (see above). But Lowick High Common does have one thing to recommend it, and that's its ability to remind you that the landscape of Cumbria has been, and in many places still is, a surprisingly productive place: given its harsh climate, its wool, lamb, beef, metals, turned wood products, minerals and, especially from our current site of interest, slate have been of national importance for centuries, and here slate quarrying still happens on a large scale: as opposed to at Honister, where slate mining was revived in 1997 largely as a (very good) tourist attraction.

The remains of the quarrying industry are worth a look, though better will be visited in the chapters on Little Langdale and Kentmere. But only on Kirkby Moor can you watch heavy machinery still pulling the stuff out of the hillsides, and reflect that this still-continuing quarrying of Lake District stone dates back to the slopes of the Langdale Pikes in the Neolithic.

Black Combe across Burlington quarries.

Gully leading up to Lowick High Common.

Kirkby Moor nowadays is giving way increasingly to the production of a new resource, wind energy, whose growing presence in Cumbria has provoked very considerable opposition. A typical sentence from a website reads: 'Wind farms could spoil substantial areas of Cumbria's natural beauty and the total electricity produced might be less than the capacity of a single nuclear powered station!' which last fact initially struck me as bleedin' obvious: a few glorified windmills can't really be compared to a nuclear reactor, I thought. But the recently-completed wind farm off the south-west of Walney Island is 130-odd turbines strong and capable of producing 370 Megawatts (MW): the Calder Hall reactor at Sellafield produced, when it was opened by the Queen in 1956, a capacity of 156 megawatts: so the outputs of big wind farms these days can be compared to more conventional power stations. When the wind's blowing, of course. With plans for another big farm on the Duddon Sands and further developments ongoing in the extant farms around St. Bees and Whitehaven, I think further wind farms around the coast are inevitable.

At the time this book goes to press the future of the Sellafield site seems certain: there will be decommissioning, phenomenal cost, leakage of nuclear waste and no more generation of power. This bleak assessment comes following a decision by Cumbria County Council in 2013 not to pursue construction of a deep water waste storage facility due to the inherent geological instability of the area (tracking enthusiasts might like to take note). So decommissioning continues, a process made more complicated by the presence of sealed rooms on the site dating back to the early days of research into both nuclear power and nuclear weapons.

One facility on site that is still operational is the THORP (Thermal Oxide Reprocessing Plant). This reprocesses spent nuclear fuel to separate the 96% uranium and 1% plutonium from the 3% of radioactive waste, which is treated and stored at the plant. The uranium is then made available for customers to be manufactured into new fuel. Work on the facility was begun in the 1970s, and went into operation in 1997 and was due to close in 2010: after making losses of something like £1bn. The facility was closed from 2005-7, following the discovery of a leak, then again in 2007-8 after an underwater hoist failed. In November 2008, Sellafield was handed over to a new consortium with a five year £6.5bn decommissioning contract. In October 2008 it was revealed that the British government had agreed to issue Sellafield an unlimited indemnity against future accidents; according to *The Guardian* "the indemnity even covers accidents and leaks that are the consortium's fault." The indemnity had been rushed through prior to the summer parliamentary recess without notifying parliament. In late 2013 the cost of decommissioning had reached an astronomical £70bn: this amount of expenditure on shoring up the site makes it extremely unlikely it'll ever be considered for electricity generation again. THORP is currently destined to close in 2018.

I recently watched an eerie, frightening documentary called *Into Eternity*. Directed and narrated by Danish director Michael Madsen, and released in 2010, it follows the construction of the Onkalo waste repository at the Olkiluoto Nuclear Power Plant on the island of Olkiluoto, Finland. The site was chosen as, 500m down into the bedrock on which the island stands, there are enormously stable geological and tectonic conditions which should endure for the envisaged lifetime of the installation, which is 100,000 years. At the time of writing the facility is still being built: the burial of spent fuel on the site, is projected to begin around 2020, and when it is full the site will be totally sealed, all access tunnels and associated infrastructure removed and the waste left for the oblivion of deep time.

That is the plan: but the builders of the facility, Finnish company Possiva Oy, had nevertheless to consider the possibility of the waste store somehow surfacing, rupturing, or being inadvertently discovered as far into the future as 100,000 years: or some ten times longer than the human archaeological record of building in stone. They had to consider, however tenuously, such eventualities as global natural or environmental catastrophe, or the total collapse of civilisation as we know it. In the case of the former, the Onkalo site could represent a major hazard if accidentally discovered by people unaware of the danger locked inside. In the case of the latter, the bunker could become viewed, if it could be accessed, as a weapon; in either case the waste could be seen as having great energy potential stored inside it, but at a perilous price of access.

They even went as far as to consider if alien visitors spotted the site from space: how could they, planning the build in the present, build warnings into the site to make it universally understandable that it is not to be tampered with? With this, the realities of long-tern deep nuclear waste storage, in mind, perhaps it is best there's to be no smiliar facility under Cumbria. I once heard and felt an earth tremor come across the Bay as I was sitting in the reading room at Lancaster University library. The area's not totally geologically stable. Pilot shale gas drilling – 'fracking', essentially a way of spending a lot of money to extract small amounts of fossil fuels from deep underground to feed the fossil fuel resources of an economy which hasn't yet been brave enough to realise how totally fossil fuel dependent it is – has recently had to be stopped near Blackpool due so seismic tremors in the area.

In the early autumn of 2007 I reached the summit of the Old Man of Coniston, glanced coastwards and was astonished to see that the chimney of Calder Hall was gone. I've never found Sellafield to be a blot on the landscape: that such a huge industrial complex can look so tiny from the mountains – and that it can also look so tiny when the hills form its backdrop – only seems, to me, to make the mountains, and their coastal plain, all the more impressive.

So it is with wind turbines, when located thoughtfully, they can enrich the cultural landscape rather than detract from it. I agree: I find them an awesome sight, possessed of a gigantic beauty, a clear sign of the continuation of the human uses of a landscape whose resources have been exploited – if that's the right word, and I'm not sure it is – for millennia.

Lambrigg wind farm.

The Bowder Stone.

Castle Crag

THERE'S NOWHERE IN Borrowdale, the historically, culturally and sceni-cally rich valley south of Derwent water, which is particularly lonely: its attractions, especially the boudering on the Bowder Stone, draw many a visi-tor year-round. But it would be a great injustice not to mention Castle Crag here. The only one of the Wainwrights under a thousand feet (and at 290m, or 951 feet, it's significantly shorter than the magic 1000), Wainwright is never-theless unstinting in his praise of the delights of the fell: "so magnificently independent, so ruggedly individual, so aggressively unashamed of its lack of inches," he says. As usual, he's right.

Given that I was going to have to climb Cat Bells some time if I was going to 'bag' all the Wainwrights, I picked a wet, cloudy, horrible Tuesday morning in February, hoping to miss the crowds and actually be able to park the car near the path onto the fells. I still struggled to park, and stopped counting after I'd overtaken a hundred people on the (admittedly spectacular) walk up to the summit: then, despite being more than ready for my sandwiches, I pressed on the mile or so to Maiden Moor, leaving the crowds behind. By the time I got to the top it was pouring down: the valley of the great Goldscope copper mine was completely hidden in scraps of cloud tearing by in strong winds. I ended

Looking up Castle Crag.

up having the sandwiches in an old level at Rigghead – it's quite eerie eating lunch in a puddle somewhere under a mountain, the supporting timbers creaking all around you, water running down behind them, daylight like a small porthole at the other end of a dark hole – before setting off downhill, when – as so often happens when you're leaving the tops – the weather began to clear. I had a beautiful wander down into Borrowdale and, feeling that I hadn't had enough summits that day, decided that a stroll up to the lowest of all the Wainwrights (and one of the two Wainwrights that aren't Birketts) wouldn't be much of an effort.

It wasn't. But I'd never really given the shortest of all the Wainwrights a second thought. Castle Crag, tiny, entirely hemmed in by the higher fells all around: what was the point? How could Castle Crag eclipse Walla Crag, or even the popular (but charmingly wooded) Latrigg?

I was completely enchanted. Castle Crag is a confusing jumble of hazel woods and old quarry faces, and I scrambled up. Scrambled is the right word: the path is made of loose slate pebbles, and there are a few interesting crags and outcrops you can traverse round or scramble up on the summit, especially around the old quarry adjacent to the small summit plateau, which is full of standing stones, miniature cairns and wierd-looking stone sculptures that generations (I'm guessing) of visitors have variously constructed or erected out of stones left behind when the quarry was abandoned.

On the summit is a war memorial which reads:

Castle Crag was given to the National Trust in memory of John Hamer 2nd

Lieut: 6th KSLI [King's Shropshire Light Infantry] born July 8 1897 killed in action March 22 1918.

It goes on to list the other men of Borrowdale who died in the same cause. Another memorial on the fell's western flank repeats some of this information in a somewhat more personal form:

The land surrounding the summit of Castle Crag was given to the nation in memory of Sir William Hamer MA MD FRCP by his wife Agnes whom this seat commemorates 1939

The views up the valley over Derwent Water's islands to Keswick and the fells beyond are magnificent, those in other directions surprisingly good considering

Looking to Derwent Water from Castle Crag.

how hemmed-in the fell feels.

Eventually, it was time to leave the summit for the wander back along Borrowdale and Derwent Water to Keswick and the car. But, seeing the words 'quarry' and 'caves' on the fell's eastern flank, I thought that rather than retrace my steps I'd head straight down the fell that way and see what I came to. The descent was more, let's say, exciting than I had bargained for, surprisingly steep in places among the hazels and little oaks, but I found a way down to the quarry, where I poked around the caves and found copious quantities of wild strawberries. I also found a sheep so deeply asleep she was completely oblivious to my photographing her and her lambs from a range of a couple of feet, which was a surreal experience. Then I remembered something I'd filed away in the back of my mind to visit when I finally got round to coming this way: Millican Dalton's cave.

Millican Dalton seems, at first glance, to have been a '60s dropout way before his time, easily dismissed as a curious eccentric with some quaint ideas which were pretty avant garde in his day, would have had a few eyebrows raised at them forty or so years ago, and which the council would quickly put a stop to these days by moving him on. But, when you seek out the cave he called home for much of the year for half a century, you can't help but begin to wonder otherwise. He's one of the Lake District's less known but great characters, and one of its great pioneering explorers from a time when the predominantly guided mountain experts of Wordsworth and the Victorians gave way to the more independent exploits of the generation of adventurers who defined the modern view of the Lakes as an all-encompassing outdoor playground.

Millican (baptised with his mother's maiden name) Dalton was born on 20 April 1867 at Nenthead, east of Alston on the Cumberland/Yorkshire/Northumberland border. His father had been an agent of the London Lead Company (LLC), but died when Millican was seven. His maternal grandfather, who worked for the LLC, and the LLC itself, ensured the family were provided for, and after Millican's grandfather's death they moved south to Middlesex in search of a comfortable suburban lifestyle. Young Millican and his brothers spent the remainder of their childhoods out in the woods and streams with a length of climbing rope, and camping in Epping Forest. Millican followed his elder brother into a city job in insurance, spending holidays camping and exploring the Lakes, Scotland and Wales, cycling, canoeing and experimenting with lightweight camping. He was an early convert to the new sport of rock climbing in the late 1880s, and an early member of the Association of Cycle Campers, now the Camping and Caravanning Club, from about 1907.

Clearly the holidays began to take precedence over the day job. Millican bought a piece of land in Essex on which to live, still commuting to the City, but dreamed of more complete freedom. He resigned his job in 1903 and moved full-time onto his plot of land, determined to find employment as an outdoor and mountain guide. He advertised and ran climbing, walking, camping and watersports holidays in the UK and the Alps, all the while gravitating more and more towards the Lakes. He based himself first at a campsite above High Lodore Farm at the south end of Derwent Water in the summer, returning to his plots of land, first in Essex and later near Epping Forest, in the winter. Contrary to some reports he did own a house on some land near Epping for many years, but he moved his southern home to Buckinghamshire in the 1920s and then really did give up bricks and mortar, living in tents all year round when he wasn't in the Borrowdale cave, although he did later build a wooden shed on his Buckinghamshire plot to provide some comfort in old age.

Millican guided parties of the hardier kinds of tourists – generally, contrary to the etiquette of the day, mixed gender parties – all over the lakes on itineraries advertised as 'CAMPING TOURS Through Lovely Scenery: ADVENTURES – NIGHT RAMBLES – BOATING – RAPID SHOOTING – BATHING – MOUNTAINEERING.' Specialities included rafting on Derwent Water and climbing on Pillar Rock or in Doves' Nest Crags, the maze of caves caused by rockfalls on the north side of Glaramara. A teetotal, vegetarian, chain-smoking caffeine addict, a manufacturer of lightweight tents, rucksacks and sleeping bags, Dalton was a larger than life character (he claimed with some authority to have invented shorts) who became a local legend.

In 1919 he led an ambitious expedition to the Austrian Alps with a number of established Lake District clients: some time between 1905 and 1914 he climbed the Matterhorn: and some time about the latter date, 1914, Millican moved more or less permanently, in the summer months and between nights out on the hills alone or with clients, into the cave in the side of Castle Crag.

More at the bottom of Castle Crag, I suppose, but you do have to climb from the path and it's much more romantic to think of the caveman perched on his eerie crag. The cave, split into two levels, the upper of which Millican called the 'Attic', still seems in a way as if its resident of a good 30 summers might just be up a fell somewhere nearby, to return at any moment. Carvings, most notably the one which reads "Don't!! Waste words, jump to conclusions!" by the cave entrance, still bear testament to Millican's time in the cave. Millican's reaction to the Second World War, the influx of evacuees to his winter home in Buckinghamshire and the compulsory blackouts aimed at baffling the German bombers, was to stay in the Lakes, and in his cave, through the winters, and he appeared in a feature in the *Daily Mirror* in January 1941, photographed outside the cave whose entrance was full of icicles as long as he was tall.

Finally he relocated to his hut in Buckinghamshire, which burnt down in the winter of 1946-7. He moved into a tent outside, in which he caught bronchitis and pneumonia and died in a local hospital in February 1947 aged 79.

Back O'Skiddaw

IN CONTRADICTION to the picturesque aesthetic of its early tourists, the Lake District is nowadays famous not because of its lakes, but because of its mountains. So here's a question: what are the four big mountains which mark the northern, southern, eastern and western edges of the Lakes?

The answer is simple: Skiddaw, Coniston Old Man, Pillar and High Street. Southwards the range of Lake District Mountains comes to an abrupt end with the Old Man, where Dow Crag dips down to Walna Scar, Dunnerdale and the Bay; westwards, Pillar's lonely magnificence looks across its little sister peak, Haycock, to the Irish Sea; eastwards, the flatness of High Street's plateau, though complemented by its more ruggedly mountainous neighbours (Ill Bell,

Frozen grass, Caldbeck Fells

Gray Crag, Eagle Crag), hints at the changing landscape towards new ranges, Shap Fells and the Howgills and Pennines.

But things are different in the north: it's as if geography somehow knows Scotland is coming, and has been struggling away, trying to keep up the altitude.

Stand on Skiddaw on a clear day and look north and east and you'll see a wilderness of big hills, admittedly only two of them over 700m (Knott and Bowscale Fell), and looking rather lowly from Skiddaw's commanding 931m; but stand on Knott or Bowscale Fell (or any of the tops you can see spread out below you looking northwards from Skiddaw) and you'll feel on top of the world. And, probably, quite cold.

MIDWINTER IN MIDSUMMER

The Uldale and Caldbeck Fells (I tend to think of the whole area as the Caldbecks, but strictly the name only applies to the eastern two thirds or so) are a superb range of mountains, especially suited to winter walking, when their more challenging aspects are magnified and when, on days when snow and ice would make, say, Sharp Edge on Blencathra too dangerous for types

Shooting hut, Lingy Hill.

like me who don't carry ropes and ice axes, they provide simply superb high level walking with far-ranging views of Skiddaw, Blencathra, the northern Pennines, the Isle of Man and across the Solway to Scotland. There are scrambles, gullies, plateaus and crags, ancient hill forts and mines and levels, in short everything you could wish for, and especially so when everything's covered in snow. I don't quite know why, but the Caldbeck Fells are to me inextricably linked with winter, proper, 'in the bleak' midwinter: and they're quite capable of feeling wintry even in the middle of June.

One midsummer's day I set out from Mosedale to climb Carrock Fell. As I made my way along the Calder to the old mine and the Cumbria Way the cloud was determinedly sticking to the hillside at around the 500 metre contour, but having inspected the old mine – where, apparently, alongside the more usual lead and copper, tungsten and even tiny amounts of gold were mined – I pressed on to the top of Grainsgill Beck, where I disappeared into thick, soaking, freezing cloud. By the time I reached the old wooden shooting hut (mentioned by Wainwright) under Great Lingy Hill I was freezing cold and numb-fingered, in spite of my exertions. I sought shelter in the hut, flicking through the visitor's book full of the comments of Cumbria Way walkers, and thawed out, poring over the map. I know it sounds impossible, but the freezing fog howling past outside was enough to make me seriously worried about stumbling into a bog somewhere along the broad saddle that leads to Carrock Fell: so I changed my mind and, back out in the cold, managed to find the top of High Pike (I nearly missed it twice) before making my way gladly down through mines and quarries to Wood Hall, and then squelched my way back to the car.

BANNERDALE CRAGS AND BOWSCALE FELL

I didn't return to the Caldbecks until after the next New Year, when one Saturday we were heading to my mother-in-law's at Kielder, were in no hurry,

Caldbeck footpath sign.

and decided a climb *en route*, not too far from the M6, might be a good idea. A quick scour of the map and Bannerdale Crags and Bowscale Fell looked in order.

Mungrisdale is beautiful in a way only the villages north of Skiddaw seem to possess: more reminiscent of remote Scottish villages than Lake District ones, sparser, tougher, a little

Thirza approaching the Bannerdale Crags scramble.

grubbier perhaps, but all the more captivating for it. Leaving Mosedale, Mungrisdale, Hesket Newmarket, Uldale or, especially, Caldbeck, heading for the winter fells and the wild country, brings with it a trepidation, a sense of loneliness and of enormous space ahead, that doesn't come when leaving other, more popular – or more pastoral – haunts. And after a day up there, coming down off the fells in the dark, cradling a well-earned pint, making the long drive in the dark back home, lying in bed remembering the day, sitting at the desk the next working day: walking these fells in winter leaves a stronger, more enduring sense of having been 'out there' than anywhere I know – even the empty Howgills. We set off from Mungrisdale and enjoyed the walk along the Glendermackin, with the long hump of Souther Fell to our left and our first objective, the east rib of Bannerdale Crags, dominating the view ahead.

At the ford across Bannerdale Beck a slight but distinct path led up over the peaty lower spur to the beginnings of the broken rock of the ridge proper at the level of the various old mine workings shown on the map: here, as elsewhere in the Skiddaw Slate group, lead was mined, as well as some copper, most successfully from 1853 until the end of the nineteenth century: as Ian Tyler's very good *Lakes and Cumbria Mines Guide* says, there are signs of the lead vein here having been "energetically tried in at least four places", and because of the site's remoteness the remains look much as they were left. The inaccessibility of some of the mines and levels shown on the face of Bannerdale Crags to the north speaks volumes of the value of lead ore – a piece of which I found later on my walk – to bygone prospectors.

The path steepened and, just before steep walking gave way to gentle scrambling, we came across a small, low-walled shelter – constructed, perhaps, by cold and windswept miners to protect their fingers from icy winds as they performed their assays up here – which proved a perfect picnic site, with views over Souther Fell to the plantations around Matterdale End, the Mell Fells, Askham Fell and the northern end of the Helvellyn group. Then the scramble continued, ending suddenly on the virtually flat summit plateau (another hundred metres or so would be nice, but you can't have everything – even Sharp Edge could do with being longer). The centrepiece of the cairn

On Bannerdale Crags.

is a piece of slate that sticks up like a fossilised Stegosaurus spike, and the centrepiece of the view is Blencathra.

Blencathra looks odd from this side for two reasons: partly because from the north it looks so uncannily the same as in the more familiar view from the south, with Sharp Edge and Foule Crag mimicking Sharp Edge and Hallsfell

On the summit of Bowscale Fell.

Edge (you tend to forget about poor Doddick Fell), nearness distorting the different scale; and partly because you get so used to seeing Blencathra in splendid isolation that it's odd to see it connected to the ground beneath your feet by the gentle sweep of Mungrisdale Common, only 250 metres lower than the top of Blencathra.

That's the end of the steep stuff on this walk, but not of the views: Bannerdale Crags and Bannerdale itself far below you present as impressive a clifftop panorama as you could wish for, and by the top of Bowscale Fell the views of Skiddaw and the Caldbecks have really opened up.

SOUTHER FELL

Souther Fell is a fine viewpoint, too, and a good place to watch the winter sunset across the saddleback of Blencathra, safe in the knowledge that the descent in the dark won't be fraught with danger. Go the long way round back to Mungrisdale and the comfort of the Mill Inn: either drop down to the River Glendermackin using the footpath at the fell's southern end, or alternatively head down to the minor road which connects Mungrisdale and Scales Farm: eschew the footpath leading down across through Mousthwaite Comb to Comb Beck, and instead take the path down across Knotts, enjoying the sunset afterglow and watching the traffic zooming along the A66 below you. I don't know which is the lonelier, silence and darkness in the valley or the view of the dual carriageway and distant Penrith from Knotts.

BINSEY

A late autumn climb of Binsey proved as difficult a climb as I've done in the Lakes, on account of genuine storm force winds: we literally had to cling to the summit trig point to stop ourselves being blown away and, the wind being easterly, the first hundred metres or so of not at all steep, very easy path back towards where we'd parked, on the road that skirts Binsey between Uldale and Bassenthwaite, had to be negotiated on hands and knees. The whole walk, there and back, had been a little over a mile, but we felt like we'd just been up Scafell.

It had been well worth it, though: the day, though windy, had been very clear, and Binsey is, as Wainwright puts is, "a viewpoint of outstanding merit." I've already raved about the view of Skiddaw and Blencathra from the Caldbeck Fells, and will again, but from Binsey you get a view of the view, as it were: the Caldbecks, with Skiddaw and Blencathra beyond. You can also see the Isle of Man – with, if you're lucky, the Mountains of Mourne in Ireland just to the north; and there's no viewpoint short of the north Cumbrian coast which makes Scotland feel closer. But, above all, again there's that view of Skiddaw and Blencathra across the Uldale and Caldbeck fells: the view that made me determined to get to know those fells better.

CALDBECK MINES

When you're not up on the hills, Uldale, Mungrisdale, Hesket Newmarket and Caldbeck are all worth a visit: all feel remote and bleak in an appealing way, here in this forgotten bottom garden of the Lake District. Caldbeck Church, St. Kentigern's, deserves a mention: its graveyard contains the rather ornate grave of John Peel, of the famous hunting song, and the less ornate grave of Mary Robinson, Mary of Buttermere, the famous beauty (if you're looking for the grave, here's a clue: the text begins, "In memory of Mary, the Wife of Richard Harrison..." John Peel, born around 1777, made a financially advantageous marriage which freed him to spend his time hunting and drinking: so passionate was he about the former that a friend said of him, "I believe he would not have left the drag of a fox on the impending death of a child or any other earthly event."

Mary, meanwhile, was the daughter of the proprietors of the Fish Hotel at Buttermere, at about the same time as John Peel. When she was about fifteen Joseph Palmer met her and extolled her beauty in his *A Fortnight's Ramble in the Lakes in Westmorland, Lancashire and Cumberland*, published in 1792. Visitors began to flock to see her in Buttermere, and in 1802 she was successfully wooed by a Colonel Alexander Hope, an MP and brother of the Earl of Hopetoun. The marriage was announced in a London paper through its

John Peel's grave.

Keswick correspondent – Samuel Taylor Coleridge, no less. Thanks to this it was soon discovered that the real Colonel Hope was abroad at the time and that Mary's husband was an imposter, and also a bigamist, being already married to a lady in Tiverton. His real name was John Hatfield, he was a bankrupt and had conned money out of several people in the area. When news of his discovery reached him he did a runner, making his way to Wales: arrested near Swansea he was tried at the local Carlisle Court of Assize and hanged. Mary later married Richard Harrison of Caldbeck, who helped her to run the inn in her parents' old age. Later in life they moved back to Richard's native Caldbeck, where Mary died on 7 February 1837.

A local saying has it that, "Caldbeck fells are worth all England else," such is the wealth of minerals and metal ores that have been mined in the area. The views and villages aside, these hills are worth visiting for, as I have said, their interest as objectives for winter walks, for the remains of mines both ancient and modern (predominantly the former) and, in a few places, for scrambles up gills and scree faces. I've already described the Bowscale scramble. Another of very different character, and with more, and more interesting mining remains, is the climb up to Thief Gills, three streams which become Roughton Gill, a tributary of a very schizophrenic river: Dale Beck, which after a mile or so becomes Branthwaite Beck; a few hundred yards further it's Parkend Beck, then Whelpo Beck, then finally Caldbeck and the River Caldew, which joins the Eden at Stanwix, the site of the old Roman fort at Carlisle.

Start at Fell Side, a mile and a bit south-east of Caldbeck. At Ingray Gill (where prospectors have found specks of gold) is a brick building housing a water intake, and a large area, to the right of the footpath, which has been fenced off and planted with deciduous trees by the National Park authority as part of a bid to encourage biodiversity. The area (it's a pretty big one) is open access land: the fences (with gates) are to keep the sheep and the fell ponies, but not the walkers, out.

Looking up Dale Beck, Iron Crag in the centre.

The walk up Dale Beck is easy and pleasant, on a good track: watch out for ponies on the hillsides and buzzards overhead. It's a good mile and a half up to the head of the valley, passing the ruins of an old smelt house, which was apparently never used, at Hay Gill, where Clints Gill, Roughton Gill and

Winter tree above Roughton Gill.

Silver Gill come pouring out of three steep ravines. Roughton Gill's huge complex of mines, including the 19th century Mexico Mine up Clints Gill, are considered important enough that the National Park authority, in partnership with English Heritage, has recently carried out a detailed survey of the area to assess how the site might best be conserved.

Queen Elizabeth I hired a group of German mining experts to mine copper around Keswick in the 1560s, and once mines in Borrowdale were well-established the miners began to look further afield for new copper, lead, even gold and silver seams. This was the origin of the Coniston mining industry, and also of metal mining in the Caldbeck Fells.

Contemporaneous documents refer to the Caldbeck mines, mined by the Company of Mines Royal between 1568 to 1630 and, while we can't be certain which mines the documents refer to, it's probably the mines around here.

Even if the Elizabethans were never here, from 1693 Edward Wright of the Company of Copper Miners in England is known to have been mining at Roughton Gill. Mining stopped after about 1730, but began again, and more profitably than before, in the early 19th century. There are various papers in the National Archives relating to these mines, including a draft lease relating to the Caldbeck mines, for a period of 21 years from June 1849, in which George William Richard, Earl of Pomfret, Sir George William Denys and Sir Francis Shuckburgh leased the mining here to a Henry Compton of Fenchurch Street, London. Another lease was made to, "James William Dixon of Sheffield, merchant and Samuel Merryweather of Caldbeck, the lessees" in 1855. The National Archives also contain quarterly reports from the mines for

Levels, Roughton Gill.

the years 1861-74, and records of the sales of Roughton copper and lead between 1852 and 1876.

The Caldbeck Fells Consolidated Lead and Copper Mining Company Ltd worked here from 1865,* but by then most of the workable metal ore had been extracted and they went bankrupt in 1876. Sporadic attempts were made at the levels thereafter, but the deepest mine, the 90-fathom mine, was bought by Carlisle City Council, who piped the water draining from it into the local mains water supply and sealed the entrance.

There's an old mining building here which served as an office and bothy, your first point of contact with the remains of the mining industry: it's all very jumbled up, and hard for the untrained eye (like mine) to date what's Elizabethan, what's comparatively modern and what's in between. I'm going to concentrate here on the obvious shafts encountered as you scramble up the gill. If you want to know more, Ian Tyler's *Lakes and Cumbria Mines Guide* is what you need to have in your hand: there's also an OS 1:2500 map, sheet 68.7, published in 1863, but this, so far, has proven difficult to get hold of.

Nearby is the entrance to the 90 fathom mine, complete with blocked man-hole cover. To the left of the old office/bothy a path climbs up and along a mound of mining waste which can be quite loose underfoot. Persevere, or make your way to the edge of the scree and clamber along the heather and rock

---

* You can see one of the company's share certificates online at the library of mining aditnow's mining document library at www.aditnow.co.uk.

at the outer edge, until the path drops down to and crosses the gill. Here is the first open shaft of the ascent, Wharton's Trial, low, narrow and waterlogged, the entrance partially obscured by a mound of mud, which could have descended from above or could be slag: poke around to your heart's content, but several better levels are dotted around the place, the best being found in the ravine by the gill, which also has the advantage of being the most obvious, and most fun, way onto Little Lingy Hill and on to Knott. The gill tumbles down in a series of waterfalls which provide easy, if damp, scrambling: it can be hard going after heavy rain.

Where Roughton Gill gives way to its upper three tributary streams, the pleasingly-named Thief Gills, and the views north really begin to open out, the sense of being about to emerge onto the open tops growing, a final waterfall and dam formed from mining spoil mark the location of what I think is Dobson's Dam trial, a low level again on your left: again a hump, this one in the floor, makes the entrance a bit tight, especially if it's been snowing, but once inside this is the shaft to explore. The water underfoot is likely to be more than ankle deep, and the passage is narrow, but it has reasonable headroom (I'm 6'4") and heads straight into the hillside, curving gently left until the circle of light at the entrance is left behind you. After a while (if you've the nerve) you find some intriguing features, including niches in the walls undoubtedly carved out by the miners as candle ledges. Further on is a spring, a little spout of water jetting out from the left hand wall of the tunnel, which explains why your socks are so wet. I must confess I ran out of nerve, exploring as I was here on my

Somewhere under Little Lingy Hill.

Above, snow ridges between Great Lingy Hill and The Knott and below, Skiddaw in cloud from Great Lingy Hill.

own, and turned back about fifty yards further. One day I'd love to come up here with Ian Tyler, who ran the mining museum at Keswick which closed, sadly, when he retired: he used to give very well regarded guided walks of areas like Roughton Gill.

Finally, you leave the streams behind and emerge onto the moor on the side of Little Lingy Hill. The first time I came here it was late January. It had been sheltered in the gill, though my hands were numb from the waterfalls and the cold air in the levels. On the top it was like stepping into the opening of *The Empire Strikes Back*. There were hare tracks in the snow, which was four or five inches deep at its thinnest and had a top surface frozen so that about every other footstep sank through into the deep grass and heather beneath: not ideal for making swift progress into the near gale force southerly wind blowing cold from between Skiddaw and Blencathra. I reached, eventually, the path up to the top of Knott and jogged up it, slipping and sliding and whooping for joy when I reached the cairn.

Drifts of frozen snow had been mounded everywhere into weird shapes shining in the crystalline afternoon sun: further afield, across the Uldale fells to Binsey and behind it the wind farm at Wharrels Hill; Aughertree Fell and Caldbeck Transmitting Station on the nameless fell behind; Mabie Forest and the hills of Dumfriesshire in the distance: closer at hand the fells around Dale Beck. North-east and east were Great Lingy Hill, High Pike and Carrock Fell, the outline of the old fort visible in the snow, the shooting hut where I'd sheltered the previous midsummer's day looking barely a stone's throw away in

Looking towards Bassenthwaite from The Knott, with Skiddaw on the left.

the clear air: beyond was Cross Fell and the snow-capped Pennines: but, above all, the splendour of Skiddaw and Lonscale Fell and, beyond, Blencathra, their tops concealed loftily in streaming cloud, the sun peering wanly through cloud over Bassenthwaite across Skiddaw's shoulder.

High Pike is another special place. Chris Bonington, who lives in Caldbeck, told the *Whitehaven News* that it's a hill "I return to after climbing some serious peak in the Himalaya or Alps and return to earth. It has the most wonderful changing moods. The light is ever-shifting across the fell making a kaleidoscope of colours, and its wildlife is fascinating."*

I stayed as long as I could, photographing and reminiscing about visits to all the places I could see, until cold and the declining sun forced me into movement. From Great Sca Fell and Brae Fell there were more views of Skiddaw and the hills around Bassenthwaite: it was dark when I got back to Fell Side, the sky was clearing and the stars were coming out. Driving home down the familiar M6 my head was full of ghostly images of white winter hills under a scouring wind.

CARROCK FELL

The Howgills have, by and large, only been of interest to shepherds and horse dealers; Black Combe and the Skiddaw Fells to shepherds, miners and, in the case of Skiddaw and her children, the Blencathra foxhounds. They are largely ahistorical, and aside from industrial remains the only words that appear on OS maps are place names.

Carrock Fell is the exception, though, with the maps proclaiming 'Fort' on the summit. This site is Iron Age, although it contains an earlier, Bronze Age burial cairn. In order to smelt iron, a useful prerequisite is iron ore, which has been mined profitably from the slopes of Carrock Fell, so maybe it's not surprising that the fort is Iron Age. It may well be that the fort, which was pretty large and whose collapsed outer walls are still very much in evidence in an oval around the summit, was destroyed by the Romans, who were keen to crush the resisting Carvetti tribe, who we met in the Helm chapter above: the Helm has its own iron age summit fort, Castlesteads, although this is pretty tiny compared to Carrock Fell's. It's also distinctly possible that the Carrock Fell fort was rebuilt by another tribe, the more peaceable Brigantes from further south, who annexed former Carvetti lands, were less troublesome to the Roman administration and who were granted the status of *civitates foederate*, which translates as something like "semi-autonomous friendly tribe from whom we don't expect a lot of trouble and who keep the local soldiers in meat and beer." So 'Iron Age' in the later Cumbrian context might mean 'Roman-ish,' or even 'dark age.'

---

* The article in question was about a series of climbs done to celebrate the 50th anniversary of the publication of Wainwright's first guide, *The Eastern Fells*, and appeared in the *Whitehaven News*, 20 May 2005.

It was always misty in Dark Age England – at least, it was if all the films about King Arthur are anything to go by. A good thing too, as if it weren't so everyone would be able to see the approach of the invading hordes of Picts/Romans/Saxons, and all the surprise would be lost. It's certainly very often misty on Carrock Fell, and windy, as is generally the case north of Skiddaw somehow, and when it is, it's easy to imagine the surly locals watching the Roman hordes marching by.

If the iron ore did attract Iron Age people, Carrock Fell's geology has retained the interests of miners and mineralogists. Skiddaw and her children are made of Skiddaw Slate, which we met in the Black Combe chapter; the Skiddaw Slates are metamorphic rocks, 'cooked' by granite, which is essentially magma which has cooled to form rock, and which is found (and mined) around Shap: it also underlies Carrock Fell. But unlike the surrounding fells Carrock Fell is largely made of gabbro, the stuff of the Skye Cuillin (and found in a layer in most oceanic crusts): gabbro is chemically identical to basalt, being cooled lava, the difference being that like granite, and unlike basalt, gabbro is formed underground. It's good for climbing, much more so than the crumbly Skiddaw Slates. And its unique (to the Lake

Above, frog on Carrock Fell and below looking up through the rain to the fort.

*Looking south from the path up from Apronful of Stones, near Mosedale and,
below, waterfall at Brandy Gill.*

District) geology means it is unusually rich in minerals. Lead and a dazzling
array of minerals (getting on for a hundred, including arsenic: it's now illegal
to remove minerals from the area without a licence) as well as tungsten, which
was mined here during both World Wars and the Korean War, when there were

shortages which pushed the prices up.

There are remains of mines worth visiting in both the valleys which divide Carrock Fell from her sisters: in the upper reaches of Carrock Beck to the north and by Grainsgill Beck, just above the confluence with the Caldew to the south; the former are more impressive, and more impressively situated, although it's the latter which are known as Carrock Mines. Either way, the mines are best visited on the way down: the best ascent of Carrock Fell by far is straight up from a jumble of erratics called 'Apronful of Stones' on the OS map as a point just north of Stone Ends, nearly due east of the summit. From here a path leads across the hillside towards Further Gill Sike, almost touching it as it turns to head straight up a shallow gully south of Scurth, eventually leaving the gully and passing briefly through a knee-deep (if you're tall) channel in the peat and coming out on the eastern summit of the fell, just a couple of minutes' amble from the hill fort. From here an easy path leads to join the Cumbria Way near High Pike, where it is your decision: left or right. An alternative, shorter route, especially in bad weather, is to head south half a mile or so earlier and to descend by Brandy Gill, which unlike most such diversions presents no significant difficulties or opportunities to get your socks soaked: in fact I'd heartily recommend it. It brings you out right on top of Carrock Mine.

Carrock Fell has one final, somewhat bizarre, claim to fame. In *The Lazy Tour of Two Idle Apprentices*, Charles Dickens tells of an ascent of Carrock Fell by himself and Wilkie Collins, while staying at Hesket Newmarket on a tour of Cumberland in 1857. Dickens tells us he'd read about the fell and had set his heart on making the ascent: infuriatingly, he doesn't tell us where from, or why.

Carrock Fell cloudscape.

Askham Fell

EARLY ONE SUMMER I walked from Kentmere up to the top of Garburn Pass, then along the western half of the Kentmere Horseshoe, up over Yoke, Ill Bell, Froswick and then up to Thornthwaite Beacon. Making my way over High Street, I skirted round The Knott, hid my rucksack at the kink of the drystone wall halfway up Rest Dodd while I popped up to the summit, then headed down to nip up on to Brock Crags and finally, in the late afternoon, pitch a tent by Angle Tarn. By sunrise next day I was standing on Kidsty Pike, then made my way north along the Roman road to Wether Hill and Moor Divock beyond.

A cursory glance at the map a few days previously had shown that following the Roman road all the way from Loadpot Hill into Penrith wasn't feasible, but there seemed to be an obvious route of the familiar green dots and dashes linking the Cockpit stone circle, which the Roman road touched, with Penrith via a little village and a pleasantly wooded looking river valley. At that time, completely under the spell of the mountains of Wainwright's *Eastern Fells*, I didn't really think much more about the last ten or so miles of the expedition that would bring me to Penrith station and home. They were just going to be the cool down exercise, the pleasant but unmemorable couple of hours to be spent running over the important points of what I'd done before collapsing onto the train. How wrong I was.

So, for starters, there was Moor Divock. Coming down from Loadpot Hill

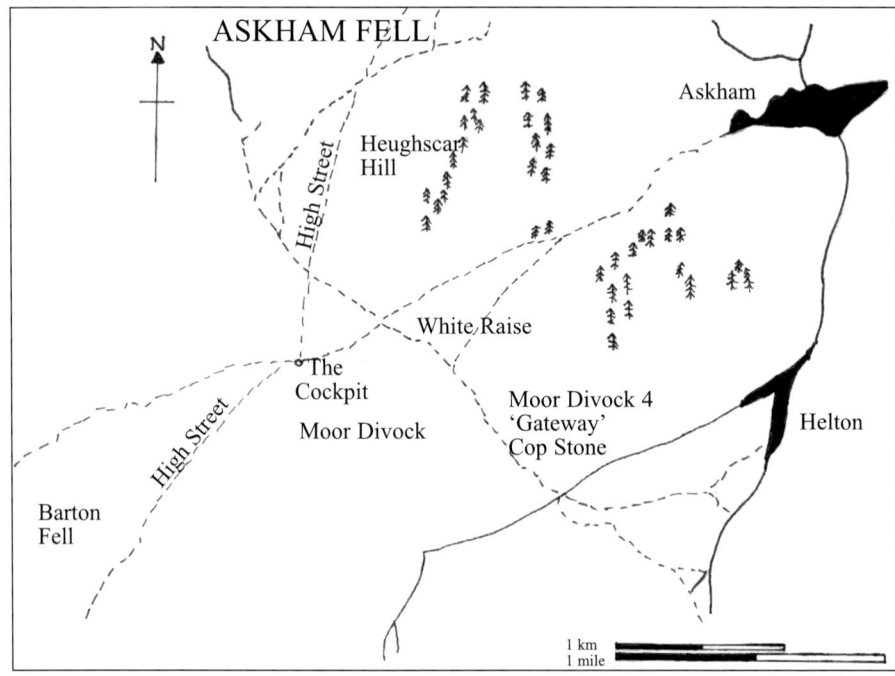

Above, winter sky, Moor Divock, and below, bilberries.

with my hands full of bilberries I reached the Cockpit, which I'd seen on the map. I was brought up close to Stonehenge and to Avebury, so am rather hard to please when it comes to stone circles, but was still a comparative newcomer to this part of the world. I'd been up most of the more popular peaks, could name pretty much every summit as seen from the tops of said peaks, and had begun to develop a list of places off the beaten track that I was intending to explore further. I hadn't really noticed from the map that Moor Divock was likely to become one of the latter. But I was astonished by three things about the Cockpit.

Firstly by the backdrop. Askham Fell is one of those places from which you can see everywhere but which is seen from nowhere. A ring of mountains surrounds it, from the Pennines round to the grassy end of the High Street hills to the fells around Keswick, especially Skiddaw, with Blencathra dominating everything (as it does, from a much greater distance, from Long Meg). Within this theatrical setting the stone circle acts as a frame for the landscape, like a prehistoric version of one of Thomas West's picturesque 'stations'. The feeling that someone else chose this as a vantage point acts as an invitation, which is amplified by the vast chasm of time between the builders of the circle and ourselves, and the vast chasm in understanding: stone circles are powerful

The Cockpit.

reminders that while it's easy to assume we know more than they did, they knew what the stone circles were for. If, that is, they were for anything in particular: but even if they weren't, their builders knew that and we don't. As the Cockpit has never been excavated, it's unknown what might be just beneath your feet.

Secondly, the circle's size surprised me. It's easy to see stone circles – Stonehenge in particular, which has a diameter pretty much identical to that of the Cockpit (about 33-34m) – as being prehistoric man showing off to us: but at the Cockpit that sense is diminished, and the puzzlement increased, by the realisation that (as Tom Clare, in *Prehistoric Monuments of the Lake District*, points out) the stones which form the circle's two concentric rings are by no means large: in fact there are bigger stones lying (apparently) naturally in the cairn field to the south. Why use small stones – and two sets of them – to mark such a big circle? The answer would probably have been laughably obvious to those who built it.

Finally, I was amazed to see that the Roman road curves around the circle: Roman roads, as a rule, are like Mrs. Thatcher – not for turning. The obvious conclusion is that whichever official was responsible for building the road made a conscious decision not to harm it, leading one to conclude that he (I think we can assume it was a he) felt at the very least respect for it. It's well-known that the Romans promiscuously added local deities to their established pantheon of worshipful beings wherever they found them: did legions, passing this way, pause to enact some sacred rite here as a thanks to a local, pagan spirit for safe passage through the hills? Was the same deity worshipped by those who'd built the circle 3,000 years or so before the Romans? The tiny fact of the curve in the road links Neolithic/Bronze Age religion (Moor Divock seems to be, on average, early Bronze Age) to Roman paganism, just as the tiny font in Martindale, which supposedly once lived on High Street at some unknown spot I'd passed early that morning, links Roman paganism with Christianity.

In order to describe the sites and sights of Moor Divock for the visitor who hasn't just spent the night somewhere up near High Street it will be necessary to start at a more likely entry point, where the Pooley Bridge bridleway leaves the dead-end road leading from Helton to Scales Farm, a very minor road off the Askham-Bampton minor road. A mile out of Helton, not long after the road has unquestionably begun to traverse the moorland, a footpath, followed almost immediately by an almost parallel bridleway, leads onto the moor, the two converging just after the Copstone. The bridleway most likely follows the route of an ancient trackway, the main, probably processional artery through what is surely a spacious ritual landscape spread before you, like those which surround Stonehenge and Avebury. But for our purposes the processional nature of the walk ahead will soon become clear, and it's best to start at the Copstone.

The Copstone, even more so than other sites on the moor, is a dilemma. It seems to be some sort of gateway: but, as we'll see shortly, there is a gateway (or at least two stones, close together, through which the way forwards passes) a little further ahead. There is literature suggesting that there was once a stone

The Copstone with Blencathra beyond.

circle here, of which the Copstone was by far and away the biggest, but if this was the case, nothing of the circle remains. It does seem to be a feature of a surviving low bank, however, and it's possible to see one or two stones sticking out of the remains of the bank having once been standing stones. On the other hand, the Copstone could equally be a strikingly-placed glacial erratic.

From here you can see our next two main objectives, Standing Stones stone circle and White Raise. The first of these is found a small stone's throw east of the bridleway 300m on from the Copstone, its distance from the bridleway throwing into doubt the bridleway's claims to being a remnant of an ancient processional route through the ritual landscape: Farrah (in *Transactions of the Cumberland and Westmorland Antiquarian and Archaeological Society*, 1st series, viii, pp. 330-2) reports an old story that Shap Avenue is rumoured to have extended as far as here. The most intriguing, indeed the only likely, and seemingly incontrovertible, remains of this ancient pathway is the above-mentioned, intriguing pair of stones which forms a gateway between the Copstone

'Gateway' stones, Moor Divock 4 and Heughscar Hill.

and the stone circle known as Standing Stones or Druids Cross, marked on the OS maps simply as 'Cairn Circle'. It may be small, but there's something about this place. Moor Divock 4, as its known to the archaeologists, is 440m north-west of the Cop stone and is 11.58m across, consisting of ten large stones set on a bank. It was excavated in the 19th century, when a burial and the remains of a vessel deliberately broken before burial were found. The small size of the site gives it a compelling intimacy: it feels sheltered, almost as if it has an imaginary roof.

Moor Divock 5 is a small circle north-north-west of Moor Divock 4, a site of interest to the archaeologist, but to the more casual visitor the next must see site is the cairn at White Raise. Messed around with by early archaeologists, and having been modified at some stage to act as a sheepfold (the 'spurs' to the north and east of the site are probably related to this former use), the original purpose of the site, conspicuously located on the top of a small rise which would not be significant in most of hilly Cumbria, was probably as a burial site, although the unmistakable remains of a burial cist are not central to the surrounding stones, which it is conjectured may mean that the cist was a later addition to a pre-existing site. When it was excavated in the 1880s the remains of a skeleton were found within.

Finally, any of a multitude of tracks takes you to the Cockpit. As I've described it above I won't say much more, except to add that you'll notice that the larger stones are on the inside of the two concentric circles, which is unusual, and that for such a large circle it's oddly inconspicuous: it's clearly visible from all three nearby junctions of bridleways, but from virtually nowhere else (a fact which puts me in mind of the situation of Stonehenge and its approach along the Avenue); the gentle spur of the end of Barton Fell means it's not really visible from most of High Street. But, again, what it loses in its visual impact from elsewhere is more than made up for by the views it commands. Further mystery, if further mystery were needed, is added by the fact that, as I've said, unlike the lowlier sites scattered across Askham Fell no one's ever excavated the Cockpit. The temptation to start tearing the turf away with my bare hands has, to date, always been tempered with a feeling that, somehow, the mystery is preferable to the knowledge. But the circle certainly has some tantalising linear relationships with some other local monuments, as listed in *A Guide to the Stone Circles of Cumbria* by Robert W. E. Farrah:

> The Cockpit has been located, together with White Raise, in an alignment with the three sister peaks of the high Pennines, Cross Fell, Little Dun Fell and Great Dun Fell in the NE, down the middle reach of Ullswater to Raise, the highest summit visible on the skyline to the SW. It is tempting to suggest that the naming of the mound White Raise and the mountain of Raise is evidence of this intent. Did the form of the mound mirror the giant-like mound of the mountain? From the Cockpit the three Pennine peaks are concealed behind White Raise, which is prominent on the near horizon. It is only on the final approach to the top of the mound that this distinctive landform of the Pennines comes into view.

A review of the site in *Transactions of the Cumberland and Westmorland Antiquarian and Archaeological Society*, 3rd series, volume 6 (2006), says that a soil core taken 65m south-east of the Cockpit shows that the site, when constructed, was on the edge of a shallow tarn, or at the very least a peat bog: it has been speculated that the fact of a tarn slowly drying and becoming a peat bog may have had some significance when it came to the siting of the Cockpit.

Great Mell Fell aligns centrally to the saddle of Blencathra from the Cockpit, and there is a barrow on Great Mell Fell which may be contemporary with the circle, and which has an alignment with Castlerigg stone circle. All clues coded into the landscape: but clues as to what we're totally ignorant.

Holme Fell

ONE OF MY FAVOURITE hill walking routes goes up the Old Man of Coniston from Walna Scar via Buck Pike and Dow Crag, out and back along the Swirl Howe ridge and then back by Goat's Water. But I honestly don't know how many times I've found myself sitting in the car in the car park where the metalled road out of Coniston meets the old Walna Scar miners' track, the car rocking in the wind, trying to peer, through the rain sluicing down the windscreen, up into the Coniston fells, trying to convince myself that heading up there is a good idea: before, inevitably, turning round and heading for a walk in Little Langdale. Aside from the

On Holme Fell.

scramble up Raven Crag to Holme Fell, described below, up which we often take people visiting the Lakes for the first time, my relationship with Little Langdale had reached the point where, as with Walney Island, I seemed to be doing it a disservice by only visiting when the weather was awful – or when I was in a hurry.

Another time, it was a hot summer Saturday evening, the sun not long sunk behind the Coniston fells. I'd spent the day cutting back and burning the laurels and rhododendrons which continually threaten to overtake the garden at Brantwood, John Ruskin's former home on the shores of Coniton Water, and I was tired, smelly, hungry and thirsty. But I'd also spent quite a lot of the day wistfully surveying the Coniston fells, it was still reasonably early. My route home took me past Black Fell, the third lowest of all the Wainwright fells

(Holme Fell then Castle Crag are lower), so I thought I'd make a quick detour and amble up it in passing. I duly left my car at the 90° bend in the road between the Drunken Duck inn and Skelwith Fold, and headed up through the trees.

I don't recall exactly how long the 233m total ascent took, but I do know that by the time I got to the surprisingly substantial summit cairn I'd dragged myself up wooded slopes so steep that I'd had to use branches, even roots, as handholds, got stuck in a gully blocked by a fallen, very prickly and almost unnegotiable pine, had filled a trainer in a bog, had got lost and had generally used a lot more calories than I'd expected to. I'd certainly earned a pint in the Drunken Duck. And the views had been a lot better than I had been expecting, especially, as Wainwright says, in the direction of Windermere; and, generally, Black Fell is a great vindication of Wainwright's theory, stated in his chapter about Pike o' Blisco but applicable to a number of fells, that "height alone counts for nothing." My wife and I once ambled out of Grasmere planning to bag Silver Howe by the directest route possible, imagining it would be a pleasant little stroll. It took me a while to get her back on the fells.

Black Fell's little sister, Holme Fell, a mere 5m lower than Black Fell at 317m, is bordered on its western side by Pierce How Beck which flows into the River Brathay just downstream of Little Langdale Tarn, having flowed through a valley reminiscent of a closed-in version of Little Langdale. A beautiful little dead-end road, somewhat dismissively signposted 'Hodge Close only' from the Hawkshead-Coniston road (the A593), is where we'll begin our exploration of Little Langdale in a chapter in the 'Dale' section later in the book. Inevitably overshadowed by Great Langdale, with its screes, pinnacles and wealth of Neolithic remains, Little Langdale is a valley of completely different character to its bigger sibling; wooded, intimate, gentle, pastoral where Great Langdale is abrupt, vast, awesome. The difference is cemented by the presence of Little Langdale Tarn, which I always think should be simply Langdale Tarn, as Great Langdale is about the only valley in the Lakes without a stretch of open water (there's not much in Eskdale, either). Langdale's picturesque Constable-ness is at odds with the extensive marks left here by slate quarrying. Most visitors – at least those who aren't intent on serious rock climbing or caving – consider these remains 'scars'; I prefer to think of them as traces of an archaeology more striking, if less compelling, than that of Great Langdale. But first, let's leave the car (or the Hawkehead-Coniston bus) and head up Holme Fell

Before you turn to the Little Langdale chapter, there's some climbing to be done – one of the best short easy scrambles in the Lakes (it's a grade 1 and a bit, depending really on how adventurous you're feeling, and has one or two surprisingly adrenaline-inducing moments). It begins at a stile just before a layby big enough for two or three cars (I've never known more than two

Scrambling on Holme Fell.

including my own to be parked there). If it's mid-summer the stile might well be hidden by chest-high bracken. Screwed to the stile is a notice asking you to keep out of the gully east of Raven Crag between 1 March and 30 June. Our route doesn't take us anywhere near this gully, but obviously please obey the sign as peregrines nest here: I've sat and watched them quarrelling with each other about the finer points of chick-rearing for over an hour on more than one occasion. They seemed oblivious to my being there.

The scramble follows a reasonably well-defined route up the tiniest gully imaginable then up a couple of more challenging faces before gradually flattening out before it reaches the grassy, in places slightly boggy, plateau near the top of Holme Fell. A path leads towards the summit to the north-east; another one leads back down Yew Band to a stile and the road a stone's throw from the layby.

From the summit you have views of Wetherlam and the back of the Old Man range, Coniston and Grizedale and, beyond Windermere, the whole panorama of Lakeland fells from the Kentmere fells round to the Langdale Pikes. To your right is Uskdale Gap, a useful way to descend to the beautiful Harry Guards Wood, Yew Tree Tarn and the main road. To your left, a fraction north of west, is Yew Band, the quickest and easiest way back to where you left the car and also a very pleasant, wooded walk. Ahead of you are two small disused reservoirs which provided water to power a funicular railway at Hodge Close quarry, explored in the Little Langdale chapter, and a peaceful place to stop and contemplate the higher things. Harry Guards Wood, the wood surrounding Yew Tree Tarn on the Hawkshead-Coniston road, is charming too, and has a good path up onto Holme Fell. But it's hard not to be struck most by the full-length view of Coniston Water – the best view of it in Wainwright's opinion. If I were you and not in a hurry I'd head to the reservoirs and thence to Hodge Close.

Scout Scar and Whitbarrow

SCOUT SCAR

I should start by qualifying what I mean by Scout Scar. Wainwright, in *The Outlying Fells of Lakeland*, says that what "all local people" refer to as Scout Scar is more correctly called Underbarrow Scar, and that Scout Scar itself is a "much smaller cliff to the south." Presumably in deference to local opinion, the 1:25,000 OS maps now name the whole clifftop Scout Scar, and who am I to argue?

Before we moved to Cumbria my wife, as a final year Liverpool medical student, was based at Lancaster Royal Infirmary but had an afternoon's teaching a week at Westmorland General. The last teaching day of the year, the doctor in charge of her group took them all up to the mushroom shelter on Scout Scar.

We moved to within ten minutes walk of Westmorland General in September three years later. I've mentioned in The Helm chapter above going for my first climb on Whitbarrow, the subject of the second half of this chapter, having picked up the business cards and headed letter paper for my then as yet non-existent freelance proofreading, editing and indexing enterprise; an entry in my diary a few days before this (when suffering from a mild bout of food poisoning) reads:

> Had a stomach ache, sat at computer all morning, took the missus lunch – it's Sunday and she's on call – tried to eat and made stomach much worse. Was sullen and morose and was going home but instead drove through Natland and

Cloudscape over Scout Scar from Natland.

Brigsteer to the viewpoint above Underbarrow. I'm sitting on the top of the cliff looking west, away from home. It's a bit hazy, and very beautiful, especially looking down on the trees. Might go to the printers tomorrow to order business cards etc., and then come back up here...

Ever since, Scout Scar has been somewhere we've taken first time visitors to the Lakes, as I can't think of a better viewpoint from which to see the hills. It's a better view than the more obvious Orrest Head, and it has the advantage of the most comprehensive and intuitive view indicator of all the various panoramas and devices scattered around the edge of the Lake District (and we are quite literally on the edge here: the National Park boundary runs across the commons about 500m south). Originally built in 1912 to commemorate the Coronation of George V, 'the mushroom' was refurbished in 1969, 'vandalised into extinction' by the time Wainwright wrote about it in 1974's *Outlying Fells*, and again restored in 2002 by the parish council to celebrate the Queen's Golden Jubilee.

The Mushroom.

The shelter itself is a stone cross-shaped windbreak shelter like a smart version of the one on top of Helvellyn, but with a bench (and somehow, no matter where you sit, the wind will manage to find you), and is roofed with a stainless steel dome, which I've read somewhere is made from the end of a milk tanker. Running around the bottom of the inside of the dome is a 360° panorama of all the fells you can see, from Ill Bell and the Kentmere fells in the north, past Whinfell and the Howgills, Farleton Fell and Arnside Knott, across the Kent estuary to nearby Whitbarrow, farther off the Coniston Fells, and the Langdales and Kirkstone.

Scout Scar deserves a place in this book for the view (and the viewpoint)

Langdale Pikes from Scout Scar. The tower is the church tower at Crook Hall.

alone, but there's a lot more to it than this. The entire area backing the Scar, Bradleyfield Allotment and Helsington Barrows, has been a Site of Special Scientific Interest for 20 years, as – along with Whitbarrow, which the second half of this chapter is about – it forms a rich upland limestone habitat virtually unique in Cumbria. English Nature says (on its website) that, "Scout and Cunswick Scars differ from Whitbarrow in being particularly noted for their open water and fen habitats and the well developed grass/heath habitat mosaic." I find this an odd claim, as to my mind (and confirmed by a glance at the map) Whitbarrow has the marshy Toby Tarn at its north end and a little pool, fenced off for the last few years, nestled by the wall south-east of Lord's Seat, whereas the tops of Scout and Cunswick Scars are dry. Maybe they mean Cunswick Tarn. But there's certainly no shortage of plant and animal life. English Nature lists an extraordinary number of rare grasses, flowers and insects which are found here, testimony to the unusual geology of limestone plateau whose crevices, folds and undulations you'll become familiar with very quickly if you stray from the path. It's beyond the scope of this chapter to go into detail about Scout Scar's flora and fauna, but I was intrigued by the mention of the leafhopper *Chlorita dumosa*, which feeds on wild thyme, and is new to Britain, described from this site in 1988 and subsequently only recorded from a single other site, in Scotland.

The grass is worth further mention. *Sesleria caerulea*, Blue Moor Grass, is a rare moorland grass found in England only on limestone uplands in the North: which means a few sites in Derbyshire, Yorkshire and the limestone of north Lancashire and Cumbria – which is one of the reasons this area, along with Whitbarrow, is a SSSI.

Rainbow from Scout Scar.

AW's walk on Scout Scar, described in *The Outlying Fells*, begins and ends at Kendal Town Hall, suggesting that Kendal's erstwhile treasurer liked to wander up here after a day's work. Isabella Lickbarrow wrote in 'On Underbarrow Scar':

> With what sincere delight I wander here;
> When from the cares and toils of life set free,
> I hail the blest return of liberty;
> And these lov'd scenes my wearied spirits cheer;
> At ease reclin'd upon this airy brow,
> The prospect stretching wide, Pleas'd I survey
> The stony slope, the hanging woods below,
> The ridges of the heath, the winding way,
> The sun-beams glitt'ring on the marshy ground,
> The cultivated farms which smile around,
> And yon far hills with mists of ev'ning grey.

As the next stanza makes clear, Scout Scar is a great place from which to watch the sunset.

The mushroom is the focal point of a broad, gently sloping heath which runs from Brigsteer Road to the limestone cliffs above Lyth Valley east-west, and St. John's, Helsington to Cunswick Fell south-north. Most of it is only slightly populated by dog walkers: the roughly triangular area of Bradleyfield (see below) between Kendal Racecourse, the mushroom and the car park on Underbarrow Road: Helsington Barrows (including the little but delightful Warriner's Wood, which belongs to the Woodland Trust, who eschew the OS

Howgills from Scout Scar.

St. John's, Helsington, and Cunswick Scar.

map's apostrophe), and Cunswick Scar, are less visited. Kendal racecourse is long disused: it was used annually as a horse racing venue from 1821 to 1839. From 1891 to 1907 it was a golf course which was closed when the present golf course on Kendal Fell expanded. The area feels remote, isolated, empty, but simultaneously the knowledge that you're only a stone's throw from Kendal makes you feel like you're walking in a park. You get the same feeling on Kendal Fell, but with the balance more townwards. It's a tension between wildness and civilisation that Capability Brown and devotees of the 18th century Picturesque tradition would have been delighted with, if only they'd have been able to leave it alone.

It's easy to assume that this high, rocky, apparently barren, useless land has always been a part of Kendal commons, used by Kendalians to supply firewood and little else, unless you count exercise and the enjoyment of the views. But in fact nothing could be further from the case. The history of this land, and of Whitbarrow and the Lyth valley, which we'll return to a little later in the book, is so complicated that only a brief summary follows.

Scout Scar, the Langdale Pikes beyond, from the Helm.

Helsington, Bradley Fields and Cunswick are all mentioned in the Domesday Book, the compilers of which showed a lot more interest in the lands of present-day southern Cumbria, formerly Lancashire North of the Sands, than they did the more 'barren' Westmorland and Cumberland. It's easy to forget just how early in British history the Domesday Book was, especially as the north in those days was, quite literally, still in the dark ages compared with the south of England.

The Danes brought many changes to Cumbria's landscape and farming practices, and many words, two of which – 'fell' and 'dale' – are the names of the first two sections of this book. Arguing that, "Cumbria...was colonized by Irish Vikings with Christians among them," in a paper called *Lost Churches in the Carlisle Diocese*, W. G. Collingwood and J. Rogers argue that Norse and Irish names appear at this time, intermingled in suggestive ways. So the Domesday Book entry for Furness gives two Norse names, Ornolf and Thorolf, and two Irish, Gilemichel and Duvan (*Dubhan*, Irish, 'the little black man') as landholders in Edward the Confessor's time. Gilemichel means 'servant of St. Michael,' a Christian name probably from Ireland.

Gilemichel also owned Bodelforde, later Bothelforde, a place now lost but possibly sited near Hawes Bridge over the Kent near Natland: the bridge is a registered National Monument, and a man-made mound nearby is thought to be the remains of a motte, although it could just be a leftover of the construction of the canal. The ford may have been where the Roman road to the fort of Watercrook crossed the river, and Bodelforde may have been a vicus settlement, a settlement of locals who had a formal arrangement to supply a local Roman fort. The land came into the possession of the Taillebois family, later the de Lancasters, barons of Kendal. The remaining history of Kendal barony, including the parishes of Helsington and Sizergh, was painstakingly transcribed by William Farrer, edited by J. F. Curwen and published in the three-volume *Records Relating to the Barony of Kendale*, in the chapter 'Helsington and Sizergh.' In 1170 William de Lancaster, the second Baron, gave to Gervase de Ainecurt (or Haencurt) Natland and "Bothelford [extending] to the brook of the gallows and to the bounds of Hoton and Stainton, with Sizaritherge."

To summarize the enormous quantity of historical detail Farrer and Curwen reproduce, the lands of Helsington belonged to the Barons of Kendal, who found that the quality of the land on the limestone plateau was, comparatively, so productive for the grazing of livestock that it was profitable enough to lease to a succession of tenants. In 1200 "Thomas le Fleming, for the health of the soul of his lady, Helwise de Lancaster, gave to the brethren of Cockersand two shillings of rent out of his land in Helsington"; Cockersands Abbey still stands, roof and all, albeit secured with a sturdy padlock, on the southern tip of the mouth of the River Lune. At this time included in the "demesne of Helsington" was "the fishery of Fors," worth "six marks" in 1273; this is the rapid/waterfall on the river Kent, known to kayakists as Force Falls, under the bridge near Sedgwick House just south-east of the A590/A591 roundabout. Pleasingly, at the time of writing there are salmon jumping up Force Falls.

In 1307 Walter de Strickland, whose son Thomas carried the banner of St. George at Agincourt, was given land at Helsington "for good services rendered in Scotland," presumably in the border wars which led to the battle of Bannockburn in 1314. In 1332 "William de TWENG, knt., granted to Walter de SKIRKELAND the waste and wood in the vill of Helsington below the sheepfold of Sir Walter towards his manor of Styritheserd." The abbey of St. Mary's at York appears to have had rights to a tithe of the profit derived from Helsington Barrows, as in 1334 "Sir Walter de Skirkland, Nicholas the reeve and Richard Wariner are bound to deliver to the abbot and convent of St. Mary's, York, three skeps of good oatmeal" or the equivalent in ready cash: Warriner's Wood presumably takes its name from Richard Wariner. The same abbey held the right to grant the living of Kirkby Lonsdale from 1240. The lands around remained in the hands of the Barons thereafter. By the 1640s the Stricklands of Sizergh still owned the land on Helsington.

Hereafter, the historical record splits the area up into three: Cunswick Scar, Bradleyfield and Helsington Barrows.

As to Bradleyfield, in 1511 "the manor of Conswyk and Bradley, held of Thomas Par, knight, by the yearly rent of one pound of pepper and one grain of pepper, worth yearly 20 marks," according to Farrer and Curwen. Par was of course the father of Queen Catherine Parr, wife of Henry VIII. The Bradleys, landowners from Lancashire, held Bradleyfield in a line of succession which ended in three co-heiresses, one of whom married into the family of the Leyburnes of Cunswick. One of the Leyburnes took part in the Jacobite rebellion of 1715, and his estate was forfeited to the crown, and sold to Thomas Crowle, one of whose heirs sold it to Sir James Lowther ('Wicked Jimmy,' who we'll meet in the Lonsdale Valley chapter), and so it passed into what would become the estate of the Earls of Lonsdale.

As for Helsington Barrows, according to Nicolson and Burn, in *The History*

Cunswick Scar from Scout Scar.

and Antiquities of the Counties of Westmorland and Cumberland (1777), there was a dispute in 1592 over rights of pasture, fishing and rights of way between Thomas Strickeland, of the Stricklands of Sizergh, and James Bellingham. Bellingham was the father of Henry Bellingham, 1st Baronet of Hilsington [sic], MP for Westmorland, and grandfather of another James, also MP for Westmorland: the line and title, died out with the second James' death at the age of 27.

The dispute in question brought before Sir Henry Curwen, Thomas Preston, Gerrard Lowther, Thomas Braythwat and Thomas Hesketh, who ordered that as "Mr. Strickland and his tenants of Levens, Syzergh and Brigster" had enjoyed the use of land at Levens, the fishing in the Kent, pasture on Helsington Barrows and Whitbarrow, and a right of way through Levens Park,

for 40 years, or for 50 in come cases, these rights should continue.

So, contrary to expectations, the allotments of Helsington and Barrowfield did not become commons by nature of their being waste land: they have in fact been considered valuable, as uplands which are suitable for grazing, something unusual in Cumbria. The highest point of Whitbarrow, as we shall see, is Lord's Seat, a name which commonly denotes a piece of high ground prized enough to have been reserved for the local Baron's personal use. And, as we'll also see below, Farrer's Allotment, the southern end of Whitbarrow's top, is still grazed by the National Trust, as is Helsington Barrows, although the beef thus produced is not the primary reason for cows being kept on Whitbarrow today. The aforementioned biological diversity of these limestone uplands has been exploited for a long time.

As for the saw above, in 1592 it was ruled that as the tenant farmers of "Levens, Syzergh and Brigster" were ruled to be able to continue to enjoy rights of grazing on the baronial lands because they had enjoyed just such a freedom for the past 40 years, so Parson and White (*History, Directory, and Gazetteer, of the Counties of Cumberland and Westmorland*) record that "the inhabitants of Kendal have an ancient privilege to walk and enjoy the prospect there presented to view." If you were wondering why no one complained about Isabella Lickbarrow unwinding and poeticizing up here of an evening, here's your answer.

In 1767, 158 acres of Kendal Fell became the first land in what's now Cumbria to be enclosed by Parliament, and was administered by the Kendal Fell Trust, which used it profitably for quarrying limestone and burning lime. There's an exceptionally well-preserved (and recently restored) twin lime kiln at Greenside, just off the top of Underbarrow Road in Kendal. Kendal, well provided with local limestone and having a canal to help distribute lime further afield, had a thriving lime industry in the 19th century and Greenside Lime Kiln is the only one in the town which survives. Signboards at the site tell you all about it.

Nowadays Bradleyfield and Helsington Barrows are mostly access land, the former in the Lake District National Park and the latter outside. Approximately half of Helsington Barrows – the southern end – is National Trust property, gifted by the Strickland Family along with Sizergh Castle and the rest of the estate to the National Trust in 1950. Cunswick Scar and the northern end of Barrowfield, surrounding Barrow Field Farm, have always been in private hands, but are well provided with footpaths. It's wonderful to be able to roam freely about the limestone on Helsington Barrows: every little dell and undulation yields something worth poking your nose into (literally, often, limestone being limestone). I also wonder, as did Wainwright in his

Opposite, sunset over Scout Scar from Natland.

Scout Scar walk in *The Outlying Fells*, where all the water goes: as on the Helm there are no streams or springs between the Scar and the River Kent, and one can only assume that limestone's cave-forming propensities are at work somewhere deep underground. I'd love to know what's down there.

Scout Scar principally means two things to me. Firstly, as I said at the beginning of this chapter, it's a place to take visitors who aren't at all familiar with the Lake District, as visibility permitting, the views are guaranteed to make people stop in their tracks. The other reason is the same as Isabella Lickbarrow's, and I suspect AW's: I can walk up here from my own front door, and every time I get here I'm still astonished that such an extraordinary place, and such a breathtaking view, are only forty minutes walk from home. It's got a great view of Whitbarrow, and few things make me happier than a view of Whitbarrow (except being there, obviously). It's the ideal way to end a long week, or indeed a long day: in summer, increasingly, it's a great way to begin one, as the wonders of technology mean I can access mobile broadband up there. The Corsican pines which are scattered across the middle of Helsington Barrows are considered unwelcome intruders nowadays, and we'll be exploring their history in the Whitbarrow section below, but I will say three things for them:

1. They provide good shade to work under
2. Their crook-like lower branches are comfortable to sit in
3. Their trunks, when fallen, are very pleasant to lie on.

All of which means that if you happen to be self-employed, happen to possess a mini laptop, mobile broadband contract and a highlighter or two, and are fed up with being bored, Helsington Barrows makes a superb environment in which to, say, write an index. Need a minute or two to clear your head before moving on to the next chapter of the book in hand? Simply go in search of the next comfortable-looking viewpoint.

Indexing on Scout Scar.

WHITBARROW

Whitbarrow cliffs in winter, Scout Scar across Lyth Valley and below, cliffs at Whitbarrow's south end form Low Fell End.

The Leyburnes of Cunswick form a convenient link between Scout Scar (well, Cunswick Scar anyway) and Whitbarrow.

I've described my first ascent of Whitbarrow, by the unusually direct route of straight up the cliff at White Scar from Raven Lodge, in the first chapter of this book. I should point out that I had genuinely missed the signs in the nearby quarry pointing out that climbing on the cliffs is not allowed: signs tend to be placed adjacent to paths, and I don't necessarily follow paths. Until 2002 there was a five year 'gentleman's agreement' with the British Mountaineering Council that there was to be no climbing on the cliffs here: the Fell and Rock

Climbing Club of the English Lake District says that the ban was put in place at the request of the landowners "due to various unbelievable activities on the crag that broke the access agreement." Quite what these unbelievable acts were I don't know, but the BMC said in early 2003 that the landowners were, alas, still not keen on letting climbers play on the cliffs. The Fell and Rock Climbing Club said that they would support a ban on climbing here from 1 March to 30 June due to the likely presence of nesting peregrines; however, "the landowners do not allow climbing at this crag." They seem to have thawed a little, but best to check with the BMC before you set off to climb.

I'm not absolutely certain where I went from the top of the cliff on that first Whitbarrow walk, but I think I found my way to the cattle shed on Farrer's Allotment, marvelling at the gaunt silver birches scattered across the limestome plateau, left carefully behind when the 1960s conifer plantations were cleared (see below). I found my way through the yews and hazels into Pether Pots and Wakebarrow, and eventually went back down via Rawsons to Mill Side and the car. Next day I drafted a marketing letter, compiled an initial list of publishers to write to offering my editing services, and then headed off to Whitbarrow again. That time I started at Row on the Windermere road through Lyth Valley, explored Township Allotment and Toby Tarn at the north end of the hill, and eventually, after getting a bit lost, mostly on purpose, found my way to the deliciously named Moon's Wood and went back to Row via the eerie Catcrag Quarry, which is more like a rock garden laid out by some of Bilbo Baggins's trolls than a quarry. I got to know Whitbarrow very well in the space of a couple of weeks, spending half of most weekdays up there and the other half working on getting the business going. Thus, slowly, both on the ground and in old books and records, I got to know Whitbarrow (Old Norse: 'white hill'. It's the limestone, you see...) as I settled into my new career as an editor and indexer.

Three of these walks especially stick in my mind. The most popular Whitbarrow walk – and, with hindsight, the most obvious, and probably the best – is the walk that Wainwright includes in his *Outlying Fells*, the walk he calls "the most beautiful in this book." I did it more or less by accident, having read about Whitbarrow Bone Cave and having, finally, taken the path that leads, from Mill Side to Farrer's Allotment, near the cave through Buckhouse Wood, done the diversion to the cave.

Spider nest on the hillside above Raven Lodge.

(I later discovered that if you follow the narrowing path past the cave you end up with a choice of fractionally dizzying but enjoyable ascents to the plateau high above Beck Head, more or less. Dead easy scrambles are always spiced up a bit by the knowledge that the tufts of grass or the little limestone blocks you're entrusting your life to aren't actually all that firmly anchored).

Looking towards the Kent Estuary in cloud.

At the time I retraced my steps from the cave to the main meandering path through the yews and, where it gradually and pleasingly shallows in gradient, picked up the pace to wander across Farrer's Allotment, then got spectacularly lost in the woods on Wakebarrow and found myself at Flodder Hall farm, by Moon's Wood, leaving myself with a long walk back along the roads before I could rejoin the public rights of way network at Raven Lodge.

Then there was a walk from North Lodge, in Low Park Wood under Whitbarrow Scar, up through the woods to Toby Tarn (which is usually a damp piece of reedy waste ground, not a tarn in the usual sense of the word). The weather was pretty wild and wooly when, after dusk, I got out of the trees and crossed the ladder/stile over the old enclosure wall, but I set off north across Township Allotment anyway, fancying a long walk back to the car through all the woods under the scar in Winster Valley in the dark. Leaving Toby Tarn the storm was rising, the kind of storm that makes you pull your hood down over your eyes, bend double and push through the wind. Sooner or later I realised I'd wandered off any obvious path, and didn't have a clue where I was. It's not a big place, Township Allotment, but when the visibility's down to ten-odd feet, it's soaking wet and you've only got a paper copy of the map (I've learnt that lesson) it seems enormous. I was pleasantly surprised to find, with numb hands, only a wet mobile screen for light and a map in several pieces, that I'd found the footpath down to Fell Edge farm, and, having dropped out of the cloud, found that if damp it was at least still and mist-free in the valley below. It was also pitch black, so I made my way back through Howe Ridding, returning to the car in the pitch dark and accompanied by the sounds of both genders of tawny owl, via Fairie's Cave, a deep, narrow, ferny gully at the foot of the cliff, from a hole in the back wall of which a stream issues over flights of little waterfalls: it's the sort of spot Millais or Holman Hunt would have painted.

And finally, a January walk on Friday evening in the dark up through Rawson's Wood to wander around in the woods on Wakebarrow, where, despite the night being moonless, there was light enough from the stars to see the path by, even under the trees: and then out onto Farrer's Allotment, where the lights of Morecambe and Heysham, Kendal and Oxenholme seemed a world away and the gaunt silver birches were like ghosts through which the shorthorn cattle wandered, startled at human presence: it was as if no one had ever been there at night, somehow. Whitbarrow's silver birches deserve mention: seen from anywhere in Winster Valley or Yewbarrow, in winter their white trunks against the white limestone cliffs and their red twigs make them look like a band of lace, or filigree, stretched around the hill.

Being further from Kendal, Whitbarrow's history is less documented than that of Scout Scar, its geological sister across Lyth Valley, but what history there is is similar: the name of the summit – Lord's Seat, a name shared with a few other summits in the area, including in Whinlatter Forest – suggests that the powers that be availed themselves of Whitbarrow's grazing in the same way as that on Scout Scar (perhaps they enjoyed the exceptional views while they were up here – you can see Snowdonia on a clear day). And, anyway, on Whitbarrow, it's more recent history which is more interesting and obvious.

It seems the Vikings were once found hereabouts: partly as Whitbarrow is a Norse name, and partly because of a sword, probably of Viking origin, found

Whitbarrow from Helsington.

buried under Whitbarrow Scar in the 1960s, which is now in Kendal Museum. The earliest historical mention of 'Witeberge' is in 1196, in reference to a fine levied that year in the King's court between Gilbert, son of Roger Fitz Reinfrid, who built Kendal Castle, and Henry de Redeman, the tenant farmer of 'Witeberge.' The reference relates to the parish of Witherslack, whose eastern boundary is at the foot of Whitbarrow Scar, as well as to Crosthwaite: Whitbarrow itself is in the parish of Crosthwaite and Lyth, but the high ground feels more intimately associated with the history of Witherslack, while Lyth is much better viewed from Scout Scar; but Witherslack has an interesting history, and as this chapter really includes the woods under Whitbarrow Scar, a brief history of Witherslack follows.

Henry de Redeman quit-claimed Witeberge (which means that he surrendered his rights to the land, while freely admitting that the surrendered rights may well not have any basis in law) in return for land at Selesat (Selside) and the right of "common of pasture of the moss between Witeberge and Levenes," i.e. the lower Lyth Valley, "to be held by Henry and his heirs by the free service of five shillings yearly." William de Lyndeseye, who died in 1282, "seised of the manors of Barton and Witherslak which Roger de Lancastre held of him by the service of a sor [i.e. one year old] sparrow-hawk (for Barton) and one penny yearly (for Witherslack)." In 1374 ownership of Witherslack parish featured in a long-drawn-out disagreement at the Coram Rege court, that is in the court presided over by Edward III (1327-77), concerning the fact that John de Lancastre had leased the land to a Michael de Haveryngtone, and when the lease passed to Michael's son John a controversy arose over who in fact owned the lease, de Lancastre or a Dame Cristiana de Gynes of Crosthwaite.

Witherslack was leased to the Pickering family from 1406, and in 1485 was one of a series of lands granted to Thomas Lord Stanley, first Earl of Derby, on 23 August, the day following Henry VII's accession – Stanley was Henry's stepfather, and is said to have retrieved the King's lost crown at the Battle of Bosworth Field on 22 August, and to have nobly placed it upon the King's head. Witherslack was let to a series of tenants, most notably a series of members of the Leyburne family, who held the manor of Witherslack Hall as well as Cunswick Hall, and Skelsmergh, north of Kendal. The Leyburnes got into trouble during and after the Civil War for refusing to denounce their Catholicism, and bought Witherslack Hall in 1653/4, along with "33 acres of arable, 37 acres of meadow and 620 acres of rocky and woody pasture, with the deer and game therein."

They remained at Witherslack Hall until the direct male line failed. The last mention of the Leyburnes at Witherslack is in 1715. One of the joint heiresses of the Leyburnes was married to Dr. Marmaduke Witham of Yorkshire, and the other heiresses died childless, so the Withams claimed the Witherslack estate.

An attempt by the Withams to recover the estate failed in 1759, and the estate was enclosed as part of the Heversham Enclosures Act in 1815, being then divided into allotments – for example Farrers', Township and Flodder Allotments. The dry limestone walls of Whitbarrow date from this time. As with the enclosure of Kendal Fell in 1767, quarrying to meet the needs of the growing town of Kendal was an important activity on Whitbarrow; and also, as on Kendal Fell, was the burning of lime for fertiliser. Witherslack was granted a parliamentary 'Inclosure Award' in 1829.

Flodder Allotment is so named because it was granted to Flodder Hall, in the Lyth Valley. Township Allotment, along with Township Plantation and White Scar Quarry, were granted to the villagers, and income derived from this land is still used to support community projects, for example providing funds for the village school, tennis courts, a bowling green, a children's playground and a small football pitch. The name of Farrer's Allotment serves as a convenient stepping-stone to the recent history of Whitbarrow.

Whitbarrow Lodge was built in the 1720s, the property of a William Bownas or Bowness, who was a tenant farmer, and it replaced the old farmhouse of High Fell End. A descendent, another William Bowness, died in 1823, and the Whitbarrow Lodge estate passed into the ownership of his daughters, who also seem to have owned Witherslack Hall, according to the records of Hart Jackson & Sons, Solicitors, Ulverston, which are in the National Archives and available online. Whitbarrow Lodge was let to tenants, then sold to William Farrer Ecroyd, a Lancashire industrialist (the firm wove worsted cloth), and MP for Preston, in 1865. His son was also named William Farrer Ecroyd, later just William Farrer (Farrer was his mother's maiden name, and when his uncle Farrer died childless his somewhat presumptuous wish that his nephew drop the 'Ecroyd' from his name was discovered in his will).

Farrer became a renowned local historian, with publications to his name that include the eight volume *Victoria History of Lancashire, Clitheroe Court Rolls, Early Yorkshire Charters, Itinerary of Henry I, Feudal Cambridgeshire* and so on. He moved to Whitbarrow Lodge permanently in 1920, enlarging the house to provide room for his copious library, and presumably Farrer's Allotment takes its name from him: Cumbria Wildlife Trust's 'Whitbarrow' leaflet says that, "On Whitbarrow these [the allotments] were named after the farms or people to whom they were apportioned, for example Farrers' [sic]," but as we've seen Whitbarrow was enclosed in 1815, and I have found no mention of Farrer being connected with Whitbarrow before 1865, so what Farrer's was originally called I don't know.

Farrer has in fact made a substantial but so far unmentioned contribution to this book: a meticulous note-keeper, while writing his histories of Lancashire, Yorkshire, etc. he compiled a vast collection of notes on Kendal Barony, which he passed to John F. Curwen, another local historian, of the family of

Curwens of Workington Hall and Belle Isle, who edited it; the compendious *Records Relating to the Barony of Kendal* was published in three volumes by the Cumberland and Westmorland Antiquarian and Archaeological Society in the 1920s, and has been the source of much of the historical information in this chapter, the Helm chapter and elsewhere.

Whitbarrow has always been forested, and there are remnants of ancient wild wood: Durham Bridge Wood, Wakebarrow, Barney Crags and Rough Hill Wood all contain ancient woodland, but most importantly most of Witherslack Woods is largely natural, and is managed (expertly, it seems to me) by Witherslack Woodlands at Halecat. But there is a considerable history of artificial planting on Whitbarrow dating back 90 years. In 1919 pine, larch, beech and sycamore plantations began to appear on the fell, due to the demand for timber created by the Great War. In 1955, the Forestry Commission leased Wakebarrow and Farrer's Allotment and planted Corsican pines on the old grazing land and red cedar amongst the native woodland. In 1965 Whitbarrow was named a Site of Special Scientific Interest: Canon G. A. K. Hervey (1893-1967), rector of Great Salkeld, founded the Lake District Naturalists' Trust, now Cumbria Wildlife Trust, in 1962, and on his death in 1967 the LDNT acquired Flodder Allotment (they own a small part of it, and have a long-term lease on the rest from the Argles family of Levens, who acquired it in the early 1870s).

In 1999 the Forestry Commission felled the Corsican Pines on Farrer's Allotment and the whole area is now access land: *The Independent* (13 September 1998) reported on the Commission's plans to fell "200,000 half-grown Corsican pines from 300 acres of Whitbarrow, a fell in the Lake District, to restore one of Britain's rarest habitats, a flower-rich, limestone grassland. The fell, home to more than 50 rare insects, is to become a National Nature Reserve, Britain's highest conservation designation." The Forestry Commission, in 2002, described the site as, "one of the most threatened areas of limestone pavement in the world." Besides being an NNR and an SSSI, Whitbarrow is also a Special Area of Conservation (SAC). I would explain the differences between these different designations, but the reader will probably thank me if I don't.

Traditional forestry techniques such as coppicing are being re-introduced to encourage diversity and, since the year 2000, shorthorn cattle have been grazed on Farrer's Allotment to speed the breakdown of the pine stumps and to keep the grassland healthy and improve its diversity: grazing helps promote the growth of herbs and grasses other than the dominant blue moor-grass: things like bird's foot trefoil, wild thyme and salad burnet, as well as other rare grasses. "We've chosen cattle in preference to sheep as they tend to be less fussy eaters, whereas sheep are more selective," says Graeme Prest of the Forestry Commission. There is little standing water on Whitbarrow – aside from Toby Tarn, described above, there's also a small tarn south-east of the Lord's Seat summit cairn, at a kink in the wall between Flodder Allotment and Wakebarrow, which was rudimentarily fenced off a few years ago but is now surrounded by a proper fence of barbed wire, and provided with a solar-powered pump which fills a nearby water trough: recently, cattle have been introduced to the Hervey Nature Reserve, and are also to be seen on Township Allotment at the time of writing, so presumably the experiment on Farrer's Allotment has been a resounding success.

Whitbarrow Scar from across a flooded Yewbarrow.

Other notable pieces of local flora and fauna are the yews and junipers, the former of which occur unusually frequently above, below and on the slopes of Whitbarrow Scar, and less frequently on the cliffs south and east of Whitbarrow, the latter being common on the summit plateau, on whose grykes small yews comically twisted into right angles by the prevailing winds are a notable feature. Wych elm and small-leaved lime, the latter very rare north of here, are also to be seen, as well as whitebeam, while the dominant natural woodland is hazel and ash, the largest and most diverse area of this kind of woodland in Cumbria. Whitbarrow is also important for its populations of ferns, butterflies and moths, as well as, apparently, *Lampyris Notiluca*, the common glow worm, amongst other things, although I've never seen an example of the latter here. There are roe deer and the occasional red deer, which stray over from Grizedale Forest; I've seen foxes and badgers, too.

After those early walks up on Whitbarrow, I started exploring further afield, getting to know the places I could see from there. The first big expedition I've already described, up Fairfield that Christmas Day: thereafter I started collecting Wainwrights, mostly those from his *Eastern Fells* book (the Helvellyn range, fells around Kentmere and Hartsop: but also the Coniston fells, Skiddaw on my birthday...). It wasn't until the following August that I revisited Whitbarrow, by which time I had half a dozen clients and enough work to keep me busy 9 to 5, Monday to Friday, and often (in fact usually) a lot longer. I wandered up the cliff path, up past the cave, and decided on a whim to carry on past the cave round the southern tip of the hill and scramble up the loose limestone at Whitbarrow's extreme south-western end. I pulled myself up past clumps of the same, rare Blue Moor Grass that grows on Scout Scar, and wandered across the strip of clifftop grass, nipped over the limestone drystone wall and through the woods onto Farrer's Allotment.

Butterflies skipped easily on the shimmering air: cattle, drowsy, begged me not to come close enough for them to have to bother moving away. Flicking flies away with their tails was too much effort already. The grass was full of grasshoppers; the air was heavy with the distant fells, as if they were about to drop off the horizon and disappear into the surrounding valleys from sheer lethargy. The easy incline up to Lords Seat seemed like a cartoon long drag to a desert oasis; I felt like gasping "water... water" throughout.

When is Whitbarrow at its best? The answer is, really, any time: in crisp, clear winter weather, when the surrounding fells (and often Lord's Seat itself) are covered in snow, as much as when the landscape is bathed in summer sun; or, if the cloud's come down, it's tipping it down and the visibility is down to ten yards, take yourself into the woods and enjoy your horizons being limited

Looking east to Whitbarrow from Yewbarrow, under a winter sky.

to a radius of a few feet. If you've got an hour, you can have a worthwhile walk on Whitbarrow. If you've got all day – or a fortnight, or a couple of years – you'll never stop learning up there. It's my favourite place in Cumbria.

Dale

WALKERS GENERALLY CONSIDER valleys as places to be passed through, as walk-ins or, perhaps more usually, walk-outs from mountains. But, as I discovered, first at Kentmere and later at Little Langdale, when forced down from the tops by the weather, the Lake District's dales are by no means places simply to be passed through. There would be no mountain ranges without the valleys that split the peaks, so that the valleys are absolutely integral to mountain scenery, and some of the Lake's most famous views – that of Wast Water, Yewbarrow, Green Gable and the Scafell group in Wasdale, or up Great Langdale to the Pikes, spring to mind – are from the valleys.

The Nab, Rampsgill and Howe Grain, Martindale, from High Raise summit cairn.

The fells are also, by and large, excepting walls and sheepfolds and the odd mine, devoid of obvious signs of human history. Not so the valleys, which tell a complicated tale of settlement, clearing, ownership, agriculture and industry.

Mallerstang

"There are few dales in Westmorland more isolated and sequestered than that of Mallerstang." William Nicholls, *The History and Traditions of Mallerstang Forest and Pendragon Castle.*

THE NORTH PENNINES NATIONAL PARK
A walk around the mountains ringing Mallerstang has already been included in this book, but here we'll explore the valley itself. As the extraordinary scenery of Mallerstang – a third Dales, a third Lakes, a third Pennines – has already been described, more or less, above, I'll try and bite my lip when it comes to the aching, and scandalously under appreciated beauty of Mallerstang. Wild Boar Fell dominates the valley, being, appropriately, more akin to a Lake District mountain than the limestone terraces of the Yorkshire side of the valley, although High Seat is in fact higher, albeit by only a metre – 709 to Wild Boar Fell's 708. As mentioned above, High Seat is in turn the fourth highest point in the Dales, after Whernside, Ingleborough and Great Shunner Fell.

Geologically, Wild Boar Fell has a millstone grit cap on layers of shales and sandstones, like the Howgills (and millstones were once made on Wild Boar Fell), whereas on High Seat the millstone cap is intermittent, and sometimes what's under the turf is either limestone or sandstone. These are some of the best limestone deposits in the world, over 1,200m thick, and containing examples of every layer of Carboniferous limestone ever classified. Geographically, Mallerstang is bordered to the south and east by the Yorkshire Dales National Park which, further west, also covers the southern Howgills (as explained in the Howgills chapter earlier in this book) and to the north by the North Pennines Area of Outstanding National Beauty (AONB). It seems extraordinary to me that this valley, with its history, its scenery, its wildlife and its centrality to what David Bellamy, in a book and accompanying television series, has called *England's Last Wilderness*, isn't part of one of the complicated schemes our governments have devised of splitting up the more outstanding areas of our country's geography, such as National Park or AONB: but it isn't.

John Dower, who, as secretary of the Standing Committee on National Parks in 1945, produced the first official report which set out what National Parks in England and Wales should be like, was of the opinion that the Howgills, along with Borrowdale, Bretherdale and neighbouring valleys deserved to be a National Park in their own right.

At the time of writing Natural England, the government's official advisor on all things environmental, is proposing to extend the Dales National Park to include the northern Howgills, Wild Boar Fell and Mallerstang, Middleton and

Barbon Fells between Kirkby Lonsdale, Sedbergh and Dentdale, and Firbank Fell, the site of Fox's Pulpit, along with other lower fells between the River Lune and the M6, and Leck Fell (which, confusingly, is in Lancashire): so the plan is for the Yorkshire Dales National Park to cover three counties.

Meanwhile the Birkbeck Fells and Whinfell, west of the M6, including the eastern section of Borrowdale, between the A6 and M6, would form part of an enlarged Lake District National Park, and a small extension south west of Kendal would add Helsington Barrows, Sizergh Fell and Lyth Valley. There's also a plan to make Orton Fell an AONB. Coincidentally, though, the day before I wrote up this chapter from some very chaotic notes the BBC reported that Cumbria County Council had decided against any expansion of the Lake District park, on the basis that it might price local people out of the housing market.

Natural England ran a consultation on the plans which ended in July 2011, so we'll have to wait and see. It seems to me that the Lake District park should probably stay as it is, that the Yorkshire Dales should be confined to Yorkshire and that a new North Pennines National Park, covering the Howgills and surrounding fells, Mallerstang and Wild Boar Fell and the already extant North Pennines AONB, as well as the relevant bits of Lancashire, should be created. But then you'd need three National Park HQs, three sets of staff, three sets of vehicles, three websites and three sets of stationery, all of which is expensive. And perhaps we shouldn't encourage people to visit every beautiful, wild upland bit of the north of England.

I do take the point about house prices, though. I used to teach Cumbrian natives at Lancaster University, most of whom reported they were most likely going to leave the area after graduation because they'd never be able to get on the housing ladder if they stayed. Conversely, though, my house is on the market, and if suddenly I found myself selling a house in a National Park and with a correspondingly higher asking price, I'd be unlikely to complain. By the time the Lake District Park Authority got round to needing a headquarters they found they couldn't afford a site within the National Park, such had been the effect on property prices. And it seems obvious to state that if this place, this whole area, were a National Park, as by rights it ought to be, this would result in more visitors, and so some of the magic might be lost.

William Nicholls, author of *The History and Traditions of Mallerstang Forest and Pendragon Castle*, a book described in more detail below, begins by saying, "There are few dales in Westmorland more isolated and sequestered than that of Mallerstang." This is still the case today. One of my wife's colleagues, on being told I was writing this book, said "Sounds great. Only don't you let him go saying Mallerstang's a sequestered spot in Cumbria and get people trampling all over it." Which is a generic problem with all books of this nature. Wordsworth and Wainwright are history's most obvious 'culprits' in this regard, celebrating the wild, lonely Lakes to such an extent that now it takes over an hour to drive from one end of Windermere to the other on any weekend in the summer. Do I really want these wild, under-visited places as full of visitors as Great Langdale or Patterdale? Of course I don't: so why am I going into print about them?

Mallerstang swift.

To answer that question comprehensively needs more space than I have here: I reckon I could fill another book trying. But briefly, it comes down to two somewhat contradictory things, selflessness and selfishness. Selflessly, I love, and am inspired by these places, and wish to share this love, as well as what I've found out concerning their pasts and presents. I feel it would be selfish not keep it all to myself.

On the other hand, I don't live in Mallerstang, so while it's all very well for me to encourage people onto the other side of the Helm, say, or up Scout Scar, it's undeniably selfish of me to publicize Mallerstang to satisfy the egotistical and financial reasons for which writers write.

ON WILD BOAR FELL

The Eden Valley has some great Norse place names – Langwathby, Appleby, Warcop – but Mallerstang is surely one of the most satisfyingly toothsome place names in the country. Its etymology is uncertain. In *The history and antiquities of the Deanery of Craven, in the county of York*, clergyman and scholar Thomas Dunham Whitaker speculates as follows: "This wild tract was,

Cairns on Wild Boar Fell.

I suppose, so called Mallard Stank, the pool of the Mallard, referring to some early expansion of the Eden." The Rev. J. Wharton, of Stainmore, told William Nicholls that, "Mallerstang [is from] Mallard Stagnum, morass of the wild duck; compare Dun-Mallard (Ullswater) and Garstang." This sounds eminently plausible to me; but Mary M. Thompson, author of *Mallerstang: a Westmorland Dale* adds that "Maller may be identical with mellor, meaning a bare hill, and Stang the Norse word for a pole. Thus Mallerstang may mean a bare hill which is a boundary mark or pole," an interesting supposition given the prevalence of tall summit cairns in the area, notably those on Wild Boar Fell and Little Fell, silent sentinels of Mallerstang.

A more recent etymology appears in Robert Gambles *Lake District Place-Names* (Hayloft, 2013), which suggests that "The first element here is obscure. It could refer to a Norse feminine personal name Malfrith or to a form of the Welsh *moel-fre* 'a bare hill', an apt description of the vast moorland above the valley. The second element, stang, is usually derived from ON *stong* 'a pole, a stake' – perhaps used as a boundary marker. Malfrith's boundary marker or the marker on a bare hill. A mysterious and unusual name for a valley."

Nicholls (pp. 10-11) says it was once known as Mallerstang Forest, in the old sense of forest being a piece of land given over as a game reserve set aside for the hunting pleasure of the nobility. So the 'Appleby Sessions Indictment Book' records that in 1665 eight men were convicted of killing a deer belonging to Anne, Countess Dowager of Pembroke, in Mallerstang Forest, and were each fined £20.

Lime Kiln from Lady Anne's Highway.

There is evidence that the Romans used Mallerstang as a thoroughfare: they had a fort at Brough, and a hoard of Roman coins was found by the old road, Lady Anne's Highway, in 1927 by a local shepherd, Peter Kerr, near Outhgill. But flint implements discovered by Annie Hamilton-Gibney at Birkett Bottom, or Watter Yat, at Mallerstang north end in 2010, and now in Penrith Museum, suggest that Mallerstang has been a thoroughfare since long before the Romans.

Not all that long after the Vikings arrived in these valleys (in round about the 9th century), Mallerstang became a strategic route for purposes of sneaking stolen cattle back to Scotland. I first read about Mallerstang in *Northern Warrior*, a historical novel set in the 14th century, whose sequel, *1314*, was the first book I edited for Hayloft. In an ingenious set piece, the hero, Andreas de Harcla of Hartley Castle near Kirkby Stephen, outwits a band of marauding Scots in the fog towards the top of Mallerstang. I was so taken by Adrian Rogan's description that I decided to go and see for myself, and so, having delivered the edited *1314* to Hayloft on the morning of Tuesday, 24 April 2007, I set out to explore Mallerstang and to climb Wild Boar Fell.

It was a cold, clear winter's day, frost on the tarmac and the peat bogs frozen underfoot. For the first and, so far, only time I met someone on the summit, a fit man in his seventies who'd just walked from Kirkby Stephen station. He soon turned back, leaving me alone with my thoughts on what must be the most interesting summit to explore in Cumbria. For one thing there's the sheer size of the summit plateau, nearly a mile long and half a mile across at its broadest (though if you're after a big summit plateau to wander about on, try Baugh Fell); and then there are the names and features scattered across the 1:25,000 OS map. The names are appropriate to a valley with such a beautiful name: High White Scar, Yoadcomb Scar, Sandtarn Riggs, Scriddles. The features: the word 'cairn' five times and, as if the cartographer was despairing of fitting everything in, 'cairns' once: these form a the distinctive line which I'm sure is related to Nine Standards in some, probably forever untraceable way, suggesting, along with the tumulus on the nab, the importance of Wild Boar Fell in prehistory; 'workings (disused),' presumably once a quarry as millstone grit is, unsurprisingly, good for making millstones, and as I said earlier in this book roughed out millstones may be seen on the eastern flank around Yoadcomb Scar; the ubiquitous trig point; the myriad pools, and Sand Tarn with its tiny island, which promise peat hags galore.

Apparently during the Second World War Wild Boar Fell was used to train tank crews from the base at Warcop how to handle tanks on steep and boggy ground. Then there's the story of Sir Richard de Musgrave and the last Wild Boar in England, told in the Nine Standards to Wild Boar Fell chapter. Then, of course, there are the views of the Howgills with the distant Lakeland fells beyond, Baugh Fell, the line of the Pennines stretching up to Cross Fell in the north, then across the valley Hugh Seat and Mallerstang Edge, with little islands of the Dales poking up, Great Shunner Fell and Whernside. All this is to say nothing of the wildlife, especially the crowd of golden plovers I saw up there one autumn.

The tangled history of the fell and the valley and the area jumbled through my mind as I wandered round the summit, tinged with the pleasure of knowing I'd left in the car a cheque as payment for the pleasure of having edited a novel set round here, the source of some of my new-found historical knowledge. It was the second cheque I'd received, the first having been for an index for a colleague from Lancaster days a couple of weeks previously. It was a moment, like the moment on Whitbarrow six months previously, when amid all the self-doubt of the last year I really felt I might succeed with my editing and indexing business. Before long I was working on another Hayloft book, *A Guide to the Stone Circles of Cumbria*, and adding both to the balance of my business bank account and to my store of knowledge about the Lake District.

It's odd somehow that on mountaintops in England history seems to have ended: quarrying, millstone making, peat cutting, even ritual activity (if that's what it was) is firmly in the past: the future holds simply a constant, or, in the case of Wild Boar Fell, less than constant stream of visitors. It's odd that mountaintops – wild, remote, natural places – should be an apparent vindication of the postmodern world's (over-) confident proclamation of the end of history. Wild Boar Fell may, however, be changed dramatically by man in the future: a preliminary investigation by Scottish Power has been carried out regarding the building of a wind farm 14 turbines strong on Greenlaw Rigg on the north western flanks of Wild Boar Fell, on land in Ravenstonedale parish but close to the border with Mallerstang, which runs across the summit plateau. Apparently the farm is unlikely to materialize at present because the landowners are not keen, but with the growth of offshore wind farms, who knows?

THROUGH MALLERSTANG
The valley's past has been chronicled in a very rare and hard to find book, W. Nicholls' *History and Traditions of Mallerstang Forest and Pendragon Castle* (1883). I'm also indebted to Mary M. Thompson's *Mallerstang: a Westmorland Dale* (Appleby, 1965), mentioned above.

We'll start at the southern end of the valley and head up towards Kirkby Stephen, for the simple reason that I don't think I've ever walked through Mallerstang the other way. Half of the valley is, of course, in Yorkshire, the border running down Hell Gill Beck from Hugh Seat, crossing the valley and ascending the other side to Swarth Fell Pike, but three things at the Yorkshire end are worth a mention.

The first is Garsdale Station, on the Settle to Carlisle line, the last railway in Britain to be constructed solely by manual labour, which runs through

Goods train on the Settle to Carlisle line in Mallerstang.

Mallerstang: the construction of the railway will be covered when we get to Outhgill, but it's worth mentioning the statin here as it makes a one-way traverse of Mallerstang using public transport possible. Currently trains run two to three hourly between Garsdale and Kirkby Stephen stations (the latter of which, be aware, is a generous mile south of Kirkby Stephen itself).

The Wensleydale Railway is still open between Redmire in Wensleydale and Northallerton, but this line used to extend to Garsdale, where it intersected with the Settle to Carlisle line at Dandry Mire just east of Garsdale station, running via stations at Hawes, Askrigg for Bainbridge (where, incidentally, there was a Roman fort: presumably transit between here and Brough was one reason the Romans used Mallerstang as a highway), Aysgarth and on through Yorkshire to the East Coast Main Line. This whole line was closed in stages between 1954 and 1992, and reopened as far as Redmire in 2003-4. There are plans to reopen the entire line as far as Garsdale, which, if it happens, will make a scenic and convenient northerly alternative to the Trans-Pennine Express.

Secondly, there's Mount Zion Chapel, a Primitive Methodist chapel built, along with 22 cottages, in 1876 for the benefit of the railway workers stationed at Hawes Junction at Dandry Mire. The chapel was painted maroon and cream, the colours of the Midland Railway, and may be the only place of worship built by railway contractors (St Gregory's, Vale of Lune, near Sedbergh, was built for, but not by, railwaymen). Nestled under the Dandry Mire Viaduct, which looks to me more like a Roman aqueduct than a Victorian viaduct, it's recently been restored and redecorated in its original livery and to me looks, as its name sounds, like something out of a spaghetti Western. Weekly services continued here up to 1999, when the 'Friends of Hawes Junction Chapel' were formed to raise funds to arrange special services and to maintain the building.

Lastly, at the junction with the B6259 Mallerstang road (which dates from the 1820s) is the excellent (and wonderfully friendly) Moorcock Inn, just the place for a wet and weary traveller at the end of a long day.

However, as this book isn't subtitled *Sequestered Spots in Yorkshire*, we'll ignore the many and tempting shake holes and caves that litter the southern end of the dale and begin our exploration at Aisgill, where the county boundary crosses the road at about the point Hell Gill becomes the River Eden. We've already heard the dubious story about Dick Turpin jumping Hell Gill Force, so we'll leave the Eden's highest waterfall behind and proceed to the main settlement in Mallerstang, Outhgill, by one of two routes, either simply along the road (there's rarely much need to worry about traffic, aside from the odd tractor) or up the path to Hellgill Bridge and then left, along Lady Anne's Way, noticing on your way that, perhaps more than any other parish in Cumbria (Longsleddale and Howgill spring to mind as rivals), Mallerstang is really a collection of strung-out hamlets and farms with very little by way of a nucleus (what geographers call a dispersed settlement: it's what happens when you need a lot of land per head of the population). The old road joins the new at a place called Boggle Green, about which I've found precisely nothing, but the name interests me because a boggle (alternate spelling boggart, Harry Potter fans might like to note) is a malevolent household fairy in northern European folklore.

But what nucleus there is, is at Outhgill. In fact, Mallerstang wasn't always a parish, but a township of Kirkby Stephen, like, for example, Kaber. I haven't been able to establish when the status of parish was conferred upon it, but can report that the population of about a hundred is too small to entitle Mallerstang to a parish council: rather, administration is performed by a parish meeting, the lowest tier of local government in England.

The former smithy has a claim to fame: now called Faraday Cottage, James Faraday, father of the scientist Michael Faraday (1791-1869), another religious non-conformist (if you want something to look up then he was a Glasite), worked as a blacksmith in Outhgill before moving to London in 1790. So, ironically, back when Mallerstang was a township, it had a shop, a post office, an inn, a smithy and a village hall (the Travers Institute, named after an incumbent of St. Mary's, Travers MacIntyre, from 1912-19: it was towards the northern end of the hamlet, and closed in the 70s): now that it is a parish it has none of these.

Two things in Outhgill are worth exploring: first the village green, on which stands a replica of the stone William Mounsey set at the source of the Eden, the stone broken by railway navvies: the inscription, translated, reads "William Mounsey, a lone traveller, commenced his journey at the mouth and finished at the source, fulfilled his vow to the genius and nymphs of the Eden on the 15th March, 1850." A little way along the road east from the green is the pinfold – the area where stray animals were penned pending their owners reclaiming them – which contains one of a series of sculptures by Andy Goldsworthy installed in pinfolds across the county. Another (very attractive) modern sculpture, 'Water Cut' by Mary Bourne, is one of ten site-specific, carved stone sculptures commissioned by the East Cumbria Countryside Project to celebrate the Millennium, all of which also function as seats, situated on public paths along the length of the Eden. It's situated on the old road north east of Hanging Lund, at about the 'L' of 'Old Road' on the 1:25,000 OS maps.

Secondly, inevitably, there's the church (opposite the former Methodist chapel). Founded in the 14th century – tradition says 1311 – by Lady Idonea de Veteripont, a descendent of the de Morvilles (Maud de Morville, granddaughter of Hugh, as in Hugh Seat, who we'll meet again at Pendragon Castle, married William de Vieuxpont, Lord of Westmorland some time before 1210: Idonea was their descendant) and the de Cliffords, who, by marriage, inherited their lands. Lady Anne, who, again, we'll meet properly at Pendragon, was a Clifford by birth. Idonea's name interests me, as the River Eden was known to the Romans as the Itouna, as recorded by Ptolemy in the 2nd century. This name derives from the Celtic word *ituna*, meaning 'water' or 'rushing' (Nicholls says he's of the opinion that the Eden is so beautiful the Saxons named it for the biblical river: beautiful it is but still somewhat optimistic if you ask me). Idonea seems to be completely unrelated to this: rather, it's a variant of a German girl's name, derived from the Old Norse Idony, of which one website says:

> Idony: English form of the Old Norse name Iðunn, which was probably derived from Old Norse Ið "again" and unna "to love." In Norse mythology Iðunn was the name of the goddess of spring and immortality.

But the similarity between Idonea and Itouna is striking, almost striking enough that it seems too much like coincidence.

St. Mary's was "RUINOUS AND DECAYED" by the time Lady Anne began to exert her influence in the area, and as a plaque above the door records she restored it in 1663. As with many chapels of the 17th century, and as with many shall churches in Cumbria, like St. John's, Helsington, or St. Gregory's, Vale of Lune (although not as much as St. Martin's, Martindale, which is of a

St. Mary's, Mallerstang.

similar age and was restored just a little earlier) it today has a collegiate atmosphere inside. It's mostly locked, but two houses nearby have keys: see the notice board for details. The interior has some Victorian stained glass and some very attractive kneelers depicting local scenes. Outside in the graveyard is a monument erected in 1998 to commemorate the 25 men, women and children who died as a result either of accident or smallpox during the construction of the railway and were buried in unmarked graves. This last, somewhat gruesome fact, combined with the story of the smashing of the engraved stone placed near the source of the Eden related in the 'Nine Standards to Wild Boar Fell' chapter, suggests that relations between the population of Mallerstang and the navvies may have been strained.

You'll also notice that people of Mallerstang all tended to live to ripe old ages. Nicholls says that around about 1810, "the inhabitants, finding it a long way to carry their dead to Kirkby Stephen, petitioned the Bishop to consecrate a burial ground near their own place of worship." The first burial was of a Margaret Moore, aged 82, in 1813. Nicholls then lists the burials on a random page of the parish register:

1823: Dec. 28, Buried Mary Ward of Outhgill, aged 91.
Elizabeth Brunskill of Cocklake, aged 86.
1824: Feb. 4, Margaret, widow of Hugh Blenkhorn. She died in Ingram in the parish of Aisgarth and county of York, aged 87.

Mar. 7, Richard Fothergill, late of Sand Pot. He died at Southwaite, aged 86
June 9, buried John Metcalfe of Aisgill, late at Hazlegill, aged 87.
Robert Atkinson of Blue grass, aged 92.
Anna Rennison, Cocklake, aged 76.
Aug. 11, Mary Brown, Tarn House, Ravenstonedale, aged 78. (pp. 42-3)

We'll leave Outhgill behind us, glancing up as we do so to Mallerstang Edge. England has only one 'named wind', the Helm Wind, a ferocious wind that sweeps down from Cross Fell to the north. Mallerstang has its own version of the same wind, which sweeps over Mallerstang Edge, and can blow (and roar) for two days or more. It blows most frequently in spring or autumn, and is accompanied by a dense bar of cloud, the 'Helm Bar', along Mallerstang Edge.

Pendragon Castle.

A chronological account of the valley's history should really start with Pendragon Castle, whose big blue castle symbol dominates the valley on the OS maps. Legend has it that it was the seat of Uther Pendragon, youngest son of one of the warlike kings of the Britain of the day, and father of the king who would unite the land, Arthur. Geoffrey of Monmouth, the 12th century monk and author of *History of the Kings of Britain* and the *Prophecies of Merlin*, relates that Uther Pendragon, father of King Arthur, received his name after seeing the portentous omen of a great dragon in the sky: he was not aware that Pendragon, 'great dragon', simply referred to a great leader. How this castle became attached to the Arthur legend I don't know, but as Lammerside Castle has a similar attachment we can guess the area had strong links to Arthurian legend from about the time Geoffrey of Monmouth was writing. Nicholson records that after the Romans withdrew their administration of the British Isles the Britons by and large refused to acknowledge the authority of the provincial Roman governors left behind, and instead restored the old tribal chiefs under the title of Pendragon, and that, "Uter was in all probability the Pendragon of the Cumbrian Cymri who long held their own against the tide of Saxons."

Nicholls noticed that Nicholson and Burn, in their *History of Westmorland*, give a different story about Uter of Pendragon Castle: they say that 'Ughtred' was the name of a Saxon warrior son of Waltlieof, Earl of Northumberland, who, though outnumbered, beat the Scots King Malcolm's army in battle, for which Ethelred gave Uchtred his daughter, the Princess Kl-iva, in marriage, and with her the counties of Northumberland and York. "Pendragon seems not to be properly the name of a man, but an epithet only, describing his warlike quality. Pen, it is well known, signifies a mountain or something that is great, and dragon hath been applied in all ages to military persons."

Nicholls was dismissive of this version of events: "The radical defect of Dr. Burns' account," he said, is "that the link is wanting what should connect Uchtred, the Saxon warrior, with the castle here." Pendragon Castle is in neither Northumberland nor Yorkshire, and it's speculation that Uter is the same name as Uchtred. He also objects that there's a story which crops up over and over about the castle, that it was beseiged by Saxons who, considering it impregnable, poisoned the well, thus killing Uter and his soldiers. Tradition also has it that Uter tried to divert the river to flow, moat-like, around both sides of the castle: but, as the saying has it,

> *Let Uther Pendragon do what he can*
> *Eden will run where Eden ran.*

Another story is that Uter's ghost, mounted on horseback, haunts Shap Fell. Pendragon Castle was, according to the historic, rather than the mythical, record, built by Ranulph le Meschin, a Norman Knight of William II and Henry I, effectively running Cumberland and Westmorland on the latter's behalf.

Another name from these years is Hugh de Morville, mentioned above. Hugh, who died about 1202, was Lord of Westmorland and Forester of Cumberland, titles which, with some others, he inherited from his father, a courtier of David I of Scotland. David took Carlisle in 1135, and with it Cumberland, which he held until Henry II retook Carlisle in 1157: presumably thereafter the allegiance of the powerful de Morvilles shifted to Henry, because Hugh was in Henry's service from 1158. In 1170 he, along with

Reginald Fitzurse, Richard Brito and William de Tracy famously overheard Henry, holding court at Bayeux and irritated at the Archbishop's claim that as he, the Archbishop, hadn't been present at the coronation, said coronation hadn't been valid, say something along the lines of "will no one rid me of this turbulent priest?" The four knights, somewhat over-zealously, crossed the channel and murdered unsuspecting Thomas Beckett in Canterbury Cathedral.

As mentioned above, Hugh Seat is named for Hugh de Morville, either because he climbed it to escape from marauding Scots, or simply because he stopped there for refreshments while out hunting. It's also said that Hugh was haunted by the profile of Wild Boar Fell on which, from Pendragon Castle, he could see the profile of the face of Thomas Beckett. If this is true, then in my opinion Hugh is one of England's lost imaginative geniuses.

The next important name connected with Pendragon is that of Lady Anne Clifford, whose descent from Hugh has been sketched above. Pendragon was attacked by Scots cattle raiders in 1342 and again in 1541, and after the latter attack it was abandoned until it passed into the hands of Lady Anne, who

Wild Boar Fell from Pendragon Castle.

rebuilt it in 1660, adding a brew house, bake house, stables and coach house.

Anne was a remarkable lady. She was born at Skipton in 1590, the only sur-viving child of George Clifford, Earl of Cumberland, who died when she was fifteen. Mortified to find that, in the days of male primogeniture, her uncle inherited her parents' estate, she was engaged for nearly 40 years in trying to claim what she felt was rightfully hers. A favourite of Elizabeth I's when she was young, she married first Richard Sackville, 3rd Earl of Dorset. After his death in 1624, she married Philip Herbert, Earl of Pembroke and Montgomery in 1630, and took the name Pembroke. Finally she inherited her parents' lands in 1643 and headed north to explore them in 1649, as the Civil War raged. Aged 60, she enthusiastically set about restoring castles – specifically those at Skipton, Appleby, Brough and Brougham as well as Pendragon – alongside, as we saw at St. Mary's, many churches and almshouses. She died in 1676 aged 86 at Brougham Castle, and reputedly Pendragon was one of her favourites. A 'Great Picture' – actually a triptych – of the family which she commissioned is now at Appleby Castle, which is a private residence.

A portrait of Lady Anne is in the Abbot Hall gallery in Kendal. She has two walks associated with her: firstly Lady Anne's Trail, which runs 100 miles from her birth place, Skipton, to Brougham where she died; secondly the Lady Anne Clifford Westmorland Heritage Trail, from Brougham to Outhgill. One other thing in connection with Lady Anne's presence in Mallerstang is impor-tant: as Nicholls says, she restored the church, and endowed it with a minister, who was also to teach the children to read and write.

Mary M. Thompson, in *Mallerstang: A Westmorland Dale* (pp. 49-50) gives an account of the traditional annual "barring out" of the schoolmaster: once a year the boys locked themselves in the schoolroom and presented the school-master with an ultimatum, asking for specified holidays, after which, once agreed and signed, school was resumed. Concerning this practice Nicholls quotes two poems, one for November, 1740, the other for September, 1794, which hint at the standard of education in the school. An excerpt from the first reads:

> *As on our beds we all profoundly slept*
> *Into our chambers great Minerva crept,*
> *With awful looks there did great Pallas stand,*
> *Her dreadful Aegis in her potent hand.*

And the second,

> *Also take care that you do punish none*
> *Until Epiphany be pass'd and gone.*
> *Sir, these demands are civil, pray consent*
> *To sign this bill and grant us merriment.*
> *For recompense whereof we will not fail*

> *To give you and your friends a glass of ale.*
> *From what is written we'll not yield one jot,*
> *It's like the Persian law that alters not.*

Thompson reports that the original school room was extremely cramped. Efforts were made throughout the 19th century to raise money for a new school, but nothing came of it. Forster's Education Act of 1870, passed to ensure universal access to education across the country, resulted in the formation of a School Board in Mallerstang in 1876 and a new school was built in Outhgill at a cost of £529. It had capacity for 48 children, but usually had about 20 pupils at any given time. It opened on 11 September 1877. Thompson relates a story that in 1943 news reached the schoolmistress that George IV was about to travel through the valley on the Royal Train on his way to Scotland. She walked the schoolchildren, "armed with little flags," to Shoregill (the few houses west of Outhgill, by the railway) to try and catch a glimpse of the King. "His majesty was in a corner seat looking across the valley to Hugh's seat. The children waved their flags and the King raised his hand in acknowledgement. As they walked back an infant burst into tears because the King had no crown on his head. 'Never mind,' said an older comforter, 'you saw the lovely door handles; they were all pure gold.'"

Oddly I haven't been able to trace when the school in Outhgill closed, but I can report that the school building was at the end of the lane that leads east past the village green, and that it was open in the 1950s.

Something else that was a long integral part of the life of Mallerstang (and

that Lady Anne, as, it seems, with everything else, took part in enthusiastically) was the annual walking of the bounds, carried out before the days of enclosure to ensure that neighbouring parishes, and neighbouring landowners, weren't slowly adopting land that belonged to the township – later parish – of Mallerstang: Nicholls tells us that the bounds were ridden on 12 July, 1865, and then again in 1906. To commemorate the centenary of this the bounds were walked again in 2006.

Big old oak tree near Lammerside Castle.

Lammerside Castle.

It's not surprising that the later residents of the vale might have been reluctant to walk the bounds: the circuit is 33 miles (53km) even before you consider the up and down. Those who took part were able to "report that our ancient bounds are still intact and there have been no incursions by perfidious neighbours in Wharton, Nateby, Kirkby Stephen – or even by those benighted folk over the Yorkshire border."

There's a fine network of roads, byways, bridleways and footpaths that can be used for walks north of Outhgill, but before we leave Mallerstang a couple of other specific places are worth mentioning. The first are the 'pillow mounds' near the river shown on the OS maps not far north of Outhgill: supposedly these are artificial medieval rabbit warrens, though this doesn't convince me: they're too big, and look like glacial drumlins to me, although I'm doubtless wrong.

Secondly there's Lammerside Castle, passed by a bridleway at the northern end of the vale past the pillow mounds. A mysterious place, about which virtually nothing is known, Lammerside presumably dates from the height of the Scots raids – the 13th or 14th century – and was doubtless a pele tower, designed to protect firstly people and secondly cattle from Scots raiding parties. It's possibly the site of the Castle Dolorous of Arthurian legend – Mallerstang's second connection with Arthur, a place where the giant Tarquin resided and where he retired to eat the local children. His brother Caradoc, another giant, had been a Knight at the Court of Uther Pendragon, but did not get on with King Arthur, and took to capturing Knights of the Round Table and taking them back to the castle. Eventually the number of prisoners – including Sir Yvain and Sir Gawain – grew so large that Arthur was forced to declare war on Caradoc, who was killed in the ensuing fight.

Lammerside today is an intriguing place, a crumbling (and faintly danger-ous) two-storey ruin with a rather substantial tree growing out of one wall. I'm ashamed to write that as I finish off this book I can't remember what kind of a tree it is and it seems a long way to go just to find out, though I am sorely tempted. If I had to put money on it I'd say it's an ash.

The fact that so little is known about what happened within these decrepit limestone walls only adds to the mystery. The only source of the story that Lammerside is the Castle Dolorous that I've managed to find is *A tour from Downing to Alston-Moor*, a posthumous work by Thomas Pennant (1726-98), the Welsh antiquarian and travel writer. It is thought, though, that it was latter-ly occupied by the Wharton family until the 17th century, when they moved to a newly rebuilt Wharton Hall, which originally dated from about the same time as Lammerside, but is more conveniently situated for a family desirous of leading something resembling a social life.

Inside an old oak near Wharton Hall.

Bretherdale

Bretherdale in winter.

In *The Outlying Fells of Lakeland* Wainwright includes a number of walks in the Shap fells, the desolate swathe of moors between Kendal's Borrowdale and Shap traversed by the old coach road, now the A6, once feared by travellers for its desolation, its vagabonds, even its wolves. It must be said AW is, to say the least, restrained in his praise of all the routes he recommends in this area. Of Howes, between Mosedale and the top of Selside Pike he writes, "Howes is not a separate fell but merely a subsidiary and undistinguished summit [of Branstree]. There is nothing exciting about it."

About the next walk, on Seat Robert between Swindale and Wet Sleddale, we're told, "it is too remote from the attractive interior of the district, and obviously nothing exciting is likely to be found... the views are extensive but dreary and unexciting." Then, the last four walks in the book are four horseshoe walks around four of the valleys between here and Kendal: Wet Sleddale ("its visual attraction has been diminished in the past decade by the construction of a massive dam"), the 'other' Wasdale ("no challenging tracks and no excitement [...] featureless desolation"), Crookdale ("does not quite measure up... all of it is grass, and most of it is wet grass [...] nowhere [...] occur any features to relieve the drab monotony of the enclosing slopes"), and finally Bannisdale ("the watershed is everywhere grassy [...] and featureless [...] the scenery is desolate and has little of beauty.") He makes no substantial mention here of Borrowdale, because it's dealt with (with well-deserved praise) in the first chapter of *Walks in the Howgill Fells*. But there, as here, AW has virtually nothing to say about the next valley north, Bretherdale.

He's not alone. Search the internet for 'Bretherdale' and you get next to nothing. Consult all the contents pages and indexes of all the books on my Lake District bookcase (7' 6" of shelves in total) and you'll bag a couple of passing mentions. The most detailed account I've found is Gareth Hayes, in *Odd Corners around the Howgills* (Hayloft, 2004), where we learn that John Dower, secretary of the Standing Committee on National Parks in 1945, proposed that the Howgills, along with Borrowdale, Bretherdale and neighbouring valleys deserved to be a National Park in their own right.

I've described the Howgills as a-historical, but compared with Bretherdale (which, to be fair, is only a few stones' throws away) they are teeming with signs of the past. Aside from the fact that the signs of the enclosures acts are clear to see (stone walls on the hills, hedges in the valleys, fences in between, piles of stones dotted along boundaries marking where vague attempts to improve the fields have been made) the landscape here gives no hint of former ownership or use. To be honest that history is fairly simple: Bretherdale was gifted by Thomas, son of Gospatrick, an Anglo-Saxon earl of Northumberland, to Byland Abbey in Yorkshire. After the Dissolution it was bought by the Whartons of Kirkby Stephen and later came into the hands of the Earls of Lonsdale, who were responsible for enclosing it.

And that's about that. But what it lacks in historical interest, Bretherdale makes up for in terms of beauty. It's certainly no Great Langdale or Wasdale: rather, it has a pastoral beauty less than that of Bowderdale or the Langdale in the northern Howgills, but, somehow, what Bretherdale lacks in scale and wildness is makes up for in sheer charm. It's just a truly special place to explore.

Park on the A6, where the bridleway leaves the road, at the layby (on the other side of the road, assuming you're driving from Kendal) with a memorial to "the drivers and crew of vehicles that made possible the social and commercial links between north and south on the old and the difficult route over Shap Fell." Walk up to Crookdale Crag and the higher, unnamed 485m summit above Greenside Crag (there's no right of way shown on the maps but there's a good, if damp after rain, path which follows the east side of the fence line), then join and follow the (these days very eroded, and as a consequence rightly closed to motor vehicles) Breasthigh Road from just past the Thunder Stone at the watershed with Borrowdale down into Bretherdale. Then walk through Bretherdale and back up to the A6 via Red Crag. A perfect little valley walk.

A couple of names adhere to nearby Tebay and deserve a mention. The first is Mary Baynes, who enjoyed the title of the 'Witch of Tebay.' She died in 1811 at the age of 90 and supposedly issued a prophesy that 'fiery, horseless carriages' would one day pass over Loups Fell, just west of the course of the West Coast Main Line. She, along with other (mostly more concrete) gems of local history are celebrated on the walls of Westmorland Services, northbound and south, a place virtually synonymous with Tebay and one that epitomizes to me the spirit of what Cumbria is, and should be, doing in the post-Foot and Mouth new millennium. Catering for tourists and passers-by as well as locals, majoring on top-quality local produce, providing jobs as well as a cracking fry-up of a morning, to say nothing of a mean barbequed burger of a sunny summer's lunchtime, made with beef or lamb from the owners' farm (and all this, don't forget, at a motorway services: they recently won an award from Egon Ronay: they've also won a million other awards, and I'm only just exaggerating). Westmorland Ltd. runs a whole spectrum of money-making activities – farm shop, café/restaurant, fuel stop, caravan park, hotel, to say nothing of the truck stop or the brilliant Rheged Discovery Centre further north, just to the west of the main Penrith motorway junction.

The whole area from the Lune Gorge up to Shap is somewhere that is passed through on the way to other places, and, mostly, you can see why: the views are great, the prehistoric remains worth seeking out, but the immediate vicinity is not overwhelming in its scenic interest and, besides, has a motorway and a major railway line running through it. That empty Bretherdale should be tucked away so close to all this frenetic 21st century journeying is as good an example as any of the diversity of place to be found in Cumbria.

Eden Valley

Practically the whole of the Eden valley, from the river's source high above Mallerstang to where it reaches the sea at Burghmarsh Point on the Solway Firth, could have made it into this book: indeed many places along it have, from the source (in the 'Nine Standards to Wild Boar Fell' chapter) to its

River Eden from Lacy's Caves.

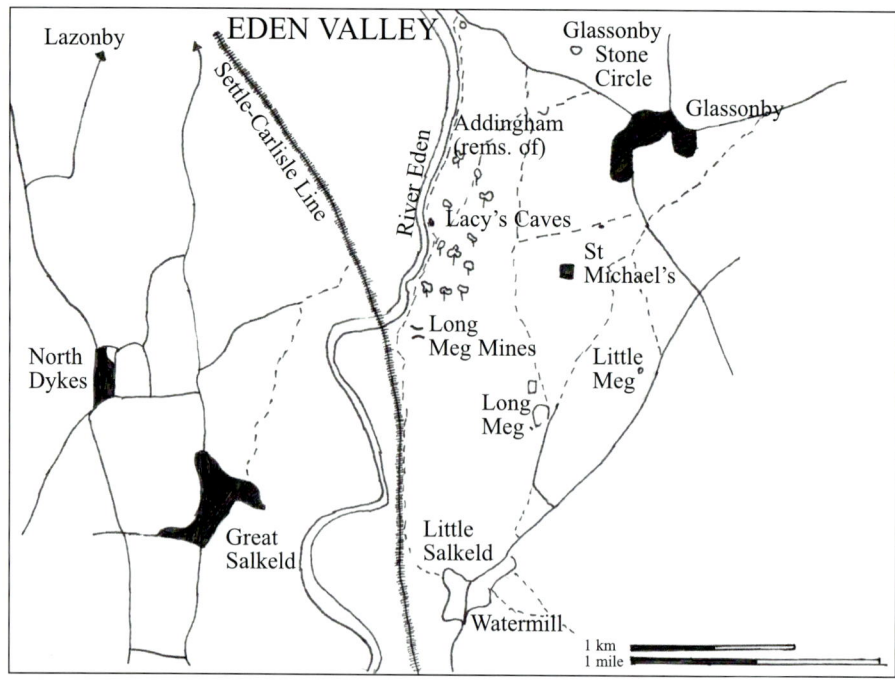

mouth, visited near the Edward I memorial in the North Coast chapter towards the end of the book. But, having to choose somewhere else along the river's long length between Kirkby Stephen and the sea to concentrate on, it has to be around Little Salkeld. I first read the name on the label of a bag of organic wholemeal flour I bought as an undergraduate in a healthfood shop in Lancaster in the 1990s, but it would be a decade before I got to the Watermill at Little Salkeld in person.

After a tour of the mill, which was restored in 1975 by Ana and Nick Jones who ran the mill until 2014, I bought a sizeable

Stream at Little Salkeld Mill.

supply of flour and other baking goods in the shop, and over lunch in the tearoom picked up one of several brochures and leaflets they printed. Most of these were (very good) recipes but the particular one in question describes a circular walk from the watermill which we did that afternoon. I can't think of a better way of exploring the area than following that walk, but it doesn't seem fair to describe it here when someone else has published it, so I'll firstly recommend you go along and buy a copy of the booklet, and second, by way of encouragement, will describe the rich human history of the area,

Walking from Long Meg towards Addingham.

chronologically. A nearly identical walk has been published in a leaflet printed by the now defunct East Cumbria Countryside Project. Incidentally at the time of going to press the watermill is recently under new ownership, but all seems business as usual.

LONG MEG

Chronologically we start at Long Meg and her Daughters, the third largest stone circle in England (after Avebury in Wiltshire and Stanton Drew near Bristol) and one of the most intriguing. Probably Bronze Age, 4500-5000 years old, the daughters are an oval ring 305 by 360 feet, while Long Meg herself is a twelve foot megalith of local sandstone, a material which will prove important later in our story of the mid-Eden valley, standing outside the circle to the south west.

Wordsworth said of Long Meg, in a letter of 6 January 1821 to his patron Sir George Beaumont: "Next to Stonehenge it is beyond dispute the most notable relick that this or any other country contains." Hyperbole certainly, and unjustified: in his notes on his poems dictated to his friend Isabella Fenwick later in

Sunset over Long Meg – notice the notch in the top of the stone.

life (in 1843) he said "When I first saw this monument, as I came on it by surprise, I might overrate its importance as an object; but, though it will not bear a comparison with Stonehenge, I must say, I have not seen any other relique of those dark ages which can pretend to rival it in singularity and dignity of appearance." Wordsworth had at least visited Castlerigg before, on a walking tour with Coleridge in 1799.

Wordsworth was familiar with Stonehenge, having slept under the stones and had a visionary experience concerning druids there during a walk from the Isle of Wight to Wales in 1793: it's a shame he never went to Avebury, which is much more like Long Meg in style, although on an altogether different scale. But clearly Wordsworth was not familiar with many other 'reliques' of a similar type or age. There are other stone circles in Cumbria which can hold a candle to Long Meg, such as Castlerigg, or even the Cockpit, given its setting. And the mis-held assumption that stone circles had something to do with the Druids continues to be widespread. The Druids were prominent during the iron age, centuries after either Stonehenge or Long Meg were built, but the rather old-fashioned street sign pointing to Long Meg from the road between Little Salkeld and Glassonby reads 'Druids' circle', a common alternative name for the circle. In fact it's quite possible Long Meg is a lot older than the late phase of Stonehenge, dating back to the very early Bronze Age, and Meg herself may well be considerably older than the circle, her daughters: if this is the case, of course, then the alignments mentioned below are the result of the circle having been constructed to reflect the placement of the megalith, rather than the

Long Meg signpost and below, Long Meg's daughters under snow.

other way round. In fact a circle with features such as these – a single entrance with portal stones, an outlier and a large open central area – could well predate the Bronze Age, making it a very early stone circle, especially this far north.

The remaining important facts about the Long Meg circle can be quickly summarised. The

stones of the circle are locally occurring glacial erratics whereas Meg, as I've said, is of local sandstone, and is the only stone on the site to have been quarried. Quarried, that is shaped, stones are rare in stone circles: what makes Stonehenge especially unique is the highly carved nature of its outer circles of sarsen stones. Long Meg herself, besides being shaped, is decorated with cup and ring marks, strikingly similar to those discovered on a boulder at Copt Howe in Great Langdale, on a route leading to the Langdale axe factory. The markings on Long Meg are, it seems to me, reminiscent of a map of circles: some day maybe I'll take this thought further.

Cup marks at Copt Howe in Great Langdale and at Long Meg.

The top of Long Meg is notched, and if you stand at the centre of the circle at sunset on the midwinter solstice the sun sets through this groove, in alignment with the summit of Helvellyn. The stone is also aligned across its long axis to the summit of Wild Boar Fell, The Nab, where there is a tumulus. All of these facts – her being sandstone, and shaped and carved, in contrast to the stones of her Daughters, her alignments, the fact of her being an outlier – suggest, to me, that she was regarded as an object of great power by the people who erected her, as well as to every generation which has left a record of its reaction to her since.

Two pairs of stones form an obvious entrance to the circle in the south west, not far from the megalith. The circle is (or was) surrounded by a ditched enclosure twice the size of the circle, invisible on the ground now but clearly seen on aerial infrared photos, which also show that the circle is the smaller top half of a figure 8-shaped feature aligned east-west, with the larger, now vanished circle surrounding the modern-day Long Meg Farm.

Finally, the best-known and the most colourful thing about the circle is the legend which tells that Long Meg was a witch directing her daughters, the stones of the circle, dancing on the Sabbath, for which sin they were turned to stone: it's said that if you count the stones and get the same number each time, the spell will be broken and the stones will turn back into witches. It's not an uncommon story about stone circles: but I must say in all honesty I've counted the stones in the circle dozens of times, and have never counted the same number twice. Neither has anyone I know, and I have made several friends try. Perhaps, subconsciously, I don't want to, just in case.

These are the significant facts concerning Long Meg: but I don't feel I've yet touched on the soul of the place. There are more spectacularly placed pre-historic monuments in Cumbria – Moor Divock, or Castlerigg, spring to mind: and what makes the view from both those places so impressive – Blencathra – is also the star of the show from Long Meg. But Blencathra is only distantly glimpsed from here, the Pennines are a lot closer and there's a much more open feeling to the landscape: despite this the prominence of Blencathra, and the knowledge of the alignment with Wild Boar Fell, means that the mountains are more present as suggestions, as facts in the minds of those who erected the stones in the distant past, which somehow makes their presence more imme-diate than if they were closer. And Meg herself is brooding, contemplative, standing aloof from but somehow protective of her daughters, like a mother huddling her ducklings at her favourite viewpoint before penning them down

Long Meg, Blencathra in the distance.

to the Eden, where there is no shortage of ducklings in early spring. Legends believed or not, there's magic at Long Meg.

I must mention that this isn't the only stone circle in the immediate vicinity: there are two more. Firstly Little Meg, at the edge of a field a little over half a kilometre north east, close to the Little Salkeld-Glassonby road, which sadly has no public access and is in a state of some disrepair, most of the stones being fallen and lying somewhat randomly scattered: and then there's Glassonby stone circle (the OS map calls it a 'cairn circle') just north of, and

clearly visible from, the road
from Glassonby to Kirkoswald,
about half a kilometre out of
Glassonby. Again there's no
public access. Little Meg has
some ring markings too.

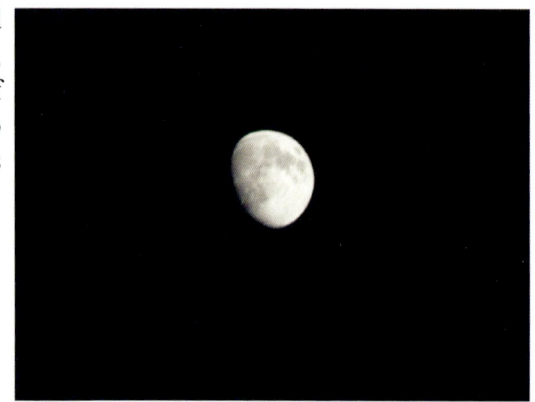

*Moon from Long Meg and below, Glassonby
stone circle.*

ADDINGHAM

Leaving the prehistoric a little, but not far behind, we move on to the intriguing church of St. Michael's (actually St. Michael and All Angels), Addingham,
a kilometre north and a little east of Long Meg. Intriguing firstly because there
aren't many churches belonging to settlements which don't exist any more:
but such is the case here. Addingham, on the riverside slope below the church,
was swept into the Eden in a flood as early as the 14th century: just some
stones still remain near a sluggish spring in the last field before the woods as
you head south down the east bank of the Eden from Daleraven Bridge – one
of the many beautiful bridges crossing the Eden, where the road nearly touches the river between Glassonby and Kirkoswald. It's strange to think that those
stark, mossed remains of a settlement have been lying there in the soft field for
seven centuries.

   The church, however, is far more impressive than the remains of the village
whose past it bears testament to, and from whose remains it was apparently
rebuilt, the original having been destroyed when the village was. A typically

River Eden from near Addingham, above, and St. Michael's Addingham, below.

squat, stout structure of local sandstone, it's exquisitely constructed and pro-portioned and despite its stoutness is more definitely a church than some fur-ther north along the Eden Valley, which, as we'll see in the chapter on the north Cumbrian coast, can feel as much like fortified strongholds. Its most interesting features are a beautiful early Saxon hammerhead cross in the churchyard, a truly striking thing which somehow manages to look more like an inquisitive cartoon child than anything else, though for some reason it also

always reminds me of a Hammerhead shark; and a Viking hog's back grave tombstone which lies in an alcove in the vestibule. There are a few other things worth a look too, including an ancient cross base, a pitch pipe which dates from 1810, and most recently, the west window, of 1973, depicting St George and the Dragon.

Left, Saxon cross at Addingham Church, below, looking up to Lacy's Caves and, to the right, spring flowers and wild garlic in Cave Wood.

LACY'S CAVES

Next we move back down to the Eden, a little south through some beautiful woodland from the remains of Addingham village, where the scant spring is still named for St Michael, to Lacy's Caves, occupying a commanding position overlooking a wide, broad and serene section of the Eden: watch out for families of ducklings in the spring.

Ducklings on the Eden and Lacy's Caves.

This auspicious location, which can be a little tricky of access if it is icy or even very wet underfoot, was picked by Colonel Sam Lacy, owner from 1790 of Salkeld Hall, as the place in which he lived out a personal fantasy of dwelling in a cave. Well, not quite: rather he employed a team of navvies, under the direction of his footman, to carve out the five chambers of Lacy's Caves, with their elegant Gothic-arched doorways and passages, from the soft

sandstone, apparently with the intention of moving there out of the hall full-time: but in reality, the caves seem to have been used as a summer party venue, as well as, possibly, a wine cellar; and rumour has it that Lacy even employed a full-time hermit to lend verisimilitude to his summer parties down by the river. Either way, the caves are a magical place to visit nowadays, picturesque enough to be quaint, beautifully situated enough to hold a certain sublimity, architecturally perfectly proportioned so that you can imagine yourself wandering through a pre-Raphaelite painting, natural enough that you can feel a bit Robinson Crusoe here. It's just a shame you're not allowed to spend the night. Toddlers will scream with delight. You'll scream as they try to pitch themselves into the river.

Lacy has another, less laudable link to another Eden highlight visited above, Long Meg and her Daughters, which, apparently he tried to dynamite – showing more orthodox, and less well-guided, sentiment than his fondness for partying in artificial caves suggest. He saw the circle as part of a Pagan past best got rid of. Legend has it that the men he assembled to perform the wicked deed were about to get to work when a thunderstorm blew up, of such violent intensity they were convinced it was a warning act of God. They fled, thus saving the circle from destruction.

LONG MEG MINES

A scant kilometre south of Lacy's Caves, through the beautiful Cave Wood – especially fine in spring, full of bluebells and carpets of wild garlic – is the latest and, undeniably, the least prepossessing of the past's legacy in this section of the Eden valley, the remains of an old gypsum mine whose skeleton is well worth a poke around (it wasn't only a gypsum mine: the mineral anhydrite was mined here from 1922). Mined between 1880 and the 1970s, the industrial remains in fact have the uncanny feeling that they were abandoned in a hurry yesterday, with mine railway carts lying about, hut doors gaping open and numerous shafts disappearing into the valley side.

ST CUTHBERT'S, GREAT SALKELD

While we're in the vicinity it would be a shame not to mention St. Cuthbert's. It's always surprised me that these two villages, Great and Little, share a name, as they're on opposite sides of the river and it's a good six miles (10km) north-south between the nearest road bridges, at Lazonby and Langwathby respec-

Carving at St. Cuthberts, Great Salkeld.

tively. The first time I went to Little Salkeld, wanting to visit the watermill, driving towards the Pennines from the M6 and only roughly knowing where I was going, I took the Great Salkeld turn off just before the Langwathby bridge on the basis that the two villages couldn't be that far apart. The round trip Great Salkeld-Lazonby-

Kirkoswald-Glassonby-Little Salkeld seemed to go on forever.

In the north coast chapter of the Coast section at the end of this book we'll meet Cumbria's other two surviving fortified churches, so here I'll just say that St Cuthbert's is the third example of a pele church, that is a church whose tower has a very practical use beyond the symbolic and ecclesiastical functions of most church towers: it functioned as a place to hide cattle, women and children

St. Cuthberts, Great Salkeld and an arch at the church.

(probably in that order) when the Scots were raiding. The three fortified towers that survive from those days are, as we'll see, fairly similar: the present-day churches they're attached to are, however, very different.

St Cuthbert's, the first of three St Cuthbert's mentioned in this book (the others are at Clifton and at Kentmere), significantly predates the other two pele churches, and the days of Robert the Bruce. Cuthbert himself, famous hermit of the Farne Isles, protector of birds and later Bishop of Lindisfarne, died in 687. His body was removed from Lindisfarne during a Viking raid in 875, and spent a few years 'wandering', so most accounts put it (I assume they mean figuratively) around the north of England before being placed in a shrine in Durham cathedral. Great Salkeld was one of the places the body rested for a while, and the first church on the site was built to house it in 880. Rebuilt in 1080, but incorporating earlier stone including many fantastically Gothic carvings around the doorway and some early grave slabs, the pele tower was added in 1380, some 75 years later than those of Burgh-by-Sands and Newton Arlosh. St Cuthbert's retains the oak cladding on the heavy iron door which leads from the nave into the tower, unlike the other two, and like Newton Arlosh it has the original very narrow door, designed to make the church easier to fortify and defend when it was full of women, children and cattle and the Scots were trying to smash their way in.

Lyth Valley

This book was written by a busy man (and latterly a busy father) running a business in a back bedroom in Oxenholme – a man therefore prone to dashing

Lyth Valley floods, 2009.

out to snatch the odd couple of hours exploring interesting-looking places on the OS map of the immediate vicinity pinned to the wall. Inevitably therefore this book features a lot of places clustered round Lyth Valley – Scout Scar and Whitbarrow, and Brigsteer Park wood – and it would be easy to ignore the valley itself. But have a look on the map and you'll notice that it's an oddity, a landscape unique in the Lake District.

Unlike the other limestone-ringed valleys of the south Lakes – Kentmere, Leven/Crake, Duddon – Lyth Valley was, for the vast majority of its history, an anachronistic, silty estuary winding deep inland. Now it's basically an entirely artificial fen, complete with dykes and drains and sluices. Perhaps, given how seemingly out of place this piece of artificially drained piece of fenland dropped into the south of the Lakes is, I should start with a bit of history explaining how the landscape came about.

G. P. Jones' *A Short History of the Manor and Parish of Witherslack* is the place to start, but allow me to summarize. Up to 1891 Witherslack was a chapelry of Beetham rather than a parish in its own right, despite being divided from Beetham by the Kent estuary. Witherslack as a name is from Old Norse and means 'the hollow of the wood.' Whitbarrow is 'the white hill.' But most of the other local names – Foulshaw, 'bird copse' – are English. Ownership before the Normans is unknown: probably no one was much bothered with the marshy swamp, salt-encrusted and platchy, and its crumbly, pitted limestone backdrop. It was part of a huge area of land granted to Ivo de Taillebois, a name we'll meet in the Martindale chapter as the first of a family who would be made Barons of Kendal by William Rufus, (see the Martindale chapter).

There's history here that predates the Conquest, though: the Witherslack sword, a Viking longsword, was found in the 1960s in a gravel bed at the foot of Whitbarrow Scar, eight feet below the surface: quite how it was unearthed I've no idea. It's now in Kendal Museum. Before we get into human history, though, what about the history of this odd man out of a landscape?

Well, it's extremely flat and very low-lying. High Heads, by a right-left kink on the main road at Lyth Moss, reaches a dizzying 24m: and then there's Dobdale Hill. If Cumbria contains Scafell Pike, England's highest peak, I wondered for a while if it also has England's lowest: Dobdale Hill has a circular 10m contour so tiny it's a testimony to the OS cartographers' dedication to accuracy they included it at all (in fact Stonea Camp, an Iron Age hill fort in the Fens, at 2m, is Britain's lowest hill).

For the following brief account I have to thank a book called *Cameos of Crosthwaite and Lyth: The Damson Valley*, written, to celebrate the millennium, by four inhabitants of the parish of Crosthwaite and Lyth, published by Titus Wilson in Kendal in 2002, and an example of the very best kind of local history.

After the erosion of the ice age much of the valley was left under the level of the Kent estuary's high tide, and in places mosses grew: these later formed peat deposits as the place slowly silted up. These became useful when the valley was enclosed under the terms of the Heversham Enclosures Award of 1815, the same Act (as all Enclosures needed Acts of Parliament) that enclosed Whitbarrow. In Lyth Valley, though, the process of making the land usable, and fertile, was a lot more complex than the general procedure on the hills, which involved walling or fencing, clearing stones and, occasionally, applying some lime or other fertiliser. Here drains had to be cut, bridges built, pump houses installed, and on top of all this extensive treatment it was necessary to reduce the acidity of the peaty soil, and its saltiness.

The result of all this effort was arable land able to produce cereal and root crops, a rare commodity in Westmorland (as was). Not surprisingly this fact made the valley, whose value was previously debatable, hot property. John F. Curwen's *Records relating to the Barony of Kendale* volume 3, titled *Crosthwaite and Lyth, Supplementary Records: Crook and Winster* (pp. 162-5) records that in 1718 the bridge over the river where the Gilpin Bridge Inn is today was in need of repair, and in 1823 (oddly after the enclosures act, when you'd have thought the major thoroughfare across the valley would have been sorted out) a new bridge was needed, suggesting that the route across the valley mouth had been a perpetual problem in the past. When the Lancaster Canal reached Kendal in 1819, a mere four years after the enclosures act was passed (and the canal was followed by the railway in 1857), however, it became easier and cheaper to import cereals and roots from further south, for example from the Fylde. So Lyth Valley is, and has been for most of its

Bridge, dyke, fences and improved fields in the Lyth Valley.

history post-1815, used for raising livestock, mostly sheep but some cattle, and of course for growing damsons.

Damsons love limestone, and a combination of this, the comparative fertility of the valley and the fact that it's a struggle growing any other kind of fruit, short of raspberries, blackberries and the odd wild strawberry this far north, have ensured that Lyth and damsons have been synonymous for a good couple of centuries, probably longer. Damson production had declined by the 1990s, but in 1996 Peter Cartmell founded the Westmorland Damson Association, a loose network of Lyth Valley damson growers who, besides selling damsons, both fresh in season and frozen, also sell damson gin and damson jam (in my opinion the finest jam of all, though de-stoning the damsons is a faff: we've recently discovered not to bother, it's easier to fish them carefully off the surface of the cooked jam). There's now an annual Damson Festival.

We first bought Lyth damsons one summer's day years before we moved from Lancaster, and then I promptly forgot all about Lyth Valley and its damsons until my first walk there, which happened by accident a couple of weeks after my first climb onto Whitbarrow. I'd walked up to Whitbarrow via Bell Rake above Low Park Wood and the beautiful gully spring of Fairies' Cave, got lost in the woods on Wakebarrow and ended up hitting the road at Flodder Hall by Moon's Wood. At this point it started raining, and being late for some kind of domestic commitment details of which now escape me I had little choice but to run back to Beck Head along the main roads. On that day I resented Lyth Valley, its straight roads and apparent monotony compared to the limestone hills, Whitbarrow and Scout Scar, the former of which I should have been on top of save for my navigational shortcomings. In those early days in the Lakes I had eyes for nothing but the tops: even with lower ones like Whitbarrow the heights were the point, and time spent in the valleys, especially 'artificial' valleys like Lyth Valley, was time wasted.

Then, one Saturday, came our first planned walk in Lyth Valley. My wife was in the early stages of pregnancy, and tired, not helped by the fact that she'd been talked into working a late shift on Friday night. She wanted to go for a wander, but preferably a gradient-free wander with a choice of decent eating establishments nearby. Given the proximity of Lyth Valley Hotel, Gilpin Bridge Inn, the Wheatsheaf at Brigsteer and the Punchbowl at Crosthwaite, the answer was obvious. Researching the history of Whitbarrow, I'd noticed an intriguing footpath which leads from the A574 at Row to a small outlying copse at Savinghill Moss, and ends there. I can only assume, but have not been able to prove, that this footpath is an old access route leading to the place where inhabitants of the valley had a right to cut peat and/or collect firewood. Be warned, as we discovered that day, the footpath is by no means the easiest to follow on the ground.

Bridge in Lyth Valley.

We had a beautiful walk through the dense mists that cling to sheltered Lyth Valley for the darker six months of the year, revelling in the winter all around us, the signs of which were forced into the foreground by the fact that there was no background: the mist saw to that. It's all too easy – and rightly so – to be so overwhelmed by the backcrop of wintry hills, whether you're viewing them from low down, or from the tops of other wintry hills, that you don't notice the signs of winter, the leaves, frozen grass blades, icy carcasses even, close at hand. But in the mist in Lyth Valley there's little else.

Slow-moving, ice-congealed waters oozed silently along drains, under bridges and through sluices. Fluffed-up birds rummaged through once-laid, now neglected hedgerows for seeds and berries they might have missed on the hundreds of foraging missions they'd already made through the same spot. Herons flapped lazily at the periphery of our vision. We got covered in mud, and laughed a lot, our laughter echoing back from the mist, and explored the enclosure landscape, seeking out signs of the great work of the early 19th century. There are the obvious bits – the dikes and ditches and bridges and pumps and sluices – and also the less obvious: piles of stones at field boundaries, remains of older fences, disused gateposts replaced by the modern galvanised ones. We quickly forgot where we were, and I found myself imagining that we were in the fens: I was born in Peterborough, and have a deep connection to that flat, artificial but somehow beautiful landscape, and Lyth Valley is, in thick mist, very familiar, although unmistakably northern at the same time, the grass being thinner, the daffodils and tulips and poplar trees not much in evidence, the weeds in the verges a different mixture. Nevertheless, suddenly it was as if I was back there, and then, just as suddenly, we were back at Gilpin Bridge Inn.

In November, with our daughter a few days old, Cumbria was hit by severe floods. We were OK, living way above the River Kent at the foot of the Helm, but we did take the pushchair down to Force Falls one afternoon and stood watching crests and boulders of water come tearing into view, only to vanish into the dark downstream a second or so later. The noise was deafening and,

Lyth Valley panorama.

with such a tiny, vulnerable person with us, the power of the river was very frightening. Next day we went to Helsington to see the floods in Lyth Valley. Drained and flood-protected it might have been: but, in the face of what the northern weather can do when it puts its mind to it, flood Lyth Valley still can.

It was a Sunday morning in March, and we'd planned to go for a family walk in Lyth Valley that day to give me a chance to collect my thoughts before writing this chapter up. My wife had been up half the night and so, when my darling daughter had been up and happily playing for an hour and a half and then started getting crochety, I decided to get said darling daughter into the car to get her to sleep and take her for a walk in Lyth Valley. I carefully calculated how long she was likely to sleep for, and drove out to Brigsteer Park wood. I loaded my sleeping infant carefully into a sling on my front, shooshed her back to sleep as I zipped her up inside my coat (not noticing, in my hurry to get her back to sleep and myself off walking, that I'd left the car with one of its doors wide open), and headed off through the woods, past the spring at Simms Well and out into the valley.

With my wife happily asleep at home, and my daughter happily asleep zipped inside my coat, I felt, somehow, more the dominant male of the family than I usually allow myself, and set off into the mists to spend some 'Quality Time' with the emerging spring. It was, after all, the vernal equinox, the first day of spring, officially.

Ramsons were, suddenly and gluttonously, through. Bluebells, too, although obviously the flowers were still weeks away. An eggshell was impaled on the end of a stick by Simms Well, clearly caught where it had fallen. Out in the valley lapwings fussed in the fields. Lark song snatched down the occasional breaths of breeze. Ducks and a pair of snipe, silent in flight, came cutting through the thin air: late Graylag geese grazed in the fields; a vole plopped down its hole in an embankment; goldfinches in the hedges, and robins, defending their territories even more aggressively than usual – even against the goldfinches. I performed a successful search for the first frog spawn of the year, and heard a woodpecker. In a small wood the carcass of a sheep was spread bizarrely far and wide, a forefoot here, a jaw there, somewhere else half a spinal column. I found the skull on a mossy tree stump. Buzzards' cries came turbocharged through the mist from somewhere up on Scout Scar, but mostly life was right in front of me, the minutiae of real nature forced into the foreground, as there was no background of hills, or of work, or of worrying about the baby, who was slumbering contentedly, stirring infrequently, down the front of my coat. I loved feeling her moving, even when she did decide that painfully pinching my chest would be a good way to stay asleep.

The fields moved by. Mist patches clung to grass clumps like mushrooms do in the autumn, and to be truthful it felt autumnal, despite it being March. Then, just before 11am, two things happened. Firstly – and this doesn't happen in autumn, and shocked me out of my fenland reverie – the sun suddenly broke up the mist, and there we were, ringed not by Boston Stump and Ely Cathedral and Fenland's signature lines of soil-draining poplars, but by Whitbarrow and Scout Scar and, in the north, glimpses of the proper Lakeland hills.

Secondly, my daughter woke up. Which I hadn't been expecting, and as I was a good half hour from where I'd left the car, and despite the fact that she was quite happy in the sling on my front, looking around at the sunlight and the trees and the birds, I doubted this happy state of affairs would last more than about 20 minutes. So I woke my wife as gently as is possible from a distance of nearly ten miles, and arranged to meet at the Wheatsheaf at Brigsteer for milk, coffee, another walk, then lunch. Then we came home and I got going on this chapter.

The next morning, Monday, I got Ruth up and dressed, and she was quite happy for a while watching me sitting at my desk, typing away. But then she got crochety and I was about to wake my wife up and hand over the baby for feeding, when I looked at her and thought, 'you're tired, not hungry.' So I loaded her into the car, where she played, happily, with the toys that clip onto the car seat, halfway to Brigsteer, then fell asleep. She slept all the way around a circular walk near Helsington Pool bridge, I had a wonderful time in the bracing spring wind under a quick grey sky, made the most of the chance to get my head round what I needed to do that week, and my wife got a bonus lie in to recharge the batteries at the start of the week. Loading Ruth back into the car woke her up, and she played happily all the way home. I later claimed the hour between her bath time and her (theoretical) bed time as an extra work hour. The joys of working freelance. And I got to see two herons, another vole and those greylag geese at the start of the week.

Little Langdale

Little Langdale from Pike of Stickle.

The Lake District was long one of Britain's major slate-producings area, its green stone providing roofs for hundreds of thousands of workers' terraced houses built during the Industrial Revolution across the country, and across the north west in particular. I've lived in six houses in the north west, all of them slate roofed. Coniston, the Skiddaw region, Honister, and Little Langdale, with its satellite valleys around Tilberthwaite, were the centres of the industry, besides smaller centres at Kentmere, Longsleddale and elsewhere. The excellent visitor centre at Honister Pass will tell you everything you could ever want to know about the Lake District's slate mining history, and allow you to go deep into the mine to see what conditions were like for the miners of yore. There's an excellent mining museum at Threlkeld, nestled under Blencathra: the one in Keswick has sadly closed. But the most impressive quarries – as opposed to mines – in the Lake District are those of Little Langdale, particularly Hodge Close and Parrock quarries and, a little further up the valley, Cathedral Quarry.

I discovered Hodge Close by accident. One Wednesday morning I finished an indexing job and decided to take the rest of the day off. I drove round the head of Windermere (the queue for the ferry was enormous) and headed for the familiar 'Hodge Close only' road, which I'd never followed to its end, always having stopped in the past to climb Holme Fell via Raven Crag. Today was no exception: I did the short scramble, wandered over to the summit and then set about exploring more thoroughly than before the top of Holme Fell.

I'd intended to climb down the eastern flanks of the fell, through Harry Guard Woods. But when I reached the disused reservoirs at the northern end of the fell I changed my mind, and followed the path along the outflow down past numerous signs of industry, mostly buildings erected for reasons now unknown, to the quarry itself. The purpose of the reservoirs is known: they provided water to power a hoist to lift blocks of unsplit slate out of the quarry.

The main quarry drops suddenly away from the car park – extremely suddenly if you stray too close to the unmarked brink while not paying attention to where you're putting your feet, as I wasn't that first time. Astonishingly well-hidden given its enormous size, Hodge Close has been disused only since the 1970s and now, a favourite with climbers, abseilers and divers, it's like a small, steep fell – Holme Fell springs to mind – in reverse, or upside down, its steep sides leading down, not up, to the 'summit' in a flooded maze of tunnels which have claimed the lives of divers who got trapped and ran out of air.

Hodge Close

There are plenty of books, not to mention museums and visitor centres in the Lakes, which can provide a much better picture of the history of mining in the Lake District than there's room for here, but briefly: according to J. D. Marshall and Michael Davies-Shiel's *Industrial Archaeology of the Lake Counties* (Michael Moon, 1969 and 1977, pp. 154-60) Sadgill Quarry in Long Sleddale, north east of the mysterious and probably prehistoric mound of Whirl Howe, was first mentioned in 1283, but it was a long time until the industry took off. Coniston slate was exported via Coniston Water from Piel Harbour in 1688. By 1753 Honister (then called Fleteworth), Tilberthwaite, Gaitswater (Goat's Water under Dow Crag) and Burlington slate quarries at

Kirkby in Furness were all producing slate. Polishing equipment was installed at Helsington Laithes in 1799, and another local polishing mill, opened in 1830, made a mantelpiece for Windsor Castle from Kendal Fell limestone. Limestone was extracted from there as early as 1656, and much of Kendal was built of stone from there and from the quarries on Whitbarrow.

Lime mortar and whitewash was made at lime kilns at similar localities. Lime burning became a major industry south of Kendal after the canal was opened in 1819 and "there is still an especially fine lime-kiln, with a double hearth, in a bank north of the Crosthwaite road, at the extremity of the built-up area" (p. 158), which has been restored and had sign boards put up. Later Farleton Fell was a major source of lime, and the remains of many kilns can be seen around Farleton and Crooklands. According to Marshall and Davies-Shiel, writing in 1977, "Hodge Close remains in use," and in fact after a few decades' silence some quarrying continues in the vicinity. Apparently 3,000,000 cubic yards of rock have been removed from Hodge Close, most of it laboriously by hand.

Quarrying is often viewed as a poor relation of mining, the remains of quarries as eyesores, but Hodge Close and Cathedral quarries belie this. As Marshall and Davies-Shiel put it, "Quarrying, as opposed to mining, is less well served in print" (p. 274) but to my mind these places are just as intriguing as mines, and unquestionably the most impressive quarry of them all is Hodge Close, although Rainsborrow Crag Quarry's lonely setting, perched high above the valley floor in Kentmere, has much to be said for it in terms of these places imparting a sense of awe.

In fact Hodge Close wasn't always a quarry: for most of its history it was a mine, the roof having been taken off some time in the 19th century: not want-

The original entrance to Hodge Close.

ing to give too much away, let's just say that the original access shaft is still there to be found and can be used to reach the flooded floor of the quarry, if you don't mind a bit of stooping and wading. Otherwise you'll have to either make the somewhat precarious descent down loose slate stones from the southern end of the quarry (the re-ascent is a lot easier) or alternatively make your way down through Parrock Quarry (see below), where you can access the huge archways between the two quarries. The remains of a railway can be seen here, and it is possible though not wholly straightforward, to scramble round either side of the water and reach the far side. In fact there's quite a lot of fun scrambling to be done around the place, and a number of pitch black above-the-water passages and chambers to be poked around in, most of them ending in spookily lapping, dripping water. There are rock climbs and abseil routes on the walls too.

In truth I find the whole place spooky: its eerieness, particularly when the weather's awful and you have the place to yourself (in which case watch your footing, as the slate gets slippery) is part of the attraction. It's one place where my childhood fear of the dark, which I conquered at about the age of eight, returns when I'm on my own, and I've never quite brought myself to swim in the stunningly blue water either: it's the thought of all the depth and machinery and the dark, deadly, twisting chambers and tunnels below that puts me off. That and the fact that it's absolutely freezing.

In Parrock Quarry.

The whole area is well worth exploring, but I will mention two more quarries in particular. Firstly Parrock Quarry, which connects with Hodge Close through the huge arches at the latter's northern end, is completely different in character from its sister. Entered from the northern end, its wooded floor, the bushes and small trees which grow from its walls and the sparkling blue of the Hodge Close lake at its end make it more reminiscent of a desert oasis than a north of England quarry: you expect to see ibexes peering down at you from the walls. Wildlife abounds, reptiles especially, and in many ways the quarry feels like a *Star Trek* set. There are some good scrambling opportunities: it's just a shame about the rubbish dump at the north end. The traverse of the stone bridge separating the two quarries is highly recommended too.

Above, the Langdale Pikes from Tilberthwaite and below, in Cathedral Quarry.

And then there's Cathedral Quarry, situated just south of the aptly named, and very beautiful Slater Bridge, to the east of Little Langdale tarn. Belonging to the National Trust, the quarry's main chamber is mostly roofed, with a huge central pillar and two arches in the main chamber, then a raised area beyond this from which lead a couple more

Above, Slater Bridge and below, Little Langdale Tarn.

passageways: again there are scrambles and climbs to be had. This is by no means a complete inventory of industrial sites worth visiting in Little Langdale, however; for example there are the quarries and levels in Yewdale Beck and Tilberthwaite Gill.

I heartily recommend getting to know the quarries of Tilberthwaite. I've never had the chance to scramble up to the higher reaches of Tilberthwaite Gill – where there are mines and levels, and one of the supposed sites of Swallowdale from Arthur Ransome's book of that name – as every time I've tried it's been raining and I've been told the gill can be very slippery in the rain. In fact this short chapter doesn't really seem to have got as far as Little Langdale, which has the beautiful Little Langdale Tarn; Blea Tarn house and its vicinity, the setting for a great deal of Wordsworth's long poem *The Excursion*; Ting Mound, a moot or meeting site of considerable antiquity;

Lingmoor Fell and the Langdale Pikes from near Slater Bridge.

Lingmoor Fell, rightly the first mountain described in Cicerone's popular *Great Mountain Days in the Lake District*; a number of beautiful bridges; the excellent Three Shires Inn... I could go on.

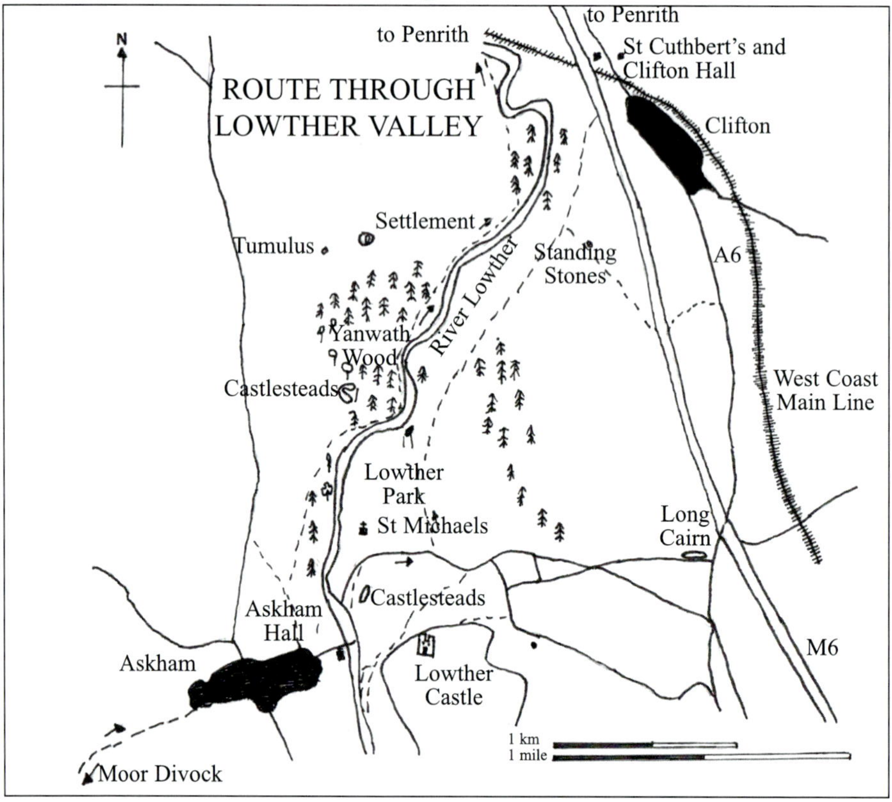

N

ROUTE THROUGH LOWTHER VALLEY

to Penrith

to Penrith

St Cuthbert's and Clifton Hall

Clifton

A6

Settlement

Tumulus

Standing Stones

River Lowther

Yanwath Wood

Castlesteads

West Coast Main Line

Lowther Park

St Michaels

Long Cairn

Askham Hall

Castlesteads

Askham

Lowther Castle

M6

1 km
1 mile

Moor Divock

Lowther Valley

In the Askham Fell chapter I've described crossing Moor Divock, after a night spent at Angle Tarn and an early morning following the route of the High Street Roman road over High Raise, Red Crag, Wether Hill and Loadpot Hill. In truth, as I said there, I hadn't really paid much attention to the details of how I was going to get from Loadpot Hill to Penrith: at that stage of my Cumbrian explorations bagging Wainwrights was everything, the remainder of the county simply space to be traversed between them. Knowing that I'd be able to see Penrith from Loadpot, it had seemed simple: head towards Penrith until I hit the River Lowther, follow said river to the outskirts of town then signs to the station.

But then came Moor Divock, and by the time I'd finished wandering around exploring all the intriguing things shown on the map, taking photos and making lists of things to research, it was a lot later than I'd intended it to be and I still had a long way to go. Reluctantly I left Moor Divock behind, determined to get a move on.

I found myself almost immediately in the enchanting village of Askham, where opportunities to not get a move on abounded. First there's the village itself, a long, thin settlement running east-west, bisected in the middle by the minor Brampton-Penrith road, with, effectively, a long thin (not very thin in places) village green running the whole way through the village. There are two village shops, two pubs – the Punchbowl and the Queens Head (the draw of which I with difficulty avoided) and, at the east end of the village, a wooded section of the River Lowther, crossed by a beautiful stone bridge (rebuilt in 1897, according to a stone on the parapet) near which, on the Askham side, are St. Peter's Church, the first of two churches mentioned in this chapter (the second being only 500 yards away), as well as Askham Hall.

St. Peter's was built in 1832, on the site of an earlier church originally dedicated to St. Kentigern. Parts of the church are much earlier: above the pulpit is a medieval corbel with a carved male head, providence completely unknown, while the baptistry on the south side was once the burial chapel of the Sandford family, Lords of the Manor of Askham from the reign of Edward III (1312-77) until 1724, when William Sandford died and the manor was sold to the Lowther family. The present St. Peter's was designed by Sir Robert Smirke, who was working on the design of Lowther Castle at the time and was asked to do the church too. Askham Hall is a 14th century pele tower converted in Elizabethan times to a comfortable country manor. It's private property and has no access, but you can get a pretty good look from the bridleway/footpath that leads north from Askham towards Yanwath Wood.

Returning to my walk: I crossed the river and made my way along the road, not realising that a much better way out of the valley from the bridge is to join

Bench in Lowther Park and, below, buzzard hunting over Yanwath Wood.

the path that leads south, climbing past a bench along the east bank of the Lowther to join the network of footpaths around Lowther Castle. My next port of call was St. Michael's, where I changed my socks (outside, naturally) and spent a while resting, refreshing my memory as to the history of the Lowther family and watching a pair of buzzards hunting over Yanwath Wood.

The Lowther family have been landowners in the area since 1283. James Lonsdale, 1st Earl of Lonsdale, born in 1736, was a notorious character known to posterity as Wicked Jimmy, among other unflattering titles. He's notorious for several things, including falling in love with the daughter of one of his Cumberland tenants, who he moved to his Hampshire estate to take her away from the gaze of the northern landowners, where she reportedly died of homesickness: the Earl, inconsolable in grief, refused to accept her death until her body, still dressed and propped up at the dining table as if ready at a moment's notice to entertain all callers, began to smell so badly that all of his domestic staff resigned.

His other celebrated act was to run up a considerable debt to his land agent, whose job, largely, was to bribe people into voting for his boss (in three elections which were held in 1857-8 he paid out over £24,000 in expenses), to beat up anyone eligible to vote who refused to promise to vote for Lowther, and to bribe and intimidate owners of any property, the title deeds of which came with a vote, into selling said property to the Earl, who thereby effectively gained opportunities to vote for himself.

When the land agent in question, whose name was John Wordsworth, died in 1783 of an illness contracted after he got lost on the fells late one night returning home on business, he left four orphaned children – Richard, William, Dorothy and John Wordsworth – and was owed a staggering £4,000 by his employer, a debt which would only be honoured after Wicked Jimmy's death in 1802, when, he having died without any (legitimate) heirs, his second cousin William, later Wordsworth's leading patron, repaid the debt with interest. Jimmy is said to have haunted Lowther for some time, before being finally exorcised: as with so many stories of ghostly exorcisms in the north of England, it was a Roman Catholic priest who finally got rid of the ghost, the locals clearly considering that the use of Latin rites was more powerful than English ones.

Askham Hall.

The Lowther family today live in Askham Hall, which as we've seen they acquired in 1724: they originally lived in Lowther Hall, rebuilt as Lowther Castle in 1806 and abandoned in the 1930s, when the combination of the Great Depression and the 5th Earl's extravagant lifestyle proved ruinously expensive. The roof was taken off in 1957, leaving the crumbling ruins, evocative of a more opulent era, that we see today. There are plans to do some restoration work to secure the ruins and to open the old castle and its grounds to the public as an attraction built in and around the gothic ruins: a 51-year lease was granted to a new charity, the Lowther Castle and Gardens Trust, in 2010: planning permission has been granted and things seem to be moving apace: while things are far from complete the garden is now open to the public every day. The Kendal Calling music festival has also relocated there in recent years. I look forward to a lot more to visit in the area in future.

But in addition to these things, there's plenty more to see around the Lowther valley. Lowther Park is a pleasant place to walk around, with a network of footpaths in and around the valley, two 'Castlesteads' iron age earth

Lowther Castle and a pheasant in Lowther Park.

works, one in Yanwath Woods (great name) and one in the woods just north of Ashkam Bridge, pleasingly close to the latest castle in the area: both are well preserved; Clifton, with Clifton Hall (another pele tower owned by English Heritage, and occasionally open to the public, although the building is accessible to the  public at all times; and the beautiful St. Cuthbert's, a tiny chapel/church with a 12th century nave, Norman doorway and beautifully carved choir stalls: Clifton was also the site of the last battle (more a skirmish) on English soil, when the Jacobite forces were fleeing pursuing troops on their way back to Scotland and, eventually, Culloden. There's an interesting and huge long cairn parallel to a minor road off the A6 between Hackthorpe and Clifton, and some standing stones in a field south of Clifton: there's the very good Bird of Prey centre in Lowther Park itself; and, of course, there's St. Michael's, Lowther.

St Michael's, Lowther

For some reason I wasn't expecting so many figures from my academic past to suddenly cluster so closely around me in the lonely quiet of the church and graveyard. The graveyard – aside from a probably 12th century cross shaft and other Viking age and later tombstones and so on which have been found here, the former of which is still in situ and the latter in the vestibule – is full of the graves of members of the Lowther family. The most obvious of these is the possibly over-the-top mausoleum erected in memory of William, the second Earl, who died in 1844: the mausoleum was erected in 1867. The church itself contains the gravestones of Wicked Jimmy (in rather pretentious, and to me somewhat schoolboy, Latin), as well as his more benevolent heir, and any number of other members of the family, including for example the tombstone of Richard Lowther (d. 1607), who was "thrice a commissioner in ye greate affaires betweene England and Scotland, all in ye time of Queene Elizabeth."

The interior has the characteristic veneer of Victorian 'restoration': the majority of the building dates from 1686 with later additions, but contains stonework, particularly the tops and bases of pillars, which, without wanting to give anything away, are much older and in the medieval grotesque tradition. St. Michael's has a unique atmosphere: it's essentially a private chapel which is also a public church, it has beautiful views, Arts and Crafts touches in addition to what I've described above, and has an atmosphere quite unlike anywhere else I've ever been: you feel like you're in an English stately home, and that when you turn round there'll be an English Heritage or National Trust

steward standing politely in a corner, asking you if there's anything else you'd like to know: and then, every time you snap out of investigating the tombstone or the ancient stone carving or whatever other feature you've been admiring, you suddenly realise that you're all alone, you're

Gargoyle in St. Michael's, Lowther and the River Lowther.

going, almost certainly, to remain all alone no matter how long you spend here, and that you can probably hear at least one species of bird of prey. The presence of the aforementioned Bird of Prey centre probably has something to do with this. I somehow, and rather selfishly, hope that St. Michael's is as quiet as it was, now that the castle and park are more open to the public. It has the same air as Lowther Castle, that of the unexpected continuation of a past age of wealth and aristocracy, but here, in the sight of God, suddenly and limitlessly made accessible to everyone, and without the abiding sense of decay that accompanies this at the ruins of the castle.

174

To finish the story of my walk: my route onwards involved following the drive down to the beautiful Low Gardens Bridge, then through the woods along the river valley to Penrith, where I took in King Arthur's Round Table and Mayburgh Henge, two more ancient circles, on the edge of Penrith, I passed the Plague Stone (which was once filled

Pines in Lowther Park and below Plague Stone, Penrith

with vinegar on market days) so that plague suffering stallholders could disinfect their fingers before accepting payment for goods, and is now found oddly situated between the main road and some retirement flats) before finally – by that stage limping slightly – reaching Penrith railway station.

Kentmere and Longsleddale

KENTMERE

The Kentmere Horseshoe – the walk from Kentmere village, up Garburn Pass, then right over Yoke to Ill Bell and Froswick, Thornthwaite Beacon and down to Nan Bield Pass before a final pull up to Harter Fell and Kentmere Pike – is

Ill Bell summit panorama

175

*Kentmere horseshoe
views, above, and
looking down from
Ill Bell, left.*

a very favourite walk of mine, especially in winter, and one day in November I set out to do the walk in reverse.

But the weather was having none of it. Half way along the path which leads diagonally up to the ridge between Shipman Knotts and Kentmere Pike, I stopped to stare up through the stinging rain at the black clouds being torn to shreds by the summit of Ill Bell and then whisked over Harter Fell a second or so later, and decided that on second thoughts I'd have to make do with an exploration of the head of the valley.

My disappointment did not last. Kentmere is full of little bits of history, and also has some Vodafone signal, which meant that, in between checking business emails from my mini laptop, I found myself sheltered in caves and under crags researching online the landscape which, swathed in the storm, was all around me.

The valley is reasonably well scattered with older (Iron and Bronze Age) settlements, especially Bronze Age: from about 1200BC the climate seems to have deteriorated and the uplands were less and less used for anything other than summer pasture. Such settlements as there are are by and large lower down the valley, either south of the present village, such as those at Hugill, east of Borrans Reservoir, or near the village, but there are some settlements at the head of the valley. This doesn't mean they were permanent settlements, however.

There's the site of a later Viking 'settlement' (so says the OS map) on Bryant's Gill. If, as is often suggested, the Vikings who arrived in Cumbria in the Dark Ages were second generation settlers from Ireland, rather than direct emigrées from Scandinavia, they may have been without the warlike characteristics more usually associated with their countrymen. Being hardy folks, they settled with their equally hardy sheep and cattle in upland areas at the heads of valleys that the indigenous farmers of the time had little use for: Kentmere is just such a place. There's another 'settlement' shown on the maps next to a sheepfold right at the head of the valley under Lingmell End, which is probably very old. There's also a cave shown on the 1:25,000 OS maps as being at a quarry north of an enclosed Bronze Age settlement at Tongue House: the cave is in fact not here but is to be found just south of Whether Fold a third of a mile or so north-northwest. It's huge but unfortunately you can only get a few yards in before an impenetrable iron grate blocks the way. It's an eerie place to be alone in a rainstorm.

Aside from settlements the other major evidence of human activity in the valley is in the form of mines and quarries, the most notable of which (to me anyway) are the door leading into a shaft on the hillside east of Browfoot between Kentmere village and Staveley, and then the massive two-tier quarry halfway up Rainsborrow Crag. On my rain-soaked first exploration of the valley I scrambled up there and, ducking round a fallen boulder the size of a Ford

Kentmere fell ponies on Harter Fell.

Transit, ate my sandwiches while scrambling round the smashed and frost-shattered chaos of the inside, climbing up and down between the chambers, very aware of the loneliness and the cold and damp. It was almost impossible to take photos because you had to stop breathing first, otherwise all you got was a picture of a cloud of breath – but, above all, I felt overwhelmed – the weight of the mountain above me, and of the length of the silence, broken only by the occasional drip of water and the distant roar of the wind overhead. I wondered how many people had been here since slate quarrying in Kentmere stopped at about the end of the Second World War. I reflected that upper

Kentmere is probably lonelier now than it has been for a few thousand years.

I haven't mentioned the final man-made feature in the valley, the reservoir. The lower valley was, as were many rivers in the area, full of bobbin, paper and other mills, and the

In the quarry on Rainsborrow Crag and Kentmere Reservoir from Harter Fell.

reservoir was built in 1848 to try and ensure a regular supply of flowing water further downstream. The reservoir came into the ownership of James Cropper papermills, which still runs in Burneside, and which is so desperate to get rid of the reservoir and the associated maintenance costs that it's trying, so far without success, to give it away.

No account of the valley's history would be complete without a mention of the Gilpin family. A Norman family who came over in 1066, they were given lands in Kentmere by King John and built Kentmere Hall. Once the Vikings had replaced the earlier upland farmers nothing much happened in Kentmere for a bit over a thousand years. Kentmere Hall, now a farmhouse, is one of the classic pele towers, built in the 13th and 14th centuries to keep the landlord's cattle out of the hands of Scots raiders.

At the time of the signing of the Magna Carta, Richard de Gilpin accompanied the Baron of Kendal to Runnymede. Returning home, Richard became famous for slaying the Wild Boar of Westmorland – a ferocious beast which had been scaring the locals – at the site of the Wild Boar Inn on the edge of what's now Windermere Golf Course, near the head of the River Gilpin, Gilpin Farm, Gilpin Mill, Gilpin Lodge, etc. As a reward the Baron granted him land in Kentmere. Richard Gilpin was immortalised in a ballad known as *The Minstrels of Winandermere*, which purports to be ancient but was supposedly written by the brother of Charles Farrish, a university friend of Wordsworth's.

The village's most famous son was the religious reformer Bernard Gilpin, who was born at Kentmere Hall in 1517. He was a Protestant preacher during

Swaledale sheep at Overend Farm, Kentmere.

Kentmere lambs and a mystery black rabbit spotted near Hartrigg.

the reign of Henry VIII, a Fellow at Queen's College, Oxford and Archdeacon of Durham: he declined the bishopric of Carlisle, was vehemently anti-Catholic and had the nickname 'the Apostle of the North.' He was in real danger of being burnt at the stake by Queen Mary: he was arrested and was facing heresy charges when, on the journey to London, he broke his leg, which delayed him, and Mary died before he got to London. Elizabeth I subsequently restored him to the position of Archdeacon. He's remembered in a memorial in St Cuthbert's Church, most of which dates from either the 17th century or from a rebuilding in 1866.

The one thing I haven't mentioned is the Brock Stone, also known as Badger Rock. A huge volcanic boulder, presumably a glacial erratic, this block in a field next to the track heading up to Garburn Pass not far out of the village is very, and justifiably, popular with scramblers

I'll end with a warning about car parking. There are some spaces by the church (£1 in the honesty box) but these are very much in demand and if you're hoping for a space you'd best be early. A nearby paddock is opened in high summer as a car park but again this can fill up. You can alternatively catch the Kentmere Rambler bus at weekends in the summer but from experience this service is subject to frequent change and timetables are hard to come by. It's operated by Stagecoach.

LONGSLEDDALE

One evening in the spring after my move to Cumbria – 2 April 2007, to be precise, a Monday and the first weekday after my birthday, which had been celebrated by buying a box set of Wainwright guides and climbing Skiddaw – my wife was working late, and I, finally, was working, editing a novel. But the deadline wasn't too

Longsleddale sign from the A6 and upper Longsleddale from the top of the fields above Sadgill.

tight, and so in the early evening rather than turn my desk lamp on I drove into Long Sleddale for the first time.

Long Sleddale is surely the most progressive of Lakeland valleys: from wide, pastoral beauty at its mouth to craggy grandeur as you slog up to Gatesgarth Pass and the quarry at Wrengill. It is also beautiful, more beautiful even than Martindale, excepting the views from Hallin Fell to the Nab, and from the Nab to Hallin Fell, and though far less impressive in terms of craggy grandeur and sweeps of hills than Wasdale (and lacking a lake) it's much more varied.

Upper Longsleddale from Cocklaw Fell.

That April evening I'd set out to climb Grey Tarn and Tarn Crag, the two peaks above the east side of the valley (ignoring Branstree, which I'm not counting as it's north of Gatescarth pass: if you want to climb Branstree I'd recommend climbing from Mardale via the old coffin trail towards Swindale and then over Selside Pike, heading back down Gatescarth Pass (pick a clear day).

The route Wainwright recommends is surely one of the best of his recommendations, the sort of route you'd stumble across by accident once in a thousand hastily planned hillwalks. It wasn't by accident that AW found it, of course, but by obsessive covering of every inch of every fell under consideration. But this route, described on page four of his Grey Crag chapter in *The Far Eastern Fells*, is brilliant. As he bluntly states "the first thousand feet is steep" but once you've slogged across the field (or up the wall, as I did, despite being neither a lady nor a "gentleman with short legs"), you come to Wainwright's "easy gully", barely distinguishable even on the 1:25,000 OS maps, and a gem of a hillwalk begins in earnest. From the top of the gully (passing through which in the slanting sunlight I felt a bit like R2D2 all alone on Tatooine) you make your way over and round Great Howe, past one of several oddly-shaped, slot-topped survey pillars scattered across the hillside which had something to do with surveying at the time Haweswater reservoir was being planned, although exactly what I'm not sure.

Anyway, next it's a fairly straightforward walk via a gate in a wall to the summit, which I reached just as the sun set over Kentmere Pike. As Wainwright points out, this point marks the head of the seven valleys of Shap Fells – Bannisdale, Borrowdale, Crookdale, Wasdale, Wet Sleddale, Swindale and Mosedale, as well as, near enough, Longsleddale itself and although it

Whirl Howe.

would be easy to bemoan that most of the Lake District view is obscured by the higher Kentmere Pike and Harter Fell, actually this forces you to look else-where and to appreciate the position of Grey Crag and its sister peak, Tarn Crag, as King and Queen of a landscape all their own. From Longsleddale Forest, south of here and on the other side of the valley, the peaks of the Lakes are seen in a different relationship to the fells eastwards: from here, glimpses of Kidsty Pike, the Scafells and the distant Coniston Fells aside, the backdrop is just Longsleddale, Kentmere and the Shap, Whinfell and Howgill fells, and you realise they deserve appreciating in their own right.

In failing light, across the well-named Greycrag Tarn on to Tarn Crag, where there's another pillar (there's a third pillar between Branstree and Selside Pike northwards in a dead straight line with the other two), and round a small sheet of water, I stayed and watched the remnants of the sunset for a few minutes, but I couldn't stay long: if I wanted to get down safely and without having to divert most of the way to the A6 – or, at least, to Stockdale Gill and then a pret-ty substantial trespass – to avoid the danger of sliding down a cliff, I had to make it back to AW's tiny gully before it was so dark I couldn't read the map. As always, I'd underestimated how long the walk would take, and hadn't brought a torch. I moved off, and as I jogged over the moor and through the bogs in the thickening dusk I had a wonderful sense of the encroaching dark-ness as encroaching danger, as if somewhere about five minutes behind me were all the wolves of gathering night, and if they were to catch up with me I'd have had it. I made it to the gully just as night proper fell, and looking down into the valley I could see nothing save a light or two down at Sadgill.

A little later, driving out of the valley past Dale End, the moon hove into view, a low moon still catching the pumpkin-orange of sunset afterglow. Longsleddale was an ancient thoroughfare that linked Shap Abbey to the religious houses further south. Yewbarrow Hall, halfway between the A6 and Sadgill, is the oldest building in the valley, having been built in 1450 by the Leyburne family, who we met as landowners in the Scout Scar and Withersack chapter. The building originally had a pele tower and has walls six feet thick. The church, St Mary's, built in 1670, was a chapel of Kendal until 1712, when Longsleddale was made a parish in its own right, and it was subjected to the ubiquitous Victorian 'restoration' by Lady Howard of Levens Hall in 1863, the Howards being Lords of the Manor until at least late in the 19th century. Some older features survive. The communion plate includes a silver chalice dated

1571, there's a carved oak door opening to a recess in the vestry bearing the date 1662, and also a spice cupboard, now located to the left of the altar, with a beautifully carved door bearing the same date, and an oak chest dated 1719.

There is a whole other Sleddale, even less visited than the valley, and that's

Swallow at Littlewood Farm under Sleddale Forest and below, in Underhill Wood.

Sleddale Forest, the moor between Kentmere and Longsleddale. Uninviting on first glimpse at the OS map, as featureless as the rest of Shap Fells, its proximity to Kendal, Staveley and the comparative metropolis of Kentmere village somehow adds to the sense of isolation up here. But in reality it's not barren at all, and I know of nowhere else in Cumbria from where you get such unique views of the Lakeland fells. You get so used to thinking of the central Lake District, and then, moving eastward, the Shap fells and Borrowdale linking the Lakes to the M6 corridor, with the Howgills and, north and south, the Eden and Lune valleys occupying the space between here and the Pennines: and whichever viewpoint you choose, be it Orrest Head, or Scout Scar or

Helsington Barrows, or the Helm, or even Helvellyn or Skiddaw, that's the way the scenery is arranged. But from Sleddale Forest everything seems muddled up. Then you drop down into Longsleddale through the beautiful, if steep, Underhill Wood.

There's more to it than views, though. From the aptly-named Craggy Wood (Craggy Plantation on the OS map) on the hillside above Staveley, to Sleddale Forest's beautiful tarns, the entirely artificial and trout filled Potter Tarn, artificially-raised and island- and heron-studded Gurnal Dubs and the incomparably named Skeggles Water at the Forest's north end ('Skeggles' sounds like the name of a P. G. Wodehouse character to me), Sleddale Forest is a wonderful place to explore, though I do suggest sticking to the walls if you want to avoid the bogs. Walk from Staveley station up through Craggy Wood, through Littlewood Farm and Birk Field to Potter Tarn, over the dam to access

Above, strange-shaped beech in Craggy Wood and, below, Potter Tarn reservoir.

186

Looking across Skeggles Water and curlew on Sleddale Forest.

land and the path to Gurnal Dubs, then a track to Black Beck. The detour up Brunt Knott is worth it for the views into the jaws of Kentmere and the top of Long Sleddale, as well as west to the other fells of south Lakeland and east to Borrowdale and the Howgills beyond. Then it's along wall edges from Dockernook Gill to Skeggles Water, where there's an astonishing sense of isolation, a loneliness hard to find inside the Lake District National Park, a loneliness I more associate with the Howgills, Baugh Fell or even the Forest of Bowland: but in those places (Baugh Fell being the exception) there are few high-level stretches of water, and here the clear waters, beached with sheep bones and bedded with peat disappearing down into darkness have an almost threateningly empty quality all of their own. You're stranded in one lonely world on the border of another, quite unknown, inhabited mostly by wide-eyed insect larvae.

Tear yourself away and either return to Staveley, using the bridleway a little to your north, or continue down into Longsleddale (good views of Swindlebank Crag and the steep valley beyond Sadgill from the top of Underhill Wood) and walk out towards Kendal. Don't underestimate how far it is through Longsleddale though, nor how little mobile reception there is down there, especially if you've agreed to phone your wife when you want a lift home. At Garnett Bridge, crossing the river then turning left will take you along Garnett Bridge Road to Burneside station in about three miles (5km).

Kentmere from Sleddale Forest.

Martindale

Martindale head in winter.

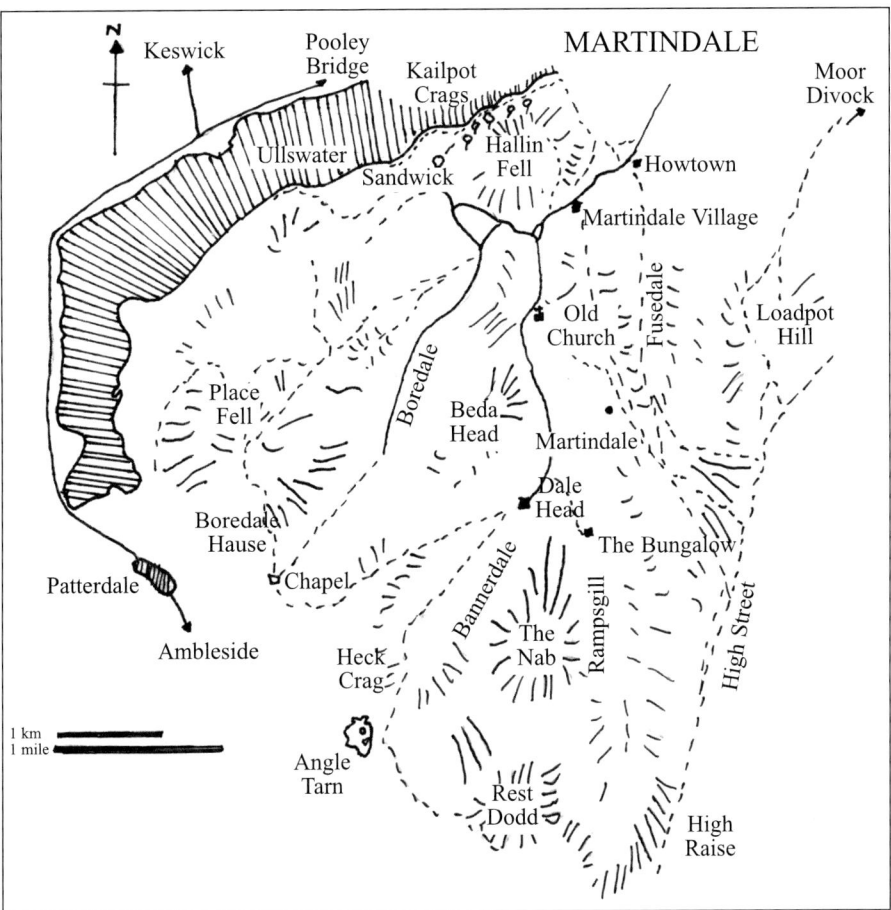

Martindale encapsulates perfectly what this book is about. It's not easy to get to: and this, combined with the fact that for most of the past eight centuries it's been a private deer forest and visitors have not been made welcome, has kept it virtually unvisited throughout its long recorded history. Wainwright wrote of it that "Keep Out notices, barricaded gates and miles of barbed wire must convey the impression even to the dullest witted walker that there is no welcome here." But despite this, or perhaps because of it, those who do make the effort are well rewarded. Even William Wordsworth, who'd happily walk from Grasmere to Keswick and back just for dinner, wrote of Martindale in his *Guide to the Lakes* that, "the views... are magnificent; yet this is only mentioned that the transient visitant may know what exists; for it would be inconvenient to go in search of them."

Well, as to the views, I'll let you go and find out for yourself. You'll notice, though, that, aside from the obvious signs of land enclosure and the odd house or barn, outside the spreadout village of Martindale – "if village it may be called," says Wordsworth, "for the houses are few, and separated from each

189

View into Martindale from the road and below, Chapel-in-the-Hause.

other... a sequestered spot indeed"– there's precious little evidence of human activity.

Which isn't to say there hasn't been human activity going on in Martindale for a very long time. There's a settlement marked on the map at Heck Beck, and while I haven't managed to find out anything about this, it does resonate tantalisingly with three other features within a two and a half mile radius on the maps. The first two are more settlements in Patterdale, one at the mouth of

Deepdale and the other at the foot of High Hartsop Dodd. The third feature is also marked on the maps, though as a place name rather than a feature: Chapel-in-the-Hause at Boredale Hause, the pass that links the two valleys. Wordsworth, with his sister Dorothy, came this way in 1805, and, walking from Sandwick on the shore of Ullswater, came through Martindale and climbed up to Chapel-in-the-Hause before climbing down into Patterdale. "Before we began to descend," he says:

> We turned aside to a small ruin, called at this day the chapel, where it is said the inhabitants of Martindale and Patterdale were accustomed to assemble for worship. There are now no traces from which you could infer for what use the building had been erected; the loose stones and the few which yet continue piled up resemble those which lie elsewhere on the mountain; but the shape of the building having been oblong, its remains differ from those of a common sheepfold; and it has stood east and west.

The ruins are still there, exactly as Wordsworth described them. This last feature of the ruin, incidentally – it's east-west alignment – will save you reaching for your compass if you're trying to decide which of the many paths that converge here is the right one to take you up to Place Fell, as it's the one leading due north.

There are two churches (really a church and a chapel) in Martindale, one of which has a history that goes back at least five or six hundred years, more likely a lot more. It's quite possible that Chapel-in-the-Hause is 1500 years old. Legend says that it was the first stone church in Britain, founded by St. Ninian, who, again, according to legend but no written source, was a Cumbrian of the mid-fourth to fifth centuries who became a monk, and founded the monastery at Whithorn in Galloway. The original church there, the Candida Casa, is supposed to be, as I've read in more than one source, the same size as the ruins at Chapel in the Hause: one day I'll go to Whithorn on a pilgrimage: but if you get there first you might like to know that Chapel-in-the-Hause's external dimensions are 27 feet east-west, 16 feet north-south, with an internal width of 8½ feet.

The only written source about Ninian is Bede, who says the southern Picts gave up "the errors of idolatry and received the true faith" from him, and who tells us he "had received orthodox instruction at Rome in the faith and mysteries of the truth. His episcopal see is celebrated for its church dedicated to St Martin, where his body rests together with those of many other saints."

He was trained by St. Martin, Bishop of Tours, hence the prevalence of St. Martin's churches connected with him. There's a well at Broughton next to the church of St. Martin dedicated to him, and the church at Whithorn is likewise dedicated to St. Martin. Patterdale is 'St. Patrick's Dale', and legend (again) has it that Patrick was a pupil of St. Ninian's. Amid dales named after the animals kept in them (mostly pigs, which are less hardy than sheep and cattle, so need the shelter of valleys – Boredale, Grizedale, Grasmere are all 'the valley of the pigs', or, in the last instance, 'lake of the pigs') – it seems odd that two valleys named for saints are found side by side. Was the reason for placing the chapel at a lonely, weather-beaten pass, aside from early monks' preferences for such places for purposes of heightened spiritual contemplation, because it was a convenient meeting place for the scattered communities of Patterdale and Martindale, of whose settlements only a handful of stones remain? Wordsworth tells us this is what the locals of his day believed, and are these low, mouldering traces of a building really once a chapel founded by Ninian 1500 years ago? We'll never know.

The recorded history of Martindale begins in 1247, when the valley belonged to the Barons of Kendal. Ivo de Taillebois was the first Baron of Kendal, appointed by William Rufus, William II and the Conqueror's brother, after the 'Harrying of the North', a military conquest to subdue the lands of the north, in 1069. His descendent William de Tailboys took the name de Lancaster, and one of his descendants, another William de Lancaster, died in 1246. The next year Henry III ordered an account of the lands of the de Lancaster family, recorded in a Public Record Office publication called the *Calendar of Inquisitions Post Mortem*, in which we find that William had left

his brother Roger de Lancaster "the whole forest of Westmorland, except Fusedale [the valley east of Martindale] and Swartfell and the head of Martindale," as these were already in Roger's possession. The same book records that in the same year the de Lancasters received "At Burton, tenants rendering 47s. 7d., a water-mill and fulling-mill, and a park worth 20s. yearly; four dales viz. – Martindale, Wamewydale, Grisdale and Glencon worth 30 pounds." Tenants are also mentioned in 1291, and tenants – presumably not the same ones – were still there in the reign of

*View across Steel End into Fusedale
from the road into Martindale.*

Elizabeth I: in a muster of Westmorland on Valentine's day 1581, 33 men and "12 footemen with Billes" are listed in Martindale. In the 1530s Lancelot Lancaster of Sockbridge grazed 300 sheep at Martindale. The Public Record Office source which tells us this reveals an interesting custom among farmers at the time: sheep which had strayed from another flock at Low Barton were to be driven back to where they'd come from, but when the same sheep strayed again it was finders keepers.

Martindale's old chapel.

The old chapel, the little cross just before Christy Bridge on the valley road on the OS maps, is, according to Charles Cox's *County Churches: Cumberland And Westmorland*, an old chapelry of Barton. About 55ft by 20ft, and "now disused save for mortuary purposes," it stands in what Cox calls "The Vale of Howgrance," Howe Grain on OS maps today, so called because it's the most fertile part of the valley. Rebuilt in 1633 on the site of a much older chapel, whose foundations can be seen outside on the south side of the current church, it was further restored in 1880, the year the new church was consecrated and the old chapel was demoted to the status of a mortuary chapel. When the original old chapel dated from is a mystery, but a certificate on the wall of the new church, from 'The Conservation Foundation Country Living Yew Tree Campaign,' which has the signatures of, amongst others, David Bellamy and Robert Runcie, states that

Martindale's new church.

the magnificent yew tree which stands just north east of the old chapel, and
which Wordsworth mentions as "still standing" (something it's still doing), is
at least 1300 years old: looking at it with my Woodland Trust Ancient Tree
Hunt hat on, I'd have said it was older.

The chapel was served by monks from Barton until the dissolution under
Henry VIII. Barton is now largely subsumed into Pooley Bridge, but its name
remains in the eminence of Barton Fell. Thereafter, it became part of Barton
parish until 1633, when the chapel was built (or the old one was rebuilt) and
it was granted a living of its own. Richard Birkett, the first to hold the living,
was inducted on 16th June (according to a sign on the wall in the antechapel),
with a stipend of £6 13s 4d. He served here for 67 years, right through the
Civil War and he died on Christmas Day 1699 aged 95. The aforementioned
sign on the antechapel wall helpfully repeats the text on his tomb, which still
stands in the churchyard just south east of the chapel, but whose top is unsurprisingly worn. Another tomb, beneath the yew, is that of Andrew Wilson,
traveller, orientalist, and man of letters. He was born at Bombay in 1830, and
died at Howtown, on the way into Martindale, in 1831. He wrote a book called
Abode of Snow, which he wrote at Bank House at Howtown, and another, *Ever
Victorious Army*, subtitled 'A History of the Chinese Campaign under Lt.-Col.
C. G. Gordon, CB, RE, and of the Suppression of the Tai-ping Rebellion',
written specially for the late General Gordon, who lost his life in defending
Khartoum. Also in the churchyard is Rev. George Woodley, perpetual curate
of Martindale, who died Christmas day 1845, aged 60. He was a poet and

essayist, a former sailor and was Bishop of Exeter before retiring to Martindale.

Apparently on the same day the new church was consecrated a wind blew the roof off the old church, which is why the old chapel was restored in 1880. From the 17th to 19th centuries, the population of Martindale was around 200. By 1900 it had fallen to 123, and today is around 80. This aside, the only significant change to the valley was during the period of the enclosures in the 18th and 19th centuries, when the valley floor was drained, flood protection – achieved by dredging gravel from the river bed and dumping it in ridges either side of, and running parallel to, the river – was installed.

Unless, like the Wordsworths, you're lucky enough to have access to a friendly boatman, or you've walked over from Patterdale, Kentmere or Mardale, nowadays you'll reach Martindale by the little road from Pooley Bridge. This road is, rather surprisingly, gritted in winter, although be aware that just before you enter Martindale proper there's a little pass between Howtown and Martindale, one of the features which conspires to make Martindale feel so lonely, and you might want to be out of Martindale not long after sunset to avoid any ice that forms on the steeper parts of the road and overwhelms the grit of earlier in the day. The top of the pass is a good place to park to climb Hallin Fell (which has a chapter earlier in the book), whence you'll find a good view of Martindale, as well as of Ullswater and the mountains beyond.

Over the brow of the hill is the new church, which is dedicated to St. Peter. It bears a superficial resemblance to the old chapel, with its stub of a bell tower, though its entrance is in the north wall, not the west end. It has a typically

Sun on Martindale Head.

Victorian interior, some lovely, very topical stained glass by Jane Gray from 1975 (there are windows celebrating Saints Ninian and Martin; John William Diggle, a former Bishop of Carlisle; and a lovely window in memory of a local woman, Ada Buxton, who died the year the windows were put in and which features a deer, a reef knot and a raven to symbolize the deer forest in Martindale, Steel Knotts, the hill behind the old chapel, and Raven Crag above Howe Grain, among others). The above-mentioned certificate concerning the yew in the old chapel graveyard is on the west wall. Don't forget to turn the lights off as you leave.

This won't be a problem in the old chapel, as it has no electricity. Having walked around the church, examined the graves and the yew and the remains of the older chapel along the south wall, and had a look at the bell, you enter into a narrow antechapel with a small vestry both to your left and right. There are two very informative notices on the wall, a donations box and some slightly damp postcards for sale. Proceed inside. Surely, this is the most beautifully evocative inside space in the Lake District? The inward-facing pews, apparently converted from the originals not long after they were first put in, give it an oddly collegiate atmosphere. The flagged floor replaced the old earth one in 1714, and the pulpit says '1634' on it.

The *pièce de resistance* is on the north side at the east end, next to the altar. Now a font, and before that a water stoup, this small, square stone bears on one side deep grooves where shepherds and others over centuries, millennia even, have sharpened their knives on it. It's thought to have been brought down from High Street, where it was placed by Roman soldiers who used the road from Windermere to Penrith as an altar to whatever spirit they believed guarded the high, cold, windy route over the mountaintops. Like the eerily beautiful green man in Kirkby Lonsdale church, it's a pretty piece of paganism in a Christian church, but its age and provenance make it for me the most amazing object in the Lake District, excepting the neolithic axes from Langdale. It's certainly among the most atmospheric, with its confused and conflicting history.

The Bungalow.

The Nab in winter.

Back outside, there's a very pleasant little climb that starts behind the old chapel up to Steel Knotts, 432 metres and a Wainwright fell, and if you descend from Brownthwaite Crag to the little path that drops down to Nettlehowe Crag you'll find yourself more or less at the little cave marked on the OS maps, which is right by the path. On the way up you'll catch glimpses of a red-roofed building by Rampsgill Beck hard by the foot of the Nab, which, again, is marked on the OS maps as 'The Bungalow'. It was built in 1910 by the Earl of Lonsdale for the use of Kaiser Wilhelm, who came here on a hunting trip, and is now available to rent as holiday accommodation from the Dalemain Estate, which now owns the deer forest. You'll also have excellent views of the post-enclosure landscape of the valley floor, with its very obviously improved fields with rule-straight edges.

By the chapel, and at Dale Head, there are signboards explaining the situation as regards access to the head of Martindale. Historically, as we've seen, Martindale was a deer forest in the ownership of the barony of Kendal. According to an inquest taken in 1619, in the reign of James I (at which time one of the agents making the inquisition was a Robert Curwen), Edward Lancaster, esquire, was in receipt of tithes from tenants in 'Martindell'. This passed from the Lancasters to the Multons of Gilsland, whose heiress passed it by marriage to the Dacres of Dacre Castle. It was then sold, in the reign of Charles II, to the Musgraves of Edenhall, who sold it to the Hasell family of Dalemain, on the far side of Ullswater, in 1679. The Dalemain estate still owns the valley and maintains the old deer herd, so that Martindale head is home to

England's largest red deer herd, and probably the only herd in the country not to have cross-bred with Sika deer.

After the formation of the National Park Martindale was one of the very few areas of open fell inside the National Park not to have open access. Theoretically, all the land outside that part of the valley floor improved during the enclosures is now open access land, since the Countryside and Rights of Way

Place Fell, frozen summit.

Act 2000, which clarified the status of access land in the National Park. The Dalemain Estate appealed against the decision to make the deer park access land, but most of their objections were dismissed. Nevertheless deer deserve privacy and respect, and these signboards show preferred walkers' routes. In particular, a direct ascent of the Nab from Dale Head is discouraged, though by prior arrangement with the Dalemain Estate permission might well be granted outside fawning season, unless stalking is planned for the day you wish to try the ascent. Alternatively, permitted routes are either up Bannerdale, past the Heck Beck settlement, up to Angle Tarn and round via Rest Dodd, up to Beda Head and round the same way, or up via Brownthwaite Crag to High Street and round by the Knott and, again, Rest Dodd. Or you could start from Hartsop or Patterdale, and get to Angle Tarn that way. It can be tempting to try and get close to the deer but please don't frighten them, particularly any time from early spring to late summer. Just take some good binoculars.

Carrying on up the road through the valley you'll come to Dalehead Farm, which has a stone inscribed 1666, the year of the Great Fire of London: Wainwright (in *Westmorland Heritage*) conjectures this is probably just a date stone. The building right next to the road on the left a few hundred yards back, just before the turning to the Bungalow, is the Fleshing House, where deer were once skinned.

Wasdale

Wasdale, strictly speaking, lies outside the remit of this book. Any day on any weekend of the year you'll find any number of the hardier sort of rucksacked and waterproof jacketed fellwalkers (though I must confess to being one of them) on the high level routes which surround what is surely the most beautiful lake in the Lakes, possibly the quintessential Lake District view (it's the one on the back of my Kendal library card): and what routes they are. Wasdale Head has by far the closest road access to Scafell Pike, the king of them all; Great Gable is also within comparatively easy reach, while Great Door on Yewbarrow and the couple of miles of screes below and between Illgill Head and Whin Rigg make for fine scrambling. The road which winds along the north western shore is a favourite haunt of couples of a certain age for whom a drive over Wrynose and Hardknott Passes, an exploration of Hardknott's Roman fort, a thermos-and-sandwiches lunch followed by a drive home via the (excellent) Muncaster Castle are excitement enough.

The thing is, though, the "most beautiful lake in the Lakes" bit aside, Wasdale is still a long drive from anywhere, and even if it's the sunniest, hottest July Saturday of the year you won't have problems parking within a stone's throw of where you wanted to. The fact that most of the hardcore walkers are staying, and have therefore parked their hired minibuses, at the youth hostel probably helps. And wherever you do leave the car, it won't cost you a penny. One word of warning, though: I've seen more than one of those couples 'of a certain age' who've decided to make their day out more adventurous by adding a walk around Wastwater to the inventory bleeding and literally in tears trying to negotiate the footpath along the shore under the screes, opposite the road. I'd suggest that going via the tops of Illgill Head and Whin Rigg, or the other way round, is in fact less effort, because the shore path essentially involves a two mile (3km) horizontal scramble. It's great fun if you set out to go scrambling: less so if you had a gentle stroll in mind. If you do opt for the uphill route, a walk via Latterbarrow, Miterdale Forest and Burnmoor Tarn has nearly as much to recommend it as the path along the top of the Wasdale screes. Why not do a circuit combining both and avoid both the picnickers and the rucksackers?

Either way, though, the walk through Low Wood by the youth hostel at the foot of the lake is beautiful: one of the most pastoral, beautiful, gentle, Ransom-esque places in the Lake District, backed by the most sublime, awesome view of them all. Climb Yewbarrow whatever you do. Middle Fell across the valley from the Youth Hostel is another good little climb.

Smardale Gill

Smardale Gill viaduct.

Smardale Gill is somewhere I didn't really take much notice of until, my daughter having come into the world, a flat, easy walk to push a pushchair along at the edge of the triangle of my beloved Howgills became an attractive idea. At which time, one very cold winter's day, I found out what I'd been missing.

It's easy to be snobbish about both nature reserves and industrial remains in the wilderness of the Lake District: less so, somehow, out here in the periphery of the Howgills, which is, in reality, much more of a wilderness than the adjacent Lake District National Park, and also than the majority of the Dales National Park, to which the southern Howgills belong. But in Smardale Gill the railway feels as old, as the cliché-ed phrase has it, as the hills: or at least as old as the various prehistoric remains which litter the valley sides.

The OS maps either side of the gash of Smardale Gill, which accomodates the old railway as it runs between Newbiggin-on-Lune on the Tebay-Kirkby Stephen road, and Crosby Garrett about three miles to the north and a long way from anywhere, are dotted with the remains of ancient structures: tumuli, settlements, pillow mounds (for more on these last see the Mallerstang chapter above). It's an odd place to find such a lot of chronologically diverse remains: you can see why people wandering around on Crosby Garrett Fell, or Smardale Fell, or even on the main bulk of the Howgills to the south, would have been grateful to retreat to the relative shelter of Smardale Gill, but given the proximity of the Eden valley to the east, and even the well-trodden route through the Lune Gorge to the south west, I can't fathom quite why they would have settled here at all. I'd more expect to find the mouldering remains of an abbey, stoic in its austere environment – like Shap Abbey – than a mix of pre-historical to medieval earthworks and an old railway line.

But the railway line was quite definitely here. The South Durham and Lancashire Union Railway, also known as the Stainmore Railway, which operated from a junction with the Stockton and Darlington Railway near Bishop Auckland to the West Coast Main Line at Tebay, existed to transport coke from the County Durham coalfields to the steel works at Barrow, although passenger trains also used the line: from east to west, the station before Smardale station was Kirkby Stephen East, and the station after was Ravenstonedale: Smardale Station itself was where School Lane meets Beck Lane just north east of Smardale Hall at the northern end of the gill.

The railway line crosses, at about its remotest point halfway through the gill, an impressive viaduct which architecturally, somehow, reminds me of Shap Abbey. Tall, even arches, an architectural feat whose beauty is all the more poignant as finding a decent point from which to view its full glory is virtually impossible. Certainly no one who ever crossed the viaduct in the days when the railway was running – between 1861 and 1952 – could have been aware that they were crossing one of the most perfectly proportioned pieces of railway architecture imaginable. I doubt many of them, in those long past days, noticed they were crossing a viaduct at all. In severe disrepair after getting on for half a century of neglect, the need to safeguard this haunting, and somewhat vertigo-inducing, piece of industrial perfection in this loneliest of places was the inspiration behind and the first project undertaken by the Northern Viaduct Trust in 1999. Among other viaducts under their care are Podgill Viaduct on the edge of Kirkby Stephen (see the Nine Standards to Wild Boar Fell chapter above).

These days, the gill is most easily explored via the railway line – via the viaduct, you might say – from the car park by the old station at the northern end, by Smardale Hall, to the A685 just west of Newbiggin-on-Lune. As I've said, it's a great walk if you happen to be pushing a pushchair: if you're feeling lucky, push the baby the whole length of the viaduct, then count on finding someone else's generous grandparents likely to offer you, baby and pushchair and all, a lift back to your own car at the far end.

Alternatively head off solo along the railway line and explore the opportunities to drop down to the gill from the railway line: they are frequent, generally steep, generally worth pursuing. The network of rights of way taking in the above-mentioned ancient remains dotting the moorlands surrounding the gill are well worth exploring too. Take a camera and see if you can get a photo of the viaduct which does it justice.

Wood

Plantation on The Rigg, Haweswater

THE LAKES, HISTORICALLY, were wooded not long after the glaciers left, only the shattered perfection of the roots of the once huge mountains standing out above the trees. Those natural woods were long ago removed by the hand of man, from the Neolithic period onwards: comparatively recently, to cut a very long and complex story ridiculously and misleadingly short, there have been attempts to reforest some of the valleys and fellsides with commercial coniferous plantations, and these attempts have been surprisingly controversial: and this story begins at Whinlatter. But commercial forests aren't the only woods in Cumbria, and this section tries to explore some of the county's diverse tree cover.

Whinlatter and Grizedale

Whinlatter, which is the focus of this chapter, is also, for reasons which will become clear, treated in what follows as the major artificial coniferous forest in the the Lakes: Grizedale, at 6050 acres, is just over twice the size of its older sister, but as Whinlatter is more centrally in the heart of the Lakes, is conspicuously closer to a major tourist hub – Keswick – and is also, contentiously,

Dodd from Keswick.

planted much higher up the sides of big hills than the other coniferous forests planted in the Lake District: for these reasons Whinlatter is a natural (or, perhaps, unnatural) starting point when it comes to thinking about Lakeland's woodland. Ennerdale would probably be a more obvious place to start, as its remoteness makes it all the more a shame it's covered by artificial forest: but it being so remote it's not as visible, and is much less visited. I should have more to say about Ennerdale in this book than I do, but I've got to stop somewhere, and the thing is that while in some respects I disagree with some of the opposition to the plantations of Whinlatter, when it comes to Ennerdale I don't: it was simply a great shame, and one that can't be reversed without decades of work rotting out treestumps and replenishing denuded and depleted soil. The afforestation of Ennerdale was less controversial than that of Whinlatter because the Forestry Commission acquired it in the 1920s, when it was already afforested, and before there was much organised opposition. In the immediate aftermath of the First World War, I guess, there was less time, and less inclination, for people to engage seriously with these issues in the context of a national timber shortage and trees were planted, something that was repeated during the next World War at Grizedale, as we'll see.

The Commission bought Eskdale and Dunnerdale in 1935. Grizedale Forest, which this chapter turns to later, has belonged to the Forestry Commission since 1937, the year after the controversy over Whinlatter. There seems to have been little public outcry over, or indeed interest in, the afforestation of Grizedale: presumably the prospect of another World War was more important to the public consciousness. But also Grizedale is a less distinctively Lake

District landscape than the area around Whinlatter pass, and was therefore less likely to occasion public outcry when forested.

Whinlatter was planted from 1919 on land that had once belonged to the Earls of Derwentwater, but which were forfeit to the Crown following the Jacobite rebellions. Charles claimed the title of 5th Earl of Derwentwater, despite his brother James, the 3rd Earl, having been stripped of the title on the occasion of his execution for his support of the 1715 uprising. Charles had been secretary to the Bonnie Prince before his 1745 attempt to regain the Scottish crown: and the 5th Earl's support of Charlie, as recorded in the beautiful folk song 'Derwentwater's Farewell', led directly to the loss of his own head. The planting of Whinlatter was one of the earliest acts of the Forestry Commission, which had at that time only just been created: the Commission came into being in 1919, as a response both to actual national timber shortages following the war effort and the realisation that should there be another World War it would be worth being prepared.

The Commission's original remit, therefore, was timber production, pure and simple: the growth of commercial (which, especially on poor-quality rocky hillsides, means coniferous) timber from commercially acquired land. Aesthetics, leisure provision, environment, wildlife: none of these issues were particularly on the cards. Post-war, land was cheap and the Commission took advantage of that fact. The 1920s were a time of brief growth, for trees as well as for the economy, then of economic depression. The 1930s were dominated by the build-up to another war: and it was, after all, in response to war that the Commission came about in the first place. Voices following in the tradition of Wordsworth – who as we'll see had much earlier lamented the blanket planting of land with just-for-profit conifers – were going to have to shout in order to make an impact.

And shout they did. The Friends of the Lake District, founded in 1934, began its life campaigning against the afforestation of the Duddon Valley, as well as campaigning for the creation of a Lake District National Park. But keeping the Forestry Commission's hands off the fells and valleys was where it began, initially with an attempt to buy back the Commission's newly-acquired land in Eskdale and Dunnerdale.

In an important book published in 1936, *Afforestation in the Lake District*, which summarises the most widespread opinion of the early history of commercial forestry in the Lake District, H. H. Symonds condemned outright the aesthetics of these conifer plantations, as well as the greed of the Forestry Commission, prepared to damage the scenery for naked profit: he criticises the scale of the plantings, the visual monotony of artificial spruce forests, and specifically, about the plantations in Ennerdale, writes that although the drop from the top of Pillar to the valley floor is only 2,200 feet:

...the canons of beauty are negligent in this arithmetic: in Nature's architecture, which has another scale, the Pillar range stands up in stupendous command. And the grandeur is an effect of contrasts, of bare slope in the lower contours and a serrated skyline of the volcanic rock above: in between is steep, broken crag, set among the colours of the fell side: here and there a vertical stream bed, or a fan of scree spilled into the grass and bracken of the lower, horizontal slopes, pulls the wide extension of the valley bottom into unity with the crag and steepness far above.

This effect of contrasts, says Symonds, has been destroyed by the treeline marching up the slope: "you are not operating in the Alps," he says, "you have not the depth and scale."

I personally think that the afforestation of Ennerdale was a terrible shame, but at the same time, I think it's worth looking at Symonds' arguments more carefully. Symonds argues the objection that while the Alps, thanks to their superior height, are capable of rising out of pine forests undaunted and undiminished to the human eye (pine forests in the Alps are, he says, "mature and magnificent after their gawky youth"), Pillar cannot; neither, by extension, could the Scafells, Gable, Old Man, all the mountainous high points (as it were) of the Lake District, none of which are much higher than Pillar: Scafell Pike is less than 300 feet higher. I agree in most places, but I do wonder if Blencathra could pull it off: and I think Skiddaw would be a lot duller to the eye than it is from around Keswick without the Latrigg and Dodd Wood plantations from which it rises. But it was indisputably shortsighted of the Forestry Commission to plant its conifers right up to the foot of one of the most majestic Lakeland mountains of them all, Pillar, even if the valley in question is one of the remotest spots in the district. Perhaps remoteness confers all the more reason to leave a place alone.

Elsewhere, for example in Grizedale Forest, where it's the views, not the terrain underfoot, which is mountainous, I think something of the elevation of Alpine scenery is conferred by your immediate surroundings on that mountainous backdrop: emerging from the shelter of the trees into the wind on Carron Crag in the middle of winter, and seeing the sweep of the Coniston fells and across past Crinkle Crags to the Langdales, then round to the Grasmere hills and finally the distant Kentmere hills, is a moment of literally breathtaking grandeur, and the foreground of treetops adds to the scale of the far hills. At Whinlatter, as would probably be the case were, say, Kentmere or the valley around Hayeswater planted, the effect of treetop after treetop after treetop running concurrently up the ridges towards the top of Grizedale Pike has a heightening effect all of its own. I wouldn't want it everywhere, but I honestly think the variety of the district would be impaired without it occurring once or twice.

The Lake District fells have frequently (and, I must agree with Symonds, somewhat ambitiously) been compared to the Alps, and of the comparison no lesser an authority than Wordsworth, in his *Guide to the Lakes*, reminds us that the history of forest management in the Lakes significantly pre-dates the early 20th century. It began in the Neolithic, when the slow process of the removal of the post-glacial, mostly pine and birch forests to make way for arable land began. Much later, for conveniences' sake let's say around 1000, the introduction of hardy breeds of sheep by Norse and Danish settlers led to the deforestation of the higher slopes. And so things remained until about the same time that the tourists began to get interested.

John Christian Curwen, landowner, was the father of Wordsworth's eldest son John's first wife and the cousin of Fletcher Christian, *Bounty* mutineer. He owned Claife Heights above the western (Hawkshead) side of the Windermere Ferry landing, and was responsible, along with another landowner, Richard Watson, Bishop of Llandaff, for the enclosure of Claife Heights and the planting on them of larch plantations in the 1790s (see Thompson, *Wordsworth's Hawkshead*, p. 131: Curwen later relented, replanting sections with native wood, something which Wordsworth credited him with in his *Guide to the Lakes*). Watson was a notorious absentee from his episcopal see in Wales, visiting once every three years: he was also an outspoken supporter of the French

Gowbarrow Park with Ullswater beyond.

monarchy during the Revolution, and was the man Wordsworth addressed an early, unpublished radical letter in support of the French Revolution to: not a man in Wordsworth's good books. Wordsworth's *Guide to the Lakes*, published in various versions between 1810 and 1835, contains a section on "Changes, and Rules of Taste for Preventing their Bad Effects" which makes its author's views on managed forestry in the Lake District very clear.

In common with later detractors, Wordsworth laments the choice of the Lake District for commercial forestry in this delightful sentence: "I would utter first a regret, that they should have selected these lovely vales for their vegetable manufactory, when there is so much barren and irreclaimable land in the neighbouring moors, and in other parts of the island, which might have been had for this purpose at a far cheaper rate." In particular he criticises the blanket planting of conifers on "the lower ground," pleading that plantations, "if introduced at all, may be confined to the highest and most barren tracts," as "interposition of rocks would there break the dreary uniformity of which we have been complaining; and the winds would take hold of the trees, and imprint upon their shapes a wildness congenial to their situation."

Wordsworth is clearly unaware of one of the northern commercial forester's chief worries, windfall risk, that is the chance of a tree planted in an exposed situation being felled by the wind before it reaches its optimal age for felling,

Trees on the flank of Harstop above Howe give an idea of what Lakeland might once have looked like, from Rest Dodd.

the reason "barren and irreclaimable land in the neighbouring moors" isn't normally used for commercial planting. But Wordsworth's main objection to conifer plantations is on aesthetic grounds: again, that they have a monotony at odds with the variety of natural beauty. "It is impossible, under any circumstances, for the artificial planter to rival the beauty of Nature [...] we shall look in vain for any of those appearances which are the chief sources of beauty in a natural wood." He goes on to concede that "in countries where the larch is a native, and where, without interruption, it may sweep from valley to valley, and from hill to hill, a sublime image may be produced by such a forest [...] But this feeling is confined to the native immeasurable forest; no artificial plantation can give it."

I disagree with Wordsworth's aesthetics here, but to get back to Symonds' comparison of the Lakes and the Alps: Wordsworth says,

> if we could recall, to this region of lakes, the native pine-forests, with which many hundred years ago a large portion of the heights was covered, then, during spring and autumn, it might frequently, with much propriety, be compared to Switzerland. [...] But the pine-forests have wholly disappeared; and only during late spring and early autumn is realised here that assemblage of the imagery of different seasons, which is exhibited through the whole summer among the Alps, – winter in the distance, – and warmth, leafy woods, verdure and fertility at hand, and widely diffused. [...]
>
> We have mountains, the highest of which little exceed 3,000 feet, while some of the Alps do not fall short of 14,000 or 15,000, and 8,000 or 10,000 is not an uncommon elevation. Our tracts of wood and water are almost diminutive in comparison; therefore, as far as sublimity is dependent upon absolute bulk and height, and atmospherical influences in connection with these, it is obvious, that there can be no rivalship. But a short residence among the British Mountains will furnish abundant proof, that, after a certain point of elevation, viz. that which allows of compact and fleecy clouds settling upon, or sweeping over, the summits, the sense of sublimity depends more upon form and relation of objects to each other than upon their actual magnitude; and that an elevation of 3,000 feet is sufficient to call forth in a most impressive degree the creative, and magnifying, and softening powers of the atmosphere. Hence, on the score even of sublimity, the superiority of the Alps is by no means so great as might hastily be inferred.

So Wordsworth does not seem to think that there is a shortage of space for valley-pine-upland-summit strata to decorate the Lakeland fells if such a transition occurred naturally, as it probably once did, before the trees were cleared for sheep, but elsewhere he does object to conifer plantations, principally, as with Symonds, because of their uniformity.

With Wordsworth in mind, John Ruskin, staying at Keswick in 1848, wrote to his friend Mary Russell Mitford, "as for our mountains or lakes, it is in vain that they are defended for their finish or their prettiness. The people who admire them after Switzerland do not understand Switzerland – even Wordsworth does not," I agree with the second half of Ruskin's opinion here, and, in terms of aesthetics, I find myself siding with him too. In Volume IV of his polemical work *Modern Painters*, Ruskin, praises the effects of conifers on mountainsides as an ingredient in great landscapes, says that what he calls redundance – that is, the sheer number of trees which can be seen in a view of mountains forested with pines, added to the effect of greater visibility of trees caused by the steepness of the slope on which they're planted – makes afforested slopes a key constituent of mountain scenery. This is provided, presumably, that a rule from *Modern Painters,* Volume II is applied, that in landscape "a forest of all manner of trees is poor, if not disagreeable in effect; a mass of one species of trees is sublime." I by no means agree with the first idea here: both up close and from afar, mixed woodlands are beautiful, especially in spring and autumn: and certainly they are to be preferred from an ecological point of view. But in the old aesthetic distinction between beauty and sublimity, so central to the way great Romantic writers wrote, mountain scenery is chiefly to be appreciated for its sublimity: and coniferous forests are, to me at least, sublime.

Lakeland is by turns beautiful and sublime, and so the Lake District benefits from the presence of both kind of forest. The scale isn't that of the Alps, but I think the effect works nonetheless. And I can't help thinking that if one of the Lake District's prime attractions is its variety of landscape and environment, and that most of those environments have in some way or other been created or altered by man, surely the addition of another kind of environment – pine forest – simply adds to the diversity? I find that the lower slopes of Skiddaw, especially Latrigg and Dodd Wood on the shores of Bassenthwaite below Skiddaw, are beautiful both to view from a distance – say from Keswick, or Catbells, or looking from the forested Dodd Wood across to Barf in Whinlatter Forest or from Barf back the other way – and close up. And I love the view of the fingers of forest reaching up Grizedale Pike as seen from Whinlatter, or from one of those charming places in the forest where the views of the hills suddenly burst in.

A book published in 1946, so with a decade's more perspective than Symonds' book, *The Lake District and the National Trust* by B. L. Thompson, says:

> the opposition [to the planting] reached such an intensity, and so captured the public mind, that it ended by almost suggesting that no conifers should be planted in the Lake District. That is an extremist view. The majority of visitors who come here find delight in conifers where they delight in moderation [...]
> I would not condemn afforestation of the right sort in the right place [...] but

let it be done in moderation, thoughtfully and intelligently, as the eighteenth century landscape designers planned the parks and great estates of our forefathers; then our descendants will continue to enjoy, as we have enjoyed, the varied beauty of the Lakes.

The Friends of the Lake District's website today says "we work to remove intrusive, monotonous non-native conifer blocks and help create mixed new native woodland, through working with the Forestry Commission, the Lake District National Park Authority and Natural England." Wonderful. Keep it up. But could you please leave Whinlatter, Dodd Wood and the higher bits of Grizedale as they are? Every single non-native conifer in Ennerdale can go, though, and good riddance. Imagine what it would look like with the valley floor covered in oaks, birches, rowans and Scots pine. Shortly before 2000 the Forestry Commission cut down the post-war Corsican pine plantations on Whitbarrow: as little as a decade later, with the help of a few cattle to root out the old tree stumps, the limestone hill's recovery was well under way.

Fungi in Castlehead Wood, Keswick.

Time was when access to most of the Forestry Commission's estate was limited to permitted paths, and fairly grudgingly granted at that. As we'll see, in more recent years the Forestry Commission has done a much better job of making Whinlatter – and Grizedale – well worth visiting for everyone, from families with pushchairs to grey-bearded twitchers to committed mountain bikers. Then there's the hi-wire complex of Go Ape, at both Whinlatter and Grizedale. I could go on about the negative history of management of forestry in Lakeland, but, looking forward not back, things look good. Especially since, in the face of overwhelming public protest, in early 2011 the government backed down from plans to sell off some of the forestry estate. The Forestry Commission is like the NHS: deeply unpopular when implemented, it is now a major source of national pride and identity.

Back to aesthetics. "Silent, gloomy forests aren't everybody's cup of tea," says AW of the Lord's Seat ascent from Whinlatter Pass described in his *The North Western Fells*: but you get the feeling, sometimes, reading his accounts

of these fells, that they might have been his: certainly he had en eye for their being well managed, as he says about Blengdale Forest in the Ponsonby Fell chapter in *The Outlying Fells of Lakeland*. The plantations on Latrigg he describes as "not always for the better" in *The Northern Fells*, but chiefly because the places the trees have been planted make the hill resemble "an experimental coiffure by a mad barber" and, besides, "the woods harbour courting couples and are not safe for solo explorers."

But the word 'gloomy' doesn't have solely negative connotations. Robert Hugh Benson, son of Edward White Benson, Archbishop of Canterbury, controversially converted to the Roman Catholic Church in 1903. Trying to sum up the many different aspects of Catholicism which attracted him, he mentions, in connection with the concept of incarnation, a vague, intangible but nevertheless vital part of the pull towards Rome, a certain kind of aesthetic experience: he sums it up by saying, "I loved twilight and mysterious music and the shadow of deep woods." That shadow of deep woods is an aesthetic

Bluebells, Hird Wood, Troutbeck Tongue and, top of page, violets.

ideal which has always moved me deeply: but the English, ideal of the woodland aesthetic has always been the broadleafed wood, the bluebelled oak forest, not the darkness under close-planted pine trees.

To me there's nothing more beautiful than bluebells in a beechwood, dap-
pled in spring sunshine, but there is something about the darkness under pine
trees that is nearly as compelling: and the darkest pine forests are the artificially planted ones. That still, phosphorescent luminosity seems to flow from an
alien world, particularly when the 'mysterious music' of the wind is roaring
through and swaying the treetops, while down below nothing stirs. Pine forests
are for me a blank canvas for the imagination, their vast dark corridors and
incessant hemming-in of the field of view a chance for the mind to wander,
along with the body, where it wishes. It's something encapsulated by a poem
of George Meredith's, *Dirge in Woods*:

> A wind sways the pines,
> And below
> Not a breath of wild air;
> Still as the mosses that glow
> On the flooring and over the lines
> Of the roots here and there.
> The pine-tree drops its dead;-
> They are quiet, as under the sea.
> Overhead, overhead

Old Park, Killington.

Rushes life in a race,
As the clouds the clouds chase;
And we go,
And we drop like the fruits of the tree,
Even we,
Even so.

And when the pinewood is planted on hill country, the horizontal monotony is tempered by vertical variation, so that, as you walk around Whinlatter, steep, twisting tracks, sudden breaks in the immediate green horizon, unexpected vistas across treetops, buzzards wheeling high overhead, the view never the same from one clearing to the next, add to the sense of extent.

Moving beyond the aesthetic, however, there's another issue in the objection to coniferous forests on the grounds that they're an obvious imposition of something artificial, a scar caused by the hand of man, on a landscape which should be left alone to be natural, to be 'wilderness': an issue which strikes right to the heart of what this book is about. There are many weapons in the arsenal of the environmental movement – to which I belong passionately – which include scientific data, environmental models and so on, but there are also cultural tools like pastoral, idealising a past which is seen as under threat, and apocalypse, where tales of the end of the world are used to dramatic effect: and then there's another, very poignant concept, that of wilderness. Symond's *Afforestation in the Lake District*'s second paragraph contains a good example of the rhetorical over use of apocalypse in support of an environmental ideal: "[this] is an apolycalyptic time. The macabre terrors of speed and of an alien thought invade the silence and grandeur of Nature's ancient places." This appeal to apocalypse, however, is in the context of this argument:

> As man civilizes, his desire for wild and primitive beauty becomes greater [...] Those instincts which crowd us together and socialize us satisfy only a part of our inherited needs: isolation, awe, and adventure, and to feel the unaltered, age-long beauty of the external world, are no less a part of a sound and satisfying life. All places of retreat and freedom, where we are not reminded of the man-made world, become of greater value to us as assimilation, crowding, and routine increase.

The Lake District, then, is a wilderness, wholly natural, a place "where we are not reminded of the man-made world." To cite a more recent example, the BBC showed the first episode of a new series, *Tales from the National Parks*, about Honister Slate Mine, in October 2011, and the episode highlights the way the language of wilderness sticks automatically to any mention of the Lake District. The programme documents the attempts of the boss of Honister

Slate Mine, entrepreneur Mark Weir, to get permission to extend the adventure activities on offer at the site to include a via ferrata and a high level zipwire on Fleetwith Pike. The latter is described as "plummeting down from one of the Lake's highest mountains in one of the park's most remote, wild landscapes." Which I'd rewrite as "descending from the 120th tallest of the 214 Wainwrights, above one of the National Park's most visited, industry-scarred and coach-infested passes."

The Friends of the Lake District were against the idea, which was at the time disallowed by the National Park committee, but on ecological grounds, as the Pike is an SSSI due to the habitats it provides to mountain flora, which would have been threatened if the via ferrata were allowed. But, according to the BBC, "The Friends... has commissioned into the unique tranquility of the area around Fleetwith Pike." I'm not sure tranquility is quite the word. Sadly Mark Weir was killed in a helicopter accident in 2011, and the via ferrata and a zip wire are now open for business.

There are numerous problems with this wilderness approach. Firstly it's simply not true: two of the things the Lakes are proudest of, Neolithic axes and Herdwick sheep, have seen to that. You'll also have to ignore the old mines and quarries, the dry stone walls, even the path under your feet if escape from signs of the hand of man is what you're looking for up in the hills. Secondly, a problem with this way of thinking is: where does it end? If we need to escape the crowding of civilisation in search of 'awe' from time to time, what does this tell us of the very essence of civilisation itself? Such viewpoints, known

Honister Pass, "one of the park's most remote, wild landscapes."

nowadays as deep ecologies, which stress the interconnectedness of the natural and human spheres and the fact that the rest of the living environment has just as much right to life and protection as the human species, tend in the end to hold up their hands in horror at the damage humans have the potential to inflict – and in many cases have inflicted – on the environment.

Often the damage is all too real: but to damn the human species because of it is not only to render the achievements of human history (art, science, religion, everything), and the achievement of evolution in bringing us about in the first place, an irrelevance, but is also to undermine faith in the only agency that can do anything about correcting environmental damage: that is, ourselves. Short of mass genocide, we have to recognise that there are a lot of people in this world, that its resources are finite and some of them are running out, and we need to get on with finding solutions not by negating ourselves and privileging the rest of the natural order above ourselves, locating the 'natural' somewhere beyond us, somewhere and something to escape to when the burden of civilisation becomes too much: but rather we need to recognise more often the extraordinary fact of human consciousness and the things it's allowed us to achieve and, with that in mind, see how we can move forward as a species.

Deep ecology does have a lot to be said for it, in particular that it fundamentally rejects postmodern ideas about the end of history and the supercession of the natural order by mankind, ideas which I, frankly, regard as nonsense, but it can very easily become too deep, equating human with bad and 'natural' with good. Wordsworth's Lake District is a sublime, empty wild: it was, "Presences of Nature in the sky/And on the earth! Ye Visions of the hills!/And Souls of lonely places!" which inspired him (and funnily those were the first lines of Wordsworth's, read on a poster on an English classroom wall, which really inspired me to read him). But there's always room for people and, more importantly, their histories in Wordsworth's lonely Lake District. Dozens of examples spring to mind but nothing shows this better than the opening lines of *Michael*:

> *If from the public way you turn your steps*
> *Up the tumultuous brook of Greenhead Ghyll,*
> *You will suppose that with an upright path*
> *Your feet must struggle; in such bold ascent*
> *The pastoral mountains front you, face to face.*
> *But, courage! for around that boisterous brook*
> *The mountains have all opened out themselves,*
> *And made a hidden valley of their own.*
> *No habitation can be seen; but they*
> *Who journey thither find themselves alone*
> *With a few sheep, with rocks and stones, and kites*

> *That overhead are sailing in the sky*
> *It is in truth an utter solitude;*
> *Nor should I have made mention of this Dell*
> *But for one object which you might pass by,*
> *Might see and notice not. Beside the brook*
> *Appears a struggling heap of unhewn stones!*
> *And to that simple object appertains*
> *A story – unenriched with strange events*
> *Yet not unfit, I deem, for the fireside,*
> *Or for the summer shade. It was the first*
> *Of those domestic tales that spake to me*
> *Of shepherds, dwellers in the valleys, men*
> *Whom I already loved; – not verily*
> *For their own sakes, but for the fields and hills*
> *Where was their occupation and abode.*

One other thing about Symonds' argument. He objects, like Wordsworth, to artificial conifer plantations on two grounds: firstly on the aesthetic ground that there isn't enough vertical room on a Lakeland mountainside for them to work aesthetically: and secondly that they have no place in the 'wild' landscape. What doesn't seem to have crossed his mind is to criticise the Alpine aesthetic for containing artificial conifer plantations on the wilderness front. There is something of a 'not in my back yard' mentality going on here, methinks.

My daughter, aged about a year, decided that because my laptop had a lid it was clearly a box, and boxes are things into which you put other, smaller things. So she put my keys on the keyboard and tried to shut the lid. When the lid wouldn't shut properly she sat on it. Hence a call to the insurance company. Human history is a bit like that. We've been playing in a very simple way with something very complex, something that we didn't properly understand, and we've broken it. But now we do have understanding: we've grown up: that's our insurance policy. We are a part of the natural order: an unusual part, unique in its self-awareness: but being human doesn't mean not being natural. The hills can be a wilderness and touched by the hand of man.

Which brings me to another problem with the wilderness argument. If Lakeland is a wilderness and the presence of anything human is an intrusion, surely humans shouldn't be going there at all? If we really want to go somewhere that takes us away from civilised society, ultimately we'll need a different National Park for everyone to have somewhere to go walking at the weekends without there being any danger of seeing anyone else. From the point of view of the wilderness, the presence of even one walker becomes an imposition. Perhaps we should fence off the whole National Park so that the wilderness can get on with the important job of being wild. I hate to think of the suffering that would cause to deer and sheep populations on the fells, though, and by extension to the rest of the interconnected ecosystem. It's expensive managing the status quo up on the hills, and it takes the tourist revenue to do it. But tourists will go walking on the hills, which causes erosion of the paths, which needs helicopter lifts of bags of boulders onto the hillsides to repair the paths, which is expensive, so needs tourist revenue...

But can I really justify, standing firmly in the romantic/post-romantic tradition with Wordsworth peering over my shoulder, enjoying man-made, deeply tampered-with landscapes as much as really wild, natural landscapes? However in reality how many truly wild, untampered-with landscapes are there anyway? Certainly none in England. How many in the world? Well, lots, at first glimpse. Another problem, though, is that with the exception of Antarctica most wildernesses already have human populations of their own. You can't really empty the Sahara of Bedouins or the Arctic of Inuits or the Northern Territory of Aborigines just because they're ruining the Western modern idealisation of wilderness.

Big though we are we're always smaller than nature, in the end, and she'll always fight back, and we'll always lose. In the blink of an eye this planet, this solar system, this galaxy won't be here anymore anyway: it's very easy to belittle our place in the natural order. I say we should be doing the opposite. Nature is always fighting back, always reasserting a presence, always adapting, growing. It needn't be a war, and we needn't be the oppressors who need removing, forcibly if needs be. Commercial use of a landscape needn't be exploitation: and, anyway, surely hillwalking is in one aspect a commercial activity anyway? Have you ever tried to count the outdoor shops in Keswick?

I thrive on a sense of finding space, escape and natural beauty – on the sense of being a wilderness fugitive in these managed, but still empty landscapes; the sense that agricultural or commercially forested land or managed moorland exists for one purpose, but that you're exploiting it for another, that is wonder, joy, exploration, thought and peace and quiet: exploiting the intentions of those who exploit for your own enjoyment is really no exploitation; instead, it's returning meaning to a space that, because it has been exploited, had previously been written off as devoid of meaning. Before the Romantics writers like Defoe were simply terrified of the Lake District's wilderness. From Wordsworth to Wainwright and beyond, writers writing about Cumbria have mostly decried tourism, while simultaneously encouraging it, stimulating public interest in a landscape prized equally for its beauty and for its sublimity. It's not their fault; both Wordsworth and Wainwright happened to be writing at a time when interest in Cumbria was on the up, and they both, Wordsworth in particular, tried to educate visitors to limit the damage; but still, 'wilderness', in Britain and Europe at least, is quite likely to be packed with tourists, for the length of every holiday season. Managed, commercial landscapes, by and large are not, and so, conversely, represent a version of escape from the commercialised 'wilderness' so apparent in Windermere, and, more so, in Grasmere. I've never been alone on the top of Helvellyn, even in a -15°C whiteout on a Tuesday in January. I've never seen anyone on Whinlatter.

Not so far from the Lake District are many other 'wild' places; the Dales, the Howgills, the Pennines. One place with fewer obvious points of comparison is Kielder Forest, the biggest forest in England. But, besides trees, Kielder has hills and streams and rivers, and history and songs, and so much wildlife: I've seen any number of badgers and foxes, barn, tawny and little owls, goshawks, marsh and hen harriers, ospreys, adders, slow worms, grass snakes, Royal fern, lichens thicker than I have seen anywhere else. There are even cormorants which roost in the pine trees along the shore of Kielder Water. The only thing I haven't seen much of there is first-hand human activity. There are ospreys too, again visible from a public hide, which made me wonder if they might be encouraged to visit Haweswater, a similarly artificial stretch of water. In spite of the current programme to reintroduce more natural, native woodland into the area, virtually the whole forest is a man-made, money-making enterprise, a wood-farm, and it's all artificial. At the time of going to press ospreys have been nesting at Foulshaw Moss – an artifically drained former confier plantation on the Kent estuary – for two years.

My top four animal sights in the Lake District have to be: first, the lonely old golden eagle who lives on Riggindale Crag not far from High Street, a mountain top best known for its Roman road and for the horse fairs once held there. The eagle is best viewed from an RSPB hide near a conifer plantation on the shores of Haweswater Reservoir. Then there are the ospreys on Bassenthwaite, best viewed from Forestry Commission hides in Dodd Wood plantation: ospreys first returned to Bassenthwaite in 1997, having been extinct in England since 1842. A chick was raised in 2001, and the same pair (they mate for life) have been breeding every year since. Liberal Democrat MP for Westmorland Tim Farron, who tabled a proposal in the House of Commons which led to the recently proposed sell-off of parts of the Forestry Commission estate being abandoned, was concerned that "if ministers decide to sell off all forests currently managed by the Forestry Commission it could mean that places such as Whinlatter Forest, a hub of wildlife overlooking Bassenthwaite Lake, would be fenced off." Then there are the Grizedale red deer, one of whom I bumped into almost literally under the huge concrete bridge where the A590 crosses the river Kent a few miles south of Kendal during the terrifying floods of late 2009. What he was doing there I've no idea: I last saw him wandering off along Nannypie Lane as if popping for a pint at the Strickland Arms. And finally, the hour we once spent standing on the bridge in

Opposite, Kielder wildlife.

the very centre of Grasmere on a bustling Easter Saturday watching an otter fishing in the river, the coachloads of tourists were utterly oblivious. None of these wildlife high points are to be found in the more classically 'wild' Lake District landscape.

To go back to deep ecology, it seems to me that nature doesn't much mind whether we're there or not or even much what we do to the landscape, so long as we give it the space and the resources to get on with things. It's often said that agriculture began with hunting: the deer found that hanging around near human settlements had advantages, such as the fact that packs of wolves tended to avoid the close vicinities of the earliest human settlements, which outweighed the increased danger of being hunted. Humans noticed this and began to leave food out for the deer, which thought it rude to decline... and so on. There's a balance to be found, and we're part of it, and finding the balance in this increasingly complex world is going to call for a lot of human ingenuity. We'd better start valuing our abilities rather than beating ourselves up over them. In their heyday of Romanticism, the search for wilderness, and sublimity, was a reaction against the long-established picturesque, which revelled in order in landscape, man-made order: but that order is in fact illusionary. Nature is always reasserting herself, and perhaps there is sublimity to be found in her continued resurgence, her resourcefulness which is the product of millions upon millions of generations, and which exists despite our impingement on the natural world.

WHINLATTER

This chapter is entitled 'Whinlatter and Grizedale', and you may well be forgiven for wondering exactly when this somewhat rambling rant is going to get there. So let us wait no longer. A 1992 Forestry Commission study called *Valuing Informal Recreation on the Forestry Commission Estate* begins by saying that:

> National forests are places for recreation of many kinds, as well as habitats for a diverse range of wildlife species, and an important factor in the character of rural landscapes. The problem in weighing the relative costs and benefits of such multiple objectives and uses is that no markets exist by which one might value the outputs of informal recreation, wildlife and enjoyment of the fine views to be found in forests.

This was the impetus behind the recent and laudable public outcry which led to the coalition government scrapping plans to sell off sections of the Forestry Commission estate, and could have been written specifically with Whinlatter in mind, for its highlights for the visitor are the facilities, the views and the wildlife, especially the ospreys. The trail guide leaflet says that the forest is run "for the nation by the Forestry Commission for recreation, wildlife, landscape design and timber production." In that order. Jolly good, although I might have put wildlife first (perhaps I am a deep ecologist at heart after all).

So what opportunities for recreation will the visitor find at Whinlatter? Well, besides the car park and visitor centre, with its inevitable gift shop; Siskins Cafe with its amazingly long menu; and Go Ape!, the 'high-wire forest adventure', there are a number of colour-coded walking routes, seven at the time of writing, ranging from a mile to five miles (8km). None of these takes in the top of Whinlatter, which is marvellous as it means no one ever goes there: Whinlatter is most easily accessed across a stile at the end of the waymarked mountain bike track at the end of Comb Plantation, marked post number 55, about 250m north west of the visitor centre, although the direct journey is a considerable struggle and involves wandering about under the Go Ape! high wire course: best to follow the green Seat How summit trail, turning left at the number 2 marker at Horsebox Crossroads: enjoy the feeling of excitement that always comes from leaving a walking route you're supposed to be following in favour of one you've chosen. Carry on to the trees' edge, cross the stile, take a short climb on your right and enjoy an easy ridge walk to the top of Whinlatter.

My recommendation from here onwards would be to take on the forest's remaining Wainwrights – Lord's Seat, Broom Fell and Barf – more or less directly, heading a fraction west of north from the summit and following the forestry fence line a little cast of the questionably named stream of Willybrag Gill to join a forest track at Aiken Beck. This will also, if you fancy, give you the chance to head to the very under-visited north western section of the forest, whose highlight is, aside from its loneliness, Spout Force waterfall – 13m high and not particularly remarkable save for the fact that it seems to spring from absolutely nowhere at all. But if heading straight on to more felltops, turn right and, following the track, taking the uphill option at any junctions, the route eventually becomes one path which breaks out of the trees 50m or so of vertical distance from the top of Lord's Seat.

Dedicated Wainwright baggers will head west and a little north to take in the slightly lower (511m to 552m) top of Broom Fell: no one else is likely to bother, which is good because it's only a pleasant half mile each way and the view is surprisingly different from that from Lord's Seat, the prominence of the fells around Keswick being lost behind and Lorton Vale and the Loweswater fells opening up instead. Back then to Lord's Seat and on to Barf for great views across Bassenthwaite to Dodd and Skiddaw and across Keswick to the geological oddities of the east side of Derwent Water. Then plunge back into the forest and navigate the maze of tracks back around the hillside to the visitor centre and car park. There's a little, twisty path that jinks between trees northwards up to the little bare-headed top of Seat How, worth a detour if you're passing for the kinds of forest views I've been praising earlier in the chapter.

Mountain bikers are welcome to use the forest trails provided they don't alarm the walkers too much. There's the Go Ape aerial walkway, but there's another at Grizedale and this chapter is already quite long enough.

Tree roots, Old Park, Killington.

There are also four marked walking trails in Dodd Wood, but the key attraction here are the ospreys: the Foresry Commission in partnership with the RSPB and the National Park run two viewpoints, a lower and an upper, between the beginning of April and when the year's brood flies away in the late summer. The upper viewpoint is 400m from the nesting site and telescopes are provided at both.

GRIZEDALE

The Forestry Commission bought Grizedale in 1937, the year after the controversy over afforestation at Whinlatter, but nevertheless the acquisition of Grizedale doesn't seem to have caused as much of a stir. It appears to have been a quick and easy acquisition, too: H. H. Symond's book *Afforestation in the Lake District* doesn't mention Grizedale, but doubtless would have done had the author been aware that the Forestry Commission was going to have its hands on it so soon.

But, covering the low, rolling Furness Fells between Windermere and Coniston Water, the area isn't as emotive as, say, Ennerdale or the slopes of Grizedale Pike, so perhaps outcry wouldn't have been very acute anyway even if it weren't for more central parts of the Lakes being planted or the threat of another World War. Also Grizedale seems always to have been forested: once naturally, but for centuries it was owned by the monks of Furness Abbey, who allowed forestry and woodland industries such as charcoal burning, as well as iron smelting, to go on, from which of course they derived an income. The charcoal burners who feature in the *Swallows and Amazons* stories were Grizedale residents in reality, and the Dog's House, the old woodman's cottage which features prominently in *The Picts and the Martyrs*, can still be visited by an easy walk southwards into the woods from the Machell Coppice car park on the east side of Coniston Water just south of Brantwood, where, incidentally, charcoal-burning still takes place. I could go on about Brantwood and its former owner John Ruskin for the rest of this book, so will merely say here that the house, gardens and other attractions are well worth visiting. In Grizedale, the most obvious remains of ironworks are about half a mile south west of Satterthwaite.

Most visitors to the forest will, however, be heading for one of the two main car parks at Grizedale visitor centre, where the useful installation of pay and display meters which take debit cards has recently taken place. The visitor centre itself is huge, and hugely impressive: based around a central courtyard are a shop and a very good and large cafe, there's also a mountain biking shop and, believe it or not, a theatre, the Theatre in the Forest. Then there's the reception for Go Ape, an aerial high-wire course through the trees for children of all ages except those under five, and in the woods nearby are often art installations. Then there's the most famous of the forest's many sculptures, a towering wooden man holding a giant axe: the last time I was there he was missing a hand and various other body parts for repair, and I hope he's had a good recovery.

The forest is full of sculptures, rock-paintings and so on: the project began in 1977, sponsored by Northern Arts. I remember stumbling across an elephant painted onto a rock in the middle of nowhere on my first visit. A map showing the locations of sculptures and the routes of the marked trails can be found at the visitor centre: the 9½ mile (15km) Silurian Way takes in all the sculptures, the Ridding Wood trail just those within an hour's circular walk from the visitor centre. The Millwood Train is a mile and a half and smooth enough for pushchairs and wheelchairs. The Grizedale Tarn trail is the best way to see the forest east of the visitor centre, the tarn itself especially beautiful on an icy winter's day, while the Carron Crag trail, the longest, takes you right to the top of the forest for fantastic views, especially of the Coniston Fells and round as far as Langdale, but also round to the north and east and out across the sea.

Then there are the mountain bike trails. There's the 10 mile (16km) North Face trail, an intricate single track trail with cambered boardwalk sections: the 14 mile (22.5km) Silurian Way cycle trail, a cycling version of the walking trail which takes in many of the forest's sculptures: the Hawkshead Moor trail, 10½ miles (17km), which takes you over to views of Coniston westwards; and Moor Top trail, which starts and ends at Moor Top car park at the forest's northern end, near Hawkshead, and is 7 miles (11km) long.

My activity of choice in Grizedale is, inevitably, wandering about exploring with an OS map in my hand and paying scant notice of where walkers are supposed to be going. This generally involves a visit to Carron Crag from wherever I've started. My first visit was especially memorable, a close, grey but slightly breezy autumn day on which I started from Satterthwaite and did a clockwise tour of places or place names which looked or sounded evocative on the map: the above-mentioned remains of ironworks; the tumbling Farra Grain Gill; Rake Close and Farra Grain Heights with its disused quarry; Mustard Hill and on up to Carron Crag, where I sketched the grey view across the pinetops as snow started to fall. I carried on across country as far as the mast and fire tower at High Man on Grizedale Moor, then threaded my way down to the visitor centre, had a look round, then headed into the eastern forest to try and find out what or whoever Potato Peg Plantation could be named after: then Grizedale Tarn, and back to Satterthwaite via a peer down Bogle Crag and the giggle-inducing Breasty Haw.

It was, to me, a day as memorable as a day on the hills in mist: but then perhaps I'm unusual in enjoying misty days on the hills, when only the map and compass give you a sense of the drama of the landscape which is actually all around you. On the day in question I disappeared knee-deep into sundry bogs and streams, got scratched and cold and wet and muddy and generally had a wonderful time. Grizedale repays further explorations than this: at its southern end particularly there's no one around and yet the forest is more natural, and much more native, than that further north.

On clear days, though, especially in winter, I think the view of the Coniston Fells from Carron Crag is hard to beat. And six year olds can make it on foot from the visitor centre, even if they might end up on your shoulders on the way back for a hot meal at the café.

Brigsteer Park

Show me a wood called 'Park' and I'll immediately start searching the OS map for a castle or big country house: I now live on a street called 'Wood Park' which was once part of the grounds of a former Royal hunting lodge. In this case we're looking for Sizergh Castle, the home of the Strickland family, who we met in the Scout Scar and Whitbarrow chapter. Presumably at one time one of the family took a shine to the wood clinging to the eastern slopes of the Lyth Valley south of the hamlet of Brigsteer, and it became known as a park: John F. Curwen's *Records relating to the Barony of Kendale* tells us that it's been called Brigsteer Park since at least 1713.

It's been worked as a coppice wood for a long time, and one can imagine hurdles and other products of coppice woods being carried out into Lyth Valley for use on the fertile fields. It fell into decline in the 1930s, and the Strickland family sold the castle and the wood to the National Trust in the 1950s. It was replanted with mixed conifers and deciduous trees in the 1960s and 70s, but in 1988 the National Trust began a more sensitive management policy, conserving remaining patches of old wood, encouraging native species to take over other areas and resuming coppicing, which is good for diversity

Path through Brigsteer Park.

and to encourage regrowth of the woodland. The 'park' aspect of the wood has been returned by allowing wide paths through the wood, which let light through to the forest floor and encourage the growth of flowers and other undergrowth. These days Brigsteer Park is a truly fairytale place, far more varied than its meagre dimensions suggest – it's not much over one kilometre long and just a few hundred metres across, but somehow the steepness of the slope makes it feel much bigger. Its focus is Simms Well, a spring at the bottom of the slope where the limestone meets the now drained valley floor.

There aren't many small and, if you like natural but managed woods in this part of the world, but Brigsteer Park is a real treat. It's best in spring, when the wood floor is awash with flowers and the trees are bursting with buds, new leaves and catkins. It makes one ponder the fact that management can be a good thing for the environment, besides the useful by-products of that management. Unusually the views are obtained by going downhill: from the top of the slope you won't see anything, as there are thick trees on both sides of the road. But burst out of the trees onto the flats of Lyth Valley early in the morning and look across to Whitbarrow as the salt breezes blow in from the sea and a lifting of the spirits is guaranteed. There are no paths leading out across the valley from the woods, but the road at the southern end is so infrequently used this doesn't really matter. The contrast between the flatness and straightness of the valley landscape and the jumbled variety of the woods goes to show that just because landscapes are managed doesn't mean they're all the same.

Crag Wood

Of all the sequestered spots celebrated in this book, Crag Wood is by far the smallest. I suppose the next smallest is probably Brigsteer Park. The smallest hill in the book (excepting Humphrey Head) is the Helm: but Crag Wood is hardly bigger than the little scrap of Underhelm Wood. It would virtually fit into Castlesteads iron age hill fort on the Helm's summit.

It's also an example of woods under the control of another major owner of woodland in Cumbria besides the Forestry Commission, the Woodland Trust. I'm a long-term member of the Woodland Trust, and have had a role in their ongoing Ancient Tree Hunt project, helping them to find and record ancient trees across the country: I've found a few gems myself in Cumbria, as well as verifying the finds of other members of the public. There are no great veteran trees in Crag Wood, though: its just an unassuming patch of woodland, less than 200m north-south and considerably less than that across the other axis.

Hidden along the Morecambe Bay coast of the Lakes on the Kent peninsula, Crag Wood nevertheless has the magic property of all small woods: it stretches space to unimaginable limits. Small it may be but you could poke around Crag Wood all day and never particularly notice you'd explored the same place twice. Or, to put it more accurately, I have poked around Crag Wood all day, on several occasions, in between bouts of working at proofreading in a hammock strung up somewhere, usually at the wood's seaward end (my job does have its advantages), and have never grown tired of it. From primroses at the narrow border between wood and sea in earliest Spring to plentiful edible mushrooms in the autumn, to the endlessly changing state of

Crag Wood (right) and Ulpha Fell from Whitbarrow with
Heysham reactors across the bay in the distance.

The pond in Crag Wood.

the rotting wrecked fishing boat just over the stile at the wood's south western corner, to the views across the estuary as the tide rushes out and rushes in again, to the summer flowers round the cluster of little pools hidden at the wood's heart, it's a place to savour a whole sunny day. Take a picnic. Go nowhere. Although a wander northwards along a short stretch of the Cumbria Coastal Way is unlike to hurt very much.

Fairy Steps

Cumbria's southern coast, petering out into Morecambe Bay's shifting sands, is often known (at least it is on the brown tourist road signs) as the Lake District Peninsulas. Really there are three peninsulas, from west to east: the Millom peninsula, bordered by the Irish Sea and the Duddon estuary; then the big one, the Barrow peninsula between the Duddon and Leven estuaries; then the Cartmel peninsula (see the Coast section) between the Leven outflow from Windermere and the Kent estuary. Then, between the Kent and the Lancashire border, is an almost-peninsula north of Leighton Moss, an RSPB nature reserve four metres above sea level pushing into the northern end of Lancashire between Silverdale and the Yealand villages.

Looked at on the map the county boundary skirts almost guiltily around the top end of the reserve, as if consciously giving it a wide berth, and oddly, though I had no idea at the time, the county boundary marks about the limits of where I got to exploring those woods and their attendant countryside back in Lancaster days, when trips to the woods around Warton Crag, especially Hyning Scout Wood and Cringlebarrow and Deepdale Woods, building shelters in the grykes and glancing across at the fells and musing on the finer points of my PhD thesis, made a welcome break from the library. Occasionally, though, driving up to Kendal to do some shopping or, later, some househunting, we'd stop in a pretty village called Beetham, which has a lovely pub, a working watermill, a paper museum and a plant nursery: and, some time, I forget when, we discovered that the local woods north of the county boundary hold a little secret we've never tired of visiting.

In my earliest explorations of this part of the world I explored from the south, simply because that's where I was, but I knew how crowded the woods and hills around Arnside and Silverdale get whenever the weather's good for walking. This is no surprise: the walking's good and the views are even better. But somehow we overlooked the Beetham woods, which are also in the Arnside and Silverdale Area of Outstanding Natural Beauty, until one Sunday afternoon, wandering off after a very large lunch at the Wheatsheaf at Beetham, we stumbled across first a ruined cottage, obviously abandoned within living memory and therefore telling a tantalisingly hidden story, in the trees where the footpath leading south-west from Beetham enters the woods heading towards Fairy Steps; and then a signpost pointing uphill (as signposts tend to in Cumbria) which proclaimed 'Fairy Steps'. Suitably intrigued, we followed.

Fairy Steps turns out to be a bit of a highlight, in the same way that the Lion and the Lamb on the summit of Grasmere's Helm Crag is. Admittedly the climb up is in no way in the same league – unless you're about five, in which case the ascent to Fairy Steps is likely to be much preferred, as you might manage it on your own feet, without recourse to anyone's shoulders – but both are culminations of a climb, both with fantastic views (though I honestly think that from Fairy Steps is better), which offer an interesting onward challenge, in this case the descent of an almost claustrophobically narrow gully down into the woods on the western side of the escarpment. There's plenty of fun scrambling and bouldering to be had in the vicinity too if you feel so inclined, and if your family is inclined to let you have a go.

Inevitably, anything with a name like Fairy Steps comes with a story, so for completeness' sake I'd better give it. The tale goes that should anyone manage to descend the steps without touching the sides, the locally resident fairies will grant any wish you care to make. I did once, successfully, make my way down without touching the sides, casting aspersions on the accepted wisdom that it's impossible: acts of fairy kindness were thereafter, sadly, absent. I later tried to get down without touching the sides with a sleeping infant on my back. I was not successful, but somehow or other I managed not to wake the baby up.

It's worth mentioning that toddlers love limestone pavements. So many little places to explore, and to hide things. Like your phone. And your car keys. But while you're there do look for a poignant reminder of history easily overlooked in the enchanted (and enchanted is the right word) environs of Fairy Steps. The route is one of the old coffin trails that cover the Lakes, in this case from Arnside and Hazelslack to the graveyard at Beetham. How the coffin-bearers negotiated Fairy Steps is a problem worth considering as you negotiate the narrow path down the escarpment, but search and you will find rings and other means by which they used to haul coffins up the scarp.

In fact these woods are a place to keep searching. Under-visited and with fantastic views, Cumbria's most southerly sequestered spot shares something in character with the limestone habitats, like Whitbarrow, further north, but is also appreciably a softer landscape, much prettier, in my opinion, than the more visited parts of the AONB on the coast, and marking the point where Lancashire, my old stamping ground, definitely takes on a different, Cumbrian slant. One of the cornerstones of this book is the idea that, no matter whether you're on the top of Scafell Pike, or on the beach at Eskmeals, or wandering across Moor Divock, or poking around Pendragon Castle, there's something definitely Cumbrian that unites all the apparently historically and geographically diverse localities that now find themselves within the county of Cumbria. The separateness of Beetham's woods from those just to the south is a fine example of this.

Coast

IF THERE'S ONE environment in Cumbria that's usually overlooked, it's not fell, or moorland, or woodland, or valley: it's the coasts, to which the last section of this book now turns. From the silty, sheltered but massively tidal creeks and estuaries of the Morecambe Bay shores, to the awe-inspiring sands where the Irish Sea comes crashing onto the flanks of Black Combe or the mouth of Wasdale, to the remnants of Hadrian's Wall where Cumbria meets Scotland, there's a lot of coastline worth exploring.

Wind turbines off Walney.

Walney Island 1

Why start with Walney Island? For one thing, the middle of the island is these days, superficially at least, just a suburb of Barrow-in-Furness (universally just 'Barrow' to the natives, who are the only people who can pronounce it right, short on the 'Ba-', long on the '-rrow'). With the possible exception of Carlisle the only large industrial town in Cumbria, as well as being home to a Naval base, Barrow, through which the shipless visitor to Walney Island (just Walney to the locals) must pass, is not exactly on the tourist radar. Given the attractiveness of the rest of the county and its towns this is hardly surprising, though I've always felt Barrow's centre to have a certain solid, Victorian grandeur. But when John Ruskin, an old man in a perilous condition of mental health, wrote in an essay called *The Storm-Cloud of the Nineteenth Century* of the view from his home at Brantwood, on the north-east shore of Coniston Water,

> From my dining-room, I am happy in the view from the lower reach of Coniston water, not because it is particularly beautiful, but because it is entirely pastoral and pure. Were a single point of the Barrow ironworks to show itself over the green ridge of the hill, I should never care to look at it more

he was expressing a distrust of industrialization along the Cumbrian coast – Sellafield has had any number of similar objections levelled at it over the years, and like Sellafield, Barrow has links to the nuclear industry, as the Trident nuclear submarines were built there, and it's likely that, in future, Trident's replacement will be too. Ruskin was also expressing a view of wilderness which I've tried to deconstruct in the Whinlatter section.

So, why begin this final section on Cumbria's coasts here? Well, this is a book about unexpectedly rewarding corners of Cumbria, and Walney is one, but what makes Walney so unexpected is that it's surely the most un-Cumbrian place in Cumbria, more so even than Lyth Valley. For one thing it is – along with its smaller companions, Sheep, Piel, Roa and Foulney Islands, which nestle like little children behind Mother Walney's protective skirts – the only island close to the Cumbrian coast. For another, if you're walking south along the island's western coast you can easily convince yourself that you're walking, say, north

Walk on Walney on a December day, with Black Combe in the background.

along the Norfolk coast, with the rigs out in the Irish Sea to the west mirroring those that would be to the east out in the North Sea if you really were in Norfolk: then you turn round, and the vista across the Duddon estuary of Black Combe and the central fells beyond comes as an awe-inspiring surprise.

Walney is also one of the few places in Cumbria that's not a museum, stately home or shop that can be enjoyed, whatever the weather, without undue hardiness. Late one December I was walking along the beach at North End Hawes on Walney on a jaw-clenchingly cold day, with a northerly gale blowing down from the Arctic and picking up some extra chill from the snow on Black Combe on its way, and it occurred to me that Walney Island had only ever been a place to visit on days like this one, when you were craving wide-open spaces and fresh air but the weather in the central Lake District was forbidding, to say the least. I like to think I'm not easily deterred by bad weather: I've climbed Helvellyn in a white out in February, albeit from Dunmail Raise, and I've been up any number of the region's bigger peaks in similar conditions. But sometimes it's just too cold, or too windy, or you're just too tired, for it to be safe venturing onto the tops, and on days like those a walk on Walney, to watch the havoc being wreaked by the incoming weather systems on the fells across the Duddon Sands, has seemed just what was needed: so much so that on the day in question I wondered if I was being unfair on Walney, using it as a refuge for my wandering instincts only when the weather's dreadful.

As night fell, Venus scudding from between gaps in cloud over the rigs out to sea, I turned back gratefully towards the car and its heater. I resolved, one day next year, to pay Walney some proper attention for once, and to come back and see if the island could repay the sacrifice of a whole spring or summer's day and night spent, not walking the hills, but treading the level sands right round the island. This would also give me the opportunity to bookend this section with two accounts, one more historical, the other more observational, about one of the least Cumbrian places in Cumbria.

There's another more compelling reason to begin here, which is that it's most likely where the human history of what's now Cumbria starts. The first people, as far as we're aware, to come to what's now Cumbria were the hunter gatherers of the Mesolithic, the 'middle stone age' (ignoring the Late Upper Paleolithic site of Kirkhead Cave on the Cartmel peninsula), and to the people of the Mesolithic the most important stone of all was flint. Their lives revolved around the uniquely knappable properties of flint, which they made into knives, scrapers, spearheads, arrowheads and the hundreds of different shaped small implements we call microliths. Flint retained its central importance until farming was introduced to Britain in the Neolithic, when the need to clear trees for agriculture led to a demand for bigger, tougher axes. The most important source of these axes in Britain was the axe 'factory' site in the gulley below Pike of Stickle in Great Langdale.

Prior to this no one had any reason to penetrate the forbidding mountain landscape, full as it was with bears, wolves and all manner of unknown and imagined dangers. But, human curiosity being what it was, people obviously did, or they'd never have found the little face of green schist in Langdale which made such beautiful axes.

However, before these axes were developed, flint was the thing, and there is no flint in the largely igneous and metamorphic rocks of the Lake District. In fact there's no flint in Cumbria at all, but there are flint reefs out on the bed of the Irish Sea, and after storms it washes up on the beaches of west Cumbria, notably on Walney Island. Given that this is the most southerly of Cumbria's flint-bearing beaches, it's not hard to conjecture that flint-knapping sites found on Walney in 1936 are among the earliest-known sites of human habitation in Cumbria. By the 1980s over 1700 flint artefacts had been recovered from North End. Even without the lure of flint, beaches were important to these mesolithic hunter gatherers because of the presence of plenteous, easily-gathered shellfish. Walney has probably been inhabited more or less constantly ever since.

The history of the island itself, however, goes back a lot further than this. The rocks that make up the central Lake District were formed in volcanic eruptions under an ancient ocean in the southern hemisphere between 500 and 450 million years ago. By the late Carboniferous period, about 290 million years ago, the area had drifted, thanks to plate tectonics, to find itself in the middle of a huge supercontinent, Pangaea. During this desert period sandstones were laid down, initially the sandstones now found around Penrith and the Eden valley; the gypsum mined at Melmerby dates from this period (see the Eden Valley chapter). Then, at the end of the Carboniferous, Pangaea began to split apart and for a brief period of time the area was covered by seawater; this soon evaporated in the heat, and the sandstone bedrocks of the Cumbrian coast, which stretch, with frequent breaks, from St. Bees to Walney, were formed, up to 400m deep in places.

Under the dunes the surface of today's island consists largely of glacial debris dumped by the glacier which flowed down the Duddon channel when the last ice age came to an end about 13,000 years ago. As the climate warmed, plants and then trees slowly returned – first juniper and dwarf birch, then pines, and gradually less hardy deciduous trees. The coastal forests were drowned during a wet phase called the 'Atlantic' around 5,200 years ago, or about 2,000 years after the earliest archaeological sites on the island were first used, but submerged remains of this forest can still be seen off the coast when the tide's out, and chunks of it wash up on the shore with the flint.

Even after the demise of flint axes and the rise of polished stone axes like the ones from Langdale, Walney continued to be important. Sandstone was used for polishing stone axes, and the Lake District historian Bill Rollinson

Beach and dunes, west coast of Walney Island, Black Combe in the distance.

has conjectured that Walney may have been used as a place from which axes were exported to Scotland and the Isle of Man. The Scandinavian settlers who gave Cumbria so many of its place names came mostly via settlements in Ireland and the Isle of Man, and it's likely many of them landed first on Walney, but from here until quite recently historical mentions of Walney Island are rare.

Speaking of place names, the Old English name for Walney was Wagneia, 'island of quicksands', and in the Domesday Book it is called Houganai, 'island of Hougun', the name given to Furness in the Domesday Book: there is a conflicting etymological claim, that it's from the Old Norse *valna ey*, meaning 'Isle of the British.' Income from North Scale, just south of the modern-day airport, is mentioned in documentation from Furness Abbey from 1247, and from the year 1558 windmills were built here – a process which continues today, as a 30 mill wind farm 4½ miles (7km) offshore was opened in 2006. There are plans to build up to 100 more; these plans are not very popular locally, as residents feel they'll ruin the views of the sunset. As I've always felt offshore wind farms have an awesome beauty all of their own I'll keep my own views quiet.

Walney's first chapel, a chapel-of-ease attached to Dalton parish, was built in the mid-16th century, with the present St. Mary's dating from 1907-8. The cornerstones of the original chapel can still be seen in the churchyard. Half the population was wiped out by the plague in 1631; it's believed that the victims were buried on the bank behind the Ferry Hotel, just north of the bridge, which was opened in 1908 to commemorate Queen Victoria's Diamond Jubilee. In 2008 Cumbria County Council spent £1 million renovating the bridge and repainting it for its centenary celebration. Today Walney has a population of approximately 13,000, making it the seventh most populated island in England.

Either end of the island now consists of nature reserves, with the built-up area in the middle. Birds regularly encountered include stonechats, mergansers, goldeneye, widgeon, lapwings, larks, pipits and birds of prey, including hen harriers, merlins and peregrines, especially in winter when they come to take advantage of the island's comparative warmth and richness in mammal life. There are day hunting barn owls too. Fieldfare, redwing, brambling and snow bunting also enjoy the warmth and shelter, and common and natterjack toads, Britain's rarest amphibians, abound, as do newts, and gulls: the south end has one of the largest colonies of breeding gulls in Europe, which apparently relocated there a century or so ago from further north in protest at the growth of the island's population after the bridge opened. Eider and shelducks breed here, and the dunes are also home to a surprising array of fungi in the autumn. BAE Systems, the shipyard based in Barrow, has an airfield between North Scale and North End Hawes, home to the Lakes Gliding Club.

Roa, Piel and Foulney Islands

Mother Walney's ducklings, these three islands are like one of those younger generations of a family whose parents are forever pointing out how unlike their siblings they are. Clustered within, very nearly, an equilateral triangle with sides a kilometre long, they're three very different places: like good children, each seems to have taken on some aspect of the mother island and made it their own defining characteristic.

Roa Island, at the southern end of the Barrow Peninsula, is linked to the mainland by a 247m causeway completed in 1846. These days the island is home to a yacht club, a rather fancy lifeboat station serving Morecambe Bay and the Irish Sea, the faded and sadly closed grandeur of the Roa Island Hotel, a tea room and the departure point of the ferry to Piel Island (there are two ferries and access to Piel can be relied on after about 10am from Easter time until the end of summer). Foulney Island is accessed from its own causeway not quite halfway along Roa Island's.

Piel, once known as Fouldrey Island – Old Norse, 'Fodder Island' – was given to Furness Abbey by King Stephen in 1127, passed back to the Crown after the dissolution and was fortified against possible attack by the Spanish at the time of the Armada. During the Civil War Cromwell's fleet sheltered here after the Royalists took Liverpool Castle. Eventually the island fell into the hands of the Duke of Buccleugh, who gave it to the people of Barrow in 1920 as a war memorial. The island's attractions are the ruins of the castle (best viewed, I think, from South End Walney's old saltworks pier) and the Ship

Piel Castle from the gull colony, South End Hawes, Walney, and below, Piel Castle from Foulney, with Walney wind turbines in the distance.

Inn, reopened following extensive renovations a few years ago.

Foulney is a small extra-tidal pile of pebbles washed one on another down the Levens channel, which was, as I've said above, connected to Roa Island by a causeway built in 1846. Foulney is a Site of Special Scientific Interest, Special Area of Conservation and Special Protection Area and prospective visitors should be aware that during the nesting season access restrictions may be

in place – particularly to Slitch Ridge, a wonderfully-named bank running north from the island's northern shore, and surely the least ridge-like thing in Cumbria – and that at this time of year dogs are not allowed. There's often a resident warden in a caravan at the seaward end of the causeway keeping an eye on things. It is very popular with terns, mostly but not exclusively Little and Arctic terns (Sandwich and Common Terns also nest here from time to time: Foulney is, strangely, the only place in north west England where Arctic Terns nest, although they also nest across North Wales, the Isle of Man and right round the Scottish coast down to Lindisfarne). Ringed Plover nest here in summer, while oystercatchers, curlews, brent geese, knot and dunlin, long-tailed duck, Slavonian grebe and thousands of eider ducks are likely to be around. Amid the salt grasses are flowering thrift and sea campion, sea kale and biting stonecrop.

In fact, Foulney is more birds on the wing and plants and views across to the Lancashire shore of the bay than it is an island: it's a blank canvas. The cause-way can be tricky underfoot on a high tide, submerged even; the gulls and terns aggressive overhead. But as a lonely place to go and sit and think about not much but the speed of the ebb and flow of the tide, and of life, in the shallow bay, there's nothing else like it. It's nowhere more than about my own height above sea level, but its always there, a little patch of grass, with a man-made tether, wavering on the edge of not existing in the vast moving muddiness of things.

Mud at low tide, Foulney causeway.

Long after dark its the finest place from which to watch the lights of Lancashire across the bay. Which makes it a uniquely memorable place, especially if you're me, and feeling nostalgic.

Eskmeals

Cumbria's southern Irish Sea coast is a collection of evocative names –
Seascale, Drigg, Saltcoats, Eskmeals, Silecroft – linked by long shingle beaches, sharing views of Black Combe inland and of Man and of gas rigs out to
sea, with only one real feature, the alliteratively tripping Esk Estuary. Half
nature reserve, half firing range – these days operated as a research and test-
ing facility by defence contractor QinetiQ – at first glance there's little more
to be said about Eskmeals. But, as with North End Walney, there's a link to
Cumbria's very earliest human past to be found around the estuary, which is
one of the reasons the place is so evocative.

The other reason is that, to stand at Eskmeals and watch a storm come rushing across the Irish Sea, bringing waves whose salt-spray surely splashes high
onto the dark bulk of Black Combe inland, and to watch the Esk feebly emp-
tying Wastwater and all the rest of the run off from England's highest hills into
the teeth of the gale, is to feel in awe of the weight of the sea before and the
land behind you. It is, for me, at the right time, the most awesome place in
Cumbria. Sharp Edge in a winter breeze excepted. The awe for me is compounded by the knowledge that people have stood here and looked at the
weather – people whose lives, in the exposed north, were very much more
lived under the weather than ours are – for a very long time. In fact it was the
storms that brought the first visitors here.

As we saw at Walney, there's no naturally occurring flint in Cumbria, but
flint – brittle, poor-quality brown stuff, but flint nonetheless – does wash up
on the beaches after storms in some places, dredged up by the waves from
reefs out on the floor of the Irish Sea. Flint was like mobile phones and car
keys to our stone age ancestors – something you always had with you – so it's
no surprise that early flint tools, and midden mounds consisting of the remains
of shellfish used to satisfy the hunger of those early knappers, have been
found, the first at Eskmeals in 1935, with further finds across the water at
Drigg. Not as old as the Late Palaeolithic antler pieces found at Kirkhead and
Lindale Low Caves described in the Cartmel chapter, but still pretty early, predominantly Mesolithic, although there were signs of human activity through
the Neolithic and perhaps into the early Bronze ages.

What the Mesolithic pioneers felt about the forbidding, wood-choked valleys and dark peaks swarming with wolves can only be imagined, but we must
guess they were curious, and had spotted features like the Langdale Pikes on
their way past across the bay, as we know that before long their Neolithic
descendents were chipping away at the rockface in Great Langdale and bringing away axes of great worth and beauty.

Of course this coast is home to Sellafield, which I think enriches the view
from Coniston's Old Man, echoing as it does those tall structures out at sea.

Pike of Stickle axe factory gully.

As I said in the Lowick High Common chapter, I missed the news in September 2007 that the cooling towers were to be demolished, and found myself standing on the Old Man wondering what on earth had happened, where the chimneys had vanished to, not long afterwards. For what it's worth, and without wanting to engage very deeply with the debate about nuclear energy, it's always seemed to me that one of Cumbria's major exports of recent (ish) times has been energy, and so-called 'alternative' energy, whether from wind, water or nuclear sources, but that long before such things existed Cumbria was a powerful source of another kind of energy, that of the language of those who have been inspired by the region's beauty to speak up for the natural world and the power that it yields in the minds of those who care for it. Once it was full of watermills; nuclear power stations are only complicated watermills.

Eskmeals Dunes nature reserve is leased by Cumbria Wildlife Trust from the Ministry of Defence and has been a nature reserve since 1970: be aware that from time to time it's closed due to live firing on the adjacent ranges, in which case red flags will make this obvious. Nearby are the excellent Muncaster Castle (fantastic grounds and the World Owl Centre) and the phenomenally well-preserved remains of a Roman bath house, part of an old Roman coastal fort: these and the reserve can be visited by a good circular walk from Muncaster Castle taking in some of the Cumbria Coastal Way. Newton Knott, a stubby little hill with the remains of an old beacon on the top, is worth taking in too. Drigg Dunes is a separate nature reserve across the estuary, in the hands of the Lake District National Park Authority.

Cartmel Peninsula

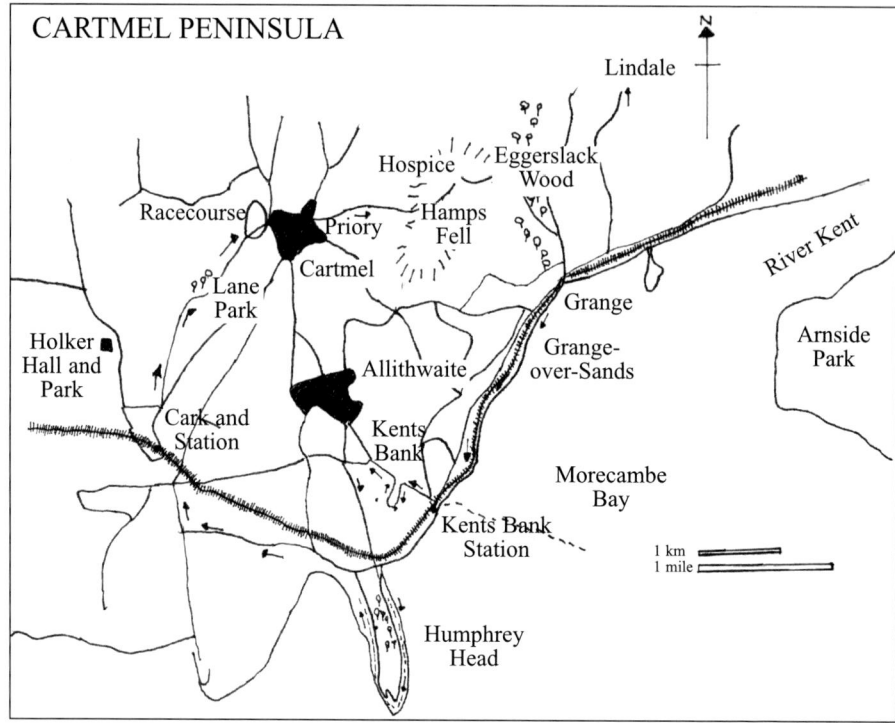

This section describes a circular walk, beginning and ending at Cark railway station and taking in Cartmel, Hampsfell, Grange over Sands, Kirkhead and Humphrey Head, the highlights of what is widely known as the Cartmel Peninsula, the strip of limestone situated between the Kent and Levens estuaries and extending out into Morecambe Bay. In many ways Cartmel is the baby sister of the next peninsula along, Furness: Thomas West wrote in his *Guide to the Lakes* of 1778 that "the only thing worthy of notice in Cartmel is the Church," but I have to disagree. Compared to neighbouring Furness, Cartmel is smaller, and has a smaller abbey, whose monks, like those of Furness, were responsible for very early iron mining in the area; it has a smaller set of limestone fells, and a much smaller main settlement, Grange compared to Barrow. But it's much prettier, and more interesting.

It would be more in the style of this book to describe these places separately, but as the walk described below is so satisfyingly complete, virtually all of it being on two long-distance footpaths, the Cistercian Way and the Cumbria

Coastal Way, and as it goes via three railway stations on the same line – Cark, Grange and Kents Bank, allowing for a great degree of flexibility – it is presented as a guided tour, and the train can be used to speed up or truncate the route as desired. Of course, the places described can all be explored individually by car; armchair-based explorers need not skip this chapter, as there is more history and description than directions in what follows. Similarly, walkers embarking from Cark should be aware that I'm assuming you have an OS map to hand. The whole walk is about thirteen miles (21km) and will take five hours at minimum, assuming fast walking, a brief sandwich at Hampsfell Hospice and a cursory glimpse into Cartmel Priory. If you're more inclined to ambling, interested in ecclesiastical history, and are planning to find something to eat in Cark, Cartmel or in Grange en route, allow a day for the whole round.

CARK TO CARTMEL

From Cark station, follow the B2572 north into the middle of Cark, and opposite the Engine Inn pub make your way along the road that leads up and to the right. Carry on until, just after leaving Cark and just after the end of the 30 limit, you reach a tarmac track leading uphill to your left. You're on the Cistercian Way, basically an alternative to the Cumbrian Coastal Way (which you'll join later) running from Roa Island to Grange, and taking in Furness Abbey and Cartmel Priory. Ahead and to your right is Hampsfell, which you'll

Cirrus clouds looking north west from the Cistercian Way leaving Cark.

Looking towards Hampsfell on the way out of Cark.

be climbing later: Cartmel is behind the trees ahead.

Follow the track past Low Bank Side, through Lane Park wood, through the beautiful field known as Seven Acres and across Cartmel racecourse into Cartmel. Pass the Village Shop, now more of a deli famous for its fabulous sticky toffee pudding – I've met Americans and Canadians who fly over every year just to stock up – and the old market cross, water pump and fish slabs, pass the second hand book shop and proceed into the grounds of the Priory.

Founded in 1190, the Priory is a beautiful, airy building both inside and out, and avoided demolition after it was dissolved in 1536 because William Marshal, later 1st Earl of Pembroke, who built and endowed the priory (and who lived in Wiltshire, at castles in Marlborough, where I went to school, and Ludgershall, where I now live), had provided for an altar and a priest for the use of the villagers inside the church. The villagers petitioned that as the church had a priest to minister to them

Cartmel Priory.

242

and that they had no other church, the old Priory church should be spared, and their petition was granted, but not before the King relieved the roof of its valuable lead. This was replaced in 1618 by George Holker, of Holker Hall, and the church was restored by the Victorians in 1830.

My two favourite features are the odd double tower, one set squarely above the crossing and the second placed at a 45° angle on top of it – apparently unique in England – and the two loaves of bread which are always to be found on a shelf on the north west corner of the crossing, paid for from an 18th-century fund left by a Rowland Briggs of Swallowmire for the benefit of the poor of the village, in return for whose gratitude he hoped they would "keep his grave unbroken up." The church also has some exceptional miserichords, which date from 1440.

CARTMEL TO GRANGE

Back in the churchyard, make your way round the east end of the church, through the gate and right to the main road. The Cistercian Way crosses the road and passes through a narrow cut onto the open fields. Follow it up onto Hampsfell, the walk's only (but surprisingly) strenuous section. Once on the top, make your way northwards to the hospice.

This isn't the only folly this walk passes – you may have spotted the 'Twr' marked on the OS map below Longlands Allotment, and we'll visit another on Kirkhead – but it is the most interesting. For one thing, the views are amongst

Lake District fells from Hampsfell

the best in Cumbria, rivalling those from Scout Scar. For another, it has a charming history; and, finally, it's a very comfortable place for a stop. The viewfinder on the roof, restored since Wainwright described it as 'unserviceable', is a bonus. Built in 1846 by George Remington, a vicar of Cartmel, for the protection and comfort of walkers, the hospice is still in tip-top condition, complete with the original boards displaying Remington's poetry, and one which explains the purposes of the hospice. I won't transcribe the poetry – if you want to read it without the walk up the fell first, you can read transcriptions in Wainwright's *Outlying Fells of Lakeland* – but the text of the other board reads:

TAKE NOTICE

All persons visiting this Hospice by permission of the owner, are requested to respect private property, and not by acts of wanton destruction show that they possess more muscle than brain. I have no hope that this request will be attended to for as Solomon says "Thou shouldest bray a fool in a mortar among wheat with a pestle yet will not his foolishness depart from him."

GEORGE REMINGTON

Quite what right Remington had to describe himself as the 'owner' of the Hospice I don't know.

When you're ready to leave the shelter of the Hospice, follow the Cistercian Way through the beautiful Eggerslack Wood and down to Windermere Road

Morecambe Bay sands from Hampsfell and, opposite, in Eggerslack Woods.

leading into Grange. If you get lost – which you probably will – don't worry, just head downhill until you find a road, and make your way into Grange.

GRANGE TO KENTS BANK

At the bottom of Windermere Road, cross the roundabout by the garage (unless you're going a few paces right into the Hazelmere tearoom or left to the station to catch the next train to Kents Bank, back to Cark or back to Carnforth), and make your way south through the Ornamental Gardens. At the far end you'll find a car park; walk through this, keeping the railway to your left, and you'll find a short tunnel which leads to the Promenade and Cumbria Coastal Way.

Turn right and head to Kents Bank. Heed the signs warning of quicksand and fast rising tides, and enjoy the information boards which tell you that pink footed geese, shelduck, pintail, oystercatcher, grey plover, knot, dunlin, bar-tailed godwit, curlew, redshank, eider, goldeneye, red breasted merganser, turnstone and ringed plover may be spotted out on the marshes. Apparently there are 'more oystercatchers, dunlin, curlew and redshank to be found in Morecambe Bay than anywhere else in Britain.'

Holme Island from Grange-over-Sands

KENTS BANK TO HUMPHREY HEAD

When you get to Kents Bank (where the right of way across the bay from Hest Bank reaches land again) follow Greaves Wood Road around to the right, up the hill past Abbot Hall Hotel. About 450m up the road is a detour which is well worth taking. On the left hand side of the road you'll find a very private-looking driveway with a sign that says 'PRIVATE DRIVE, NO PARKING NO TURNING PLEASE.' Walk confidently across to a gate which allows access to Kirkhead.

Make your way up to Kirkhead Tower, another folly which I haven't been able to find out anything about, other than that its gothic-ness suggests the early 19th century. On your map you'll see a cave marked just down the hill to your west. Reaching it is not for the faint-hearted – or faint-footed – but it's worth the effort.

Kirkhead Cave is one

Kirkhead Tower and, below, birds on the mudflat from Humphrey Head.

of two places in Cumbria – the other being Lindale Low Cave a few miles to the north – where there's evidence of Palaeolithic human activity, suggesting that people may have been here long before the Mesolithic people we, figuratively speaking, met searching for flint on Walney Island and at Eskmeals: specifically, a piece of antler from Kirkhead Cave was carbon dated in 2002 to between 13,050 and 12,400 years old.

Make your way back to Greaves Wood Road and follow the Cumbria Coastal Way to the north end of Humphrey Head. Now you could simply skip Humphrey Head and continue back along the Cumbria Coastal Way to Cark, most likely turning right at the T-junction to take you through Flookburgh, but this would be a shame.

Humphrey Head to Cark

Instead of turning right at the narrow gate leading past the outdoor centre carry on along the shore and then along the path through the delightfully stunted Humphrey Head Wood until you reach Humphrey Head Point, from where you have three choices: follow the fence up to the trig point on the top and carry on back to the Cumbria Coastal Way; make your way up the western shore back to the coastal way; or, preferably, go up to the trig point, enjoy the universally interesting view, and then go back down to the point and along the western shore, where you'll find the 'Natural Arch' and the rather disappointing 'Holy Well' promised on the OS map.

The well, which oddly is signposted from the B5277 Kents Bank to Flookburgh road, was used by monks from Cartmel Priory to heal the sick (the water contains salicin, a bitter-tasting chemical similar to aspirin and found in willow bark). Mentioned in West's *Guide to the Lakes* of 1778, a modern sign warns not to drink the water. Having disregarded this I can report that it tastes a little bitter, a little salty, faintly medicinal – you wouldn't want to drink lot of it – and as far as I can tell does neither harm nor good.

If you are not put off scrambling around limestone hillsides, you can

Cave entrance on Humphrey Head and, opposite, Cartmel Peninsula skies.

now make your way up the cliff from under a yew tree just north of a cave-like tangle of fallen rocks to find another, low, double-doored cave, where apparently the last wolf on England was killed, making it a nice double of Wild Boar Fell.

All that remains now is to make your way back to Cark, using the Cumbria Coastal Way for all or some of the distance, or going round via the New Embankment if you're feeling brave, though be warned: as Wainwright says in the chapter on Humphrey Head in *The Outlying Fells*, "wandering on the mud is not recommended if your wife makes you clean your boots, as some do." How times change.

North Coast

View across the Solway Firth from Silloth.

I can't remember now what part the car needed, but anyway it needed something, it was half way through Friday afternoon and there was no way the thing was going to be drivable by Monday. But the garage in question was run by the man who'd taught my wife to drive, who simply loaned us the company's Audi A6 for the weekend. 'It's done so many miles,' he said 'don't worry about putting on a few more over the weekend.' So on Saturday we headed off on for the first of a few, but probably not enough, explorations of the far north coast of Cumbria. It sticks in my mind partly because, though we've rarely spent our weekend days exploring places by car, when we have we've always enjoyed it – there seems to be so much time, hard to find in the week, to talk – but mostly because completely by accident we stumbled across a string of places which simply demanded more to be found out about them.

Beech avenue, looking across the B5032 between Silloth and Abbeytown, Skiddaw beyond.

An obvious feature of the cultural history of the borders are the pele towers, fortified farmhouses in which the lower storey was designed as a safe place to barricade cattle when the Border reivers came reiving. Sometimes, failing the presence of a pele, local churches were used: when, I imagine, it became apparent that reivers weren't interested in such niceties as not stealing from, or setting fire to, churches, some churches were built as both churches and pele towers: there are three in Cumbria that I'm aware of, two in the north, while the other, Great Salkeld, is in the Eden valley, and is described briefly in the Eden valley chapter.

There's also a 'pele vicarage', built, like Cumbria's pele churches, in the early 14th century, at Corbridge just east of Hexham in Northumberland. But it must be said that the idea of the locals hiding their cattle, women and children in a church and feeling the need to barricade said church securely is a particularly striking one. Both churches described here belonged to Holme Cultram Abbey, one from the 12th and one from the 14th centuries, and so the abbey, which has a tragic recent history, will need a visit too.

St John's, Newton Arlosh

As mentioned in the Martindale chapter, one of the early proponents of Christianity in what's now Cumbria was St. Ninian, an enthusiastic founder of churches who's said to have built the first church at what's now Newton Arlosh, to celebrate his safe return from Rome, where he went to receive an education in Christianity. Whether this is true is far from certain, as the 'Newton' half of the name suggests the current settlement and its church were built to replace something, the something in question being a port called Skinburness, situated on the southern edge of the mouth of the odd double estuary of Moricambe, the last inlet of the Cumbrian coast before the Eden, which last marks the northern

St. John's, Newton Arlosh.

boundary of both the county and of England. Skinburness was developed by Edward I in 1301, the king having used it as a port from which to keep Carlisle supplied while it was harrying, and being harried by, Scots cattle raiders and, more seriously, Robert the Bruce.

Edward gave Skinburness to the Abbot of Holme Cultram, together with the right to hold a market on a Thursday and an annual festival a fortnight long. The Bishop of Carlisle went one further, granting the Abbot leave to build a church there. But Skinburness succumbed to a series of violent storms shortly thereafter, and despite the monk's efforts – the 'sea dyke' shown on the OS maps probably dates from this time and represents an attempt to hold back the floods – a church, dedicated to St. John, was finally built at the settlement which replaced Skinburness, Newton Arlosh, 'the new town on the marsh,' under a new charter dated 11 April 1304. It's likely this was a formality and that the church was already being built when the charter was granted.

Assuming the pele tower was built at the same time as the rest of the church, this makes Newton Arlosh's fortified tower older than that at St Michael's Burgh by Sands. Great Salkeld church is much earlier than these, but its pele tower is later, dating from 1380. Pevsner says that Newton Arlosh's tower dates from 'shortly after 1304', St Michael's is 'mid 14th century' and St Cuthbert's is 'late 14th century.'

Holme Cultram Abbey was sacked during Robert the Bruce's 'Great Raid' of 1322: no early records pertaining to St John's seem to have survived that raid, and thereafter not much of the church's history survives.

What is certain is the strength of its fortifications. The walls are hugely thick, as you'll notice when you enter by the main door, which is only 31 inches wide, making forcing an entry difficult, something which gives the interior a cave-like, almost claustrophobic quality. Tradition states that whichever newly-wed emerges from the church first after a marriage ceremony will wear the proverbial trousers in the relationship. The door from the nave to the vaulted basement under the tower is similarly proportioned, a second defence should attackers gain entrance to the nave, with an iron-framed door clad in oak. All in all it goes to show how readily the two forms of church and pele come together, especially since not every community could afford more than one stone building: so you build your church of stone, to the glory of the eternal God, and as the parable commands: and you're incidentally relieved that this means the reivers can't come and burn the thing down. Even the windows are high in the walls and very narrow, to make it difficult to fire flaming arrows and other weapons through. The spiral staircase is only wide enough to let one person move up at a time: and the church bells fortuitously doubled as alarm bells.

Holme Cultram was dissolved in 1538 and by 1580 it was reported that St. John's Church had fallen into disrepair and so it remained until 1843, when it was restored. The graveyard seems to have remained in use, though: there is, for example, a tombstone with a skull and crossbones dated 1737. It was restored under the direction of local architectress Sara Losh of Arlosh Hall, when a sizable extension was added to the north side (effectively a transept, but unusually one bigger than the nave), and in 1893 the interior was rearranged, the altar having been moved to the north wall of the extension, where it is today, and the box pews introduced in 1843 were removed. Sara Losh also added a number of internal carvings and the eagle on the roof ridge: the font, however, is older, older probably than the rest of the church, and is thought to have been brought from Holme Cultram.

ST MICHAEL'S, BURGH BY SANDS

St Michael's shares some similarities with the church at Newton Arlosh, and is in many ways better-preserved in the sense that it retains more of its original shape and layout. It's lost its original door, however – which means it's very fortunate, and surprising, that St John's, and St Cuthbert's, Great Salkeld, have their origi-

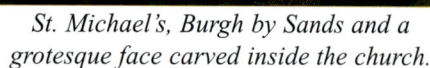

St. Michael's, Burgh by Sands and a grotesque face carved inside the church.

nals still intact: you'd have thought a main door two and a half foot across would be amongst the first things to go in a fortified church when there are no longer bands of Scots rampaging around the countryside. But then old habits die hard: St Michael's military connections go back a long way, it being built on the site of, and from the stones of, one of the central buildings of an old Roman fort, Avallava, on Hadrian's Wall. The spookily-nosed pagan head in the east wall of the chancel inside the church is testimony to the church's origins, and is one of not many Roman remains inside a Cumbrian church that I'm aware of, the font at Martindale being an exception: so that both of these churches, St John's and St Michael's, have tenuous links to Martindale.

It's also about the only evidence on the ground the casual observer will find of Hadrian's Wall, the last five or so miles of which ran along the south coast of the Solway. Archaeologists will show you where the milecastles, fortlets, vallum and the wall itself were, and they're marked on the OS maps, but except occasionally, when sections which are now under marshland are briefly uncovered as the mudbanks shift, you won't find anything except St Michael's remaining of Hadrian's Wall. This can prove something of an anticlimax to those who've made the whole journey from east to west.

The earliest church on this site was probably early 12th century: there was certainly one in existence about 1200, when the living was given to Holme Cultram. The north aisle was added early in the 13th century, when the door was moved to the new aisle and the old doorway filled in with sandstone blocks. There was once a second tower above the east end – Newton Arlosh church's pele tower is also at the east end – and the nave has been lengthened at the east end at some point. The church happens to contain five particularly clear mason's marks, three of which can also be identified at Holme Cultram and one in the outside wall of the choir of Carlisle Cathedral. The pele tower is probably the earliest of the three surviving church peles and is very similar to that at Newton Arlosh. There was once a fortified vicarage near the east end of the church too.

The high point in the church's history came in 1307, when Edward I died of dyssentry at Burgh on his way to fight the Bruce's army. The body was laid in the church for a while before being carried to Westminster Abbey, as is commemorated by an impressive memorial on Burgh marsh, a little over a mile north of the village, in a forlornly beautiful spot on the marches which feels about as much in Scotland as England, where the Eden and the Esk join the Solway Firth.

HOLME CULTRAM

Holme Cultram Abbey, founded in 1158 as a daughter abbey of Melrose Abbey – just east of Galashiels in south eastern Scotland – shares something with Cartmel Abbey, in that after the Dissolution it escaped demolition by virtue of the fact that there was no parish church, like those described above, to replace it. Most of the original abbey church's surroundings have vanished – the existing church is only six bays long, to the original nine – but the distinctive eagle-topped, and eagle-shouldered west front remains, like an old

Holme Cultram Abbey and gravestone at Holme Cultram.

chaplain emeritus lamenting how things were back in the day. Sadly though I've never seen Holme Cultram's proud and reflective remains in any state other than as a burnt-out wreck, they having been set on fire by a local teenager who, having stolen half a bottle of vodka's worth of cash from the abbey in 2006, later returned having consumed said half bottle of vodka and set fire to the place, and was later sentenced to four years in prison. The fire spread rapidly, and took the roof, the pews, fortunately not the windows which were removed in time, but most tragically the abbey's centuries of records, right back to the cartulery, the document containing details of the monastery's foundation.

It was only a few months after the fire that we first visited. I wanted, as we were passing, to have a look at the farm on the site of the abbey's former cooperage, Abbey Cooper Farm (or Abbey

Cowper Farm) as I have a niece called Abbey Cooper, and we were shocked to see the state of the gutted church. It was a damp, grey day and the smell of wet burnt timber hung heavy everywhere you went.

West Cumbria Archaeological Society were doggedly engaged in carrying on some archaeological work trying to determine the layout of the former abbey buildings, and villagers kept coming up to us strangers utterly spontaneously to talk about the fire. They all seemed to be in a state of deep grief. All praised the Vicar, David Tembey, for his positive attitude in finding an alternative place of worship and then getting on with the job of finding money for the restoration, which at the time of going to press I believe to be complete. I can't wait to actually set foot inside.

Walney Island 2

As mentioned earlier I resolved, one cold, wet winter's late afternoon, during a short, brisk dusk walk up the beach from Earnse Bay after a Christmas shopping excursion, to make some proper time to do Walney Island justice the following spring or summer.

Then came the perfect opportunity – admittedly a little earlier in the year than I'd had in mind, 21 March, the first day of spring, though in reality it had been spring for a fortnight. It hadn't rained for three weeks, the snowdrops were well over and the daffodils out, birch sap had finished running, bluebells and ramsons were coming through, the weather forecast was still almost impossibly good for the time of year. Next day my wife was working a shift at Barrow hospital from 8 to 4pm, finishing just in time to give me a lift home. After a quick brunch at Hazelmere in Grange-over-Sands she dropped me off at Grange Station, and I got on the next train to Barrow and gazed out of the window at the bright haze still clinging tenaciously to the marshes stretching to Humphrey Head.

I found myself studying the map once again, and checking through the *Swallows and Amazons* style equipment list I'd written in my notebook, making sure I hadn't forgotten anything; and, before I knew it, we were passing Dalton, through brick-lined cuttings and past the backs of terraced houses. I had a three second glimpse of Furness Abbey, long enough to think of Wordsworth and his schoolfriends, who used to ride out here from Hawkshead. A passage in *The Prelude* makes reference to Shakespeare's "Bare ruin'd quires, where late the sweet birds sang":

> *With whip and spur we through the chauntry flew*
> *In uncouth race, and left the cross-legged knight,*
> *And the stone-abbot, and that single wren*
> *Which one day sang so sweetly in the nave*

> *Of the old church, that, though from recent showers*
> *The earth was comfortless, and, touched by faint*
> *Internal breezes – sobbings of the place*
> *And respirations – from the roofless walls*
> *The shuddering ivy dripped large drops, yet still*
> *So sweetly 'mid the gloom the invisible bird*
> *Sang to itself that there I could have made*
> *My dwelling-place, and lived for ever there*
> *To hear such music.*
>
> (Wordsworth, *Prelude* (1805), II: 116-28)

I was too far away to have been able to see a wren, but this didn't matter as it had been an "invisible bird" to Wordsworth in the 1790s: I did see a kestrel hovering above the south wall of the nave, which I took for a good omen. Furness Abbey is made of the same red sandstone underlying Walney Island, probably quarried at Ormsgill on the mainland north of the Walney bridge.

I've always liked Barrow, mostly I think because it reminds me of Liverpool, my favourite city and the only big city I've ever lived in. I think it's partly because they're both port towns, partly because they both share a sense of decayed Victorian grandeur and a tendency to perpetual wind, mist and drizzle, both borne aloft by the relentlessly sunny dispositions of their inhabitants: and partly that wherever you are there will be the sound of seagulls. From the station I made my way as directly as possible towards the huge BAE

Looking south down the channel, east coast of Walney, from North End Hawes.

Systems sheds which I knew were near the bridge, and was pleased to find myself walking down Collingwood Street, named presumably after W. G. Collingwood, man of letters, founding father of much of our knowledge of the history of the Lake District, secretary to Ruskin and father of Dora Altouynan, the mother of the children who inspired *Swallows and Amazons.*

Crossing the bridge, a cold wind was blowing up the channel from the north, and it had got mistier – foggy, even. I wondered if it was too early in the year, after all for a night on Walney but pressed on. Over the bridge, I followed the road north for about two thirds of a mile, looking at the boats dried out on the mud, and came to the place where the road turns inland towards Cow Tarn Lane and the west coast, and the footpath that leads between the high water mark and the houses of North Scale begins.

Although suburban garden fences are just a few yards through the queach to your left and boatsmans' and lug worm diggers' footprints and tyre tracks stud the sticky, dayglo orange mud, it only takes a few yards before you start to feel that familiar, longed-for thrill of being somewhere wild. Lapwings and oyster-catchers start to appear here and there along the shore, and before long you pass a sign telling you that you're entering the nature reserve. Then the foot-path, which has become a bridleway, strikes out across the channel to the mainland and you press on along the increasingly muddy shore, which is becoming more and more indented with tiny creeks, and more and more suggestive of the Essex marshes. The undergrowth to landward is thinner but deeper, and soon begins to look more inviting than the deepening mud.

At the point where, just south of the south end of Walney Island Airfield (which belongs to BAE and was a gunnery school in the Second World War), a footpath heads inland to meet the end of Red Ley lane, and I follow it inland for a few yards, guessing that there would be another path leading away towards the airfield fence before too long. I was right. Soon I was stooping through the undergrowth along the fence, the shore a stone's throw to my right, odd disused brick structures of uncertain design among the trees over the fence to my left. I was scouring the ground looking for signs of the rare nat-terjack toads which breed around here when a movement caught the corner of my eye and I looked up. A pair of barn owls soared silently away over the tree-tops. I followed them through the trees for a hundred yards or so, hoping for a photograph, catching momentary glimpses but nothing more, before decid-ing to give up and leave them in peace.

Suddenly the trees and scrub behind the airfield fence came to an end, and just as abruptly so did the path. Looking out over the apparently deserted tri-angular tarmac of the runway, I squeezed myself along between the high fence and stands of catching, whip-like miniature willows and then, more alarming-ly, between a lower fence of ordinary stockproof wire netting backed by a double row of rolls of razor wire on my left and a seamless barrier of hawthorn

Reeds, North End Marsh, Walney.

to my right. It was not terribly comfortable, but before long the bushes gave way to thick grass and gorse, patches of reeds swaying nearer the shore, and the going got a lot easier. I followed, alternately, an old, low, straight dike and the high water mark and – aside from a place where the path wound through reeds and suspiciously deep-looking mud, the dike disappeared and the high water mark was blocked by a complex set of switchbacking creeks and pools, through which I to'd and fro'd for a few minutes – I got along pretty fast through the reeds. The creeks of North End Marsh got wider, the reed beds continuous, the sun began to make an occasional fleeting appearance through

Drainage ditch, North End Marsh.

the haze. A drain from the runway led out into the biggest creek so far. I came to an odd area of overgrown tarmac right on the shore where, incongruously, I startled a pheasant, and spotted a barn owl nesting box, then a barn owl pellet, then another barn own.

As suddenly as the airfield ended, the dunes began. The grazing sheep were an unexpected sight, the dozens of kinds of seabird less so. Alternately following the shore then making my way up into the dunes, I got to the northern tip of the island when, with perfect timing, like Proserpine released from Hades, the equinoctial sun finally cleared the haze and bathed all of Scarth Hole, the Duddon sands and Black Combe beyond in warmth and light. Spring was here. I got out my stove and made an instant soup (why do you only ever want these outdoors?), ate some biltong and biscuits, and generally soaked in the views.

The sunlight was slanting towards late afternoon as I made my way along the firm sands of the north west shore, admiring the plume of cloud blowing off Black Combe and, from the tops of the dunes, the handsome skyline of

Barrow, its churches and town hall and shipyards. I scouted out a few likely-looking holes in the dunes in which to spend the night, then decided it was too early to stop moving for the day just yet, so headed down to

Footprints in sand, north west coast of Walney Island and dunes, north end of Walney with Black Combe in the distance.

Centre of Barrow from across the marshes on Walney Island.

Earnse Bay, the starting point of many a winter walk, through North Walney and across the waste land at Park Vale into Vickerstown.

There are a few towns in Britain that were built by companies – Lever Brother's Port Sunlight and Cadbury's Bournvillle spring to mind – but as far as I can think there's only one named after a company. Vickers, originally Sheffield steel founders, bought the Barrow Shipbuilding Company in 1897, and was later bought by current owners BAE Systems. The main roads through the middle are Central Drive and Ocean Road, but the other streets are named after ships built at the yard: *Euryalus, Natal, Strathnaver*. Everyone, from kids to old dears with poodles, seemed to want to stop to talk about something, from the warmth of the evening sun, to the glare of the evening sun in their eyes, to their little sister's lack of skill on a bicycle. No one seemed to

Sunset over the Irish Sea.

find it at all odd to find a 6' 4" skinny blond chap wandering around with a bulging rucksack on his back, not even the girl in the off licence on Amphitrite Street where I stopped to buy some beer to take the edge off the loneliness that always seems to accompany the first hour or so after sunset when I'm sleeping out alone.

I made my way down Ocean Road and back north on Biggar Bank Road then along the tarmac footpath that passes the golf club, stopping just short of Earnse Bay to watch the sun set. Then, feeling a bit like a penniless pirate who's spent all his doubloons on grog and has to sleep rough down under the docks, I made my way past the snug-looking dwellings on West Shore retirement park, past a few late dog walkers, past a couple of families with campervans, through the waste land between the airfield and the shore, and back to the freshwater pools at the south end of the nature reserve. Poking about in the dusk, I found one of the sites I'd spotted earlier, a kind of valley in the dunes

Campfire in the dunes.

that led up to a cleft beyond which was a pool studded with islands and Canada geese, and on whose left was a tributary valley just big enough for the camp of a solitary Robinson Crusoe. I pulled some stones together for a fireplace, went down to the tide mark and collected armfuls of driftwood, lit a fire, cracked open a beer, set my dinner of beef stew, in my titanium kettle suspended from a forked stick, to heat above the flames. I phoned my wife.

I spent the evening reading a novel about Fletcher Christian, feeding the fire, creeping over to the pool to watch the dim shapes of birds and the lights of Barrow, wandering down to the beach to feel the freshening wind. About nine I dimly heard voices on the breeze, and scouted down to the pool to see the lights of head torches away at the far end: people from one of the campervans collecting water, to wash up after their barbeque, I guessed. About ten I wandered down to the beach one last time. The tide was in, the breakers roaring on the shore. There were a couple of lights on ships and rigs on the Millom gas fields. To the south were the warning lights on Walney Wind Farm, which I'd be passing the next morning.

I sat down and looked at the stars and thought of the mesolithic hunters, the early frontier-pushers who came here for flint and shellfish and who will have looked north at the hills, as I had done earlier, and wondered what was among them. Back then, of course, a lot of trees and swamp, and bears and wolves. But also a landscape of mythic importance, one to be filled with stone circles, standing stones, thunder stones and rock art, one that would yield the precious green tuff for stone axes. Perhaps the group who found the tuff at Langdale came here on their way to stock up with flint. Then I went back, pulled the fire apart and got into my bivi bag. Five minutes later, I heard voices and saw lights flashing over the dunes just across my little valley. A procession of half a dozen people, kids from Vickerstown I guessed, came blundering by, sticking to the maram-topped ridges, passing within ten feet of me, but I'm pretty certain they had no idea I was there. Ten minutes later they came back past the other side of my little camp, and I heard the leader say "careful, it gets steep here." Clearly they'd done this plenty of times before. A few minutes later, when my heart had stopped pounding, I was asleep.

I woke a few times in the night, often feeling a little chilly, then, after five minutes of tossing and turning, was quite warm enough to go back to sleep. Once I woke with a start, convinced I'd heard somebody, but it was only a puff of wind which had got in somehow and set the carrier bag with the empty beer cans in it rustling. I spent a glorious hour from about five, dozing, listening to the lapwings, snipe and geese calling to each other, watching it get lighter, and once or twice fancied I could hear natterjack toads calling, though it was really too early in the year. By six I'd been down to the pool, said "good morning" to the geese and had made a cup of tea, and by quarter to seven had shaken sand out of everything, packed (it's so much quicker not having a tent to take down), scattered the ashes of the fire, dumped the unburnt log ends on the shingle under the high tide mark, and covered where it had been with sand. After a last look at the birds on the pool I was off.

It was a glorious, breezy morning. I pushed a bag of rubbish into the bin at

Goldeneye, Walney Island marshes.

Earnse Bay and headed south, passing World War II concrete lookout emplacements and Sunday paper-carrying dog walkers. One Dalmatian seemed particularly interested in me, and his owner explained "he's wondering where your dog is." He seemed impressed that I'd spent the night out on the dunes, and pleased that I was enjoying his island so much.

Soon, just as when heading north on Walney, I was alone again. Past Bent Haw the road, Thorny Nook Lane, heads off inland to Biggar, and much of the time you've the choice of walking along the beach or along the top of a low, unstable-looking dirt cliff, intermittently anchored with concrete defences. I mostly chose the latter, enjoying the gulls and skylarks and the cormorants apparently trying to dry their wings while standing in the spray from the surf on the beach. Great circle planes from North America overtook me overhead, heading for London and Europe. At Hillock Whins, a dizzying thirty foot or so above sea level (and about as high as Walney gets) I found a sheltered cleft in the hillside, made more tea and heated strips of smoked sausage and halves of pitta bread on my stove. I'd hoped to find water in the pool shown on the map just behind the little postage stamp of access land here, but it was choked up with reeds.

Walney Lighthouse.

Down at South End, you feel like you're on a different island. The topography is similar to North End, albeit with more field and less dune, but there are buildings – a ruined farm, the lighthouse, the Nature Reserve HQ buildings, more World War II concrete structures, including what look to be gun emplacements, and the birds are different. North End is all geese and oyster-catchers and eider ducks, down here it's skylarks and gulls. Lots of gulls: herring gulls and greater and lesser black backed gulls, Walney having a third of the UK population of the latter at nesting time. It's still the biggest gull nesting site in Britain, although, as signs in the various bird hides scattered around tell you, it's declined somewhat in recent years, due to predation from foxes, which were first seen on the island in the 1980s. The problem has been compounded by a drop in the rabbit population, thanks to myxamatosis in the 1990s – from which, oddly, the rabbit population has failed to recover – and a reduction in the number of eider ducks nesting nearby, all of which make potential prey for foxes scarcer (this is the UK's most southerly eider duck nesting site, incidentally). Then there have been changes in the density of the grass on the nest site, probably also linked to the decline in the rabbit population, which apparently the gulls have not found to their liking. Then there's the closure of the old landfill site at Low Bank, which was a favourite scavenging ground for gulls.

Starlings, Walney Island.

That the delicate interplay of such seemingly trivial environmental changes can have such a dramatic effect on a natural system such as the gull colony here makes you realise how enormous and irrevocable are the thousands of changes mankind has wrought throughout the Lake District and the areas surrounding it; indeed, throughout the world.

There are still an awful lot of gulls here, enough to make wandering around here alone a slightly intimidating experience. Gulls aren't exactly shy and will think nothing of dive-bombing you if you get too near a nesting site – even, as it would be at this time of year, a prospective nesting site. It's generally a lot quieter if you go around on the beach.

Further differentiating South End from North End are the views. The backdrop is not Lakeland fells but Lancashire hills, Morecambe Bay, Blackpool

Tower, and the foreground is dominated by two things, one ancient, one modern. Inland is Piel Castle, the ruined point of departure for boats to Furness Abbey's lands in Ireland and the Isle of Man, a wonderfully Gothic structure like a better-preserved Kendal Castle, now in the care of English Heritage. Then, out to sea, is the massive wind farm. Built by Denmark's Dong Energy, the 130-odd turbines are capable of producing 370 megawatts – enough, as far as I can tell, to power most of the county when it's windy, which it usually is. Walney is said to be the breeziest coastal site in Britain. I did say it was always windy in Barrow.

Once I'd reached the south point – which, like the tip of North End Hawes, is curled a little behind the rest of the island, making Walney from the air look a bit like a giant seahorse – I passed a ruined pier which once belonged to Walney's salt works. Salt was discovered here by accident in the 1880s during excavations looking for coal deposits, and mined until 1909. Right next to the pier is Seasalter trout farm, built on the remains of another extraction site, this time gravel beds.

Shortly beyond this you reach South End Nature Reserve's car park and visitor centre, where the round-Walney walker, confronted with a sign saying "All visitors to obtain a permit and a trail leaflet from the car park," will hurry his or her tired legs along until certain not to have been spotted leaving the area leafletless.

The old salt works pier with Piel Castle beyond.

From here on I saw more people every hour than on the rest of the walk combined, if you make an exception of my detour into Vickerstown the evening before. There's a steady stream of cars making for the gull colony, and once you pass the huge caravan park a mile or so further on the traffic only increases. It's satisfying to the searcher after sequestered spots that the rest of the walk back to the bridge, the pretty village of Biggar excepted, is the dullest part of the walk, and the miles begin to drag fractionally as the BAE sheds draw slowly nearer. Before long I was walking back through Vickerstown, and as I approached the bridge passed a bus stop at precisely the same moment as a bus with 'Hospital' displayed on its front. By the time I'd jumped on and extracted my wallet from the depths of my rucksack I was halfway across the bridge; by the time I'd sat down I was back on the mainland, feeling strangely deflated that my journey had come so abruptly to an end.

It wasn't quite the end, though. From South End car park onwards the road I'd followed had been part of the Cistercian Way, the long(ish) distance footpath that also features in the Cartmel Peninsula chapter of this book, and as the adventure had really begun with a glimpse of Furness Abbey, one of the greatest abbeys of medieval England, it was the obvious place to kill the couple of hours before my lift home was ready. It was a peaceful and reflective way to end the weekend, following English Heritage's little guidebook, feeling the remaining warmth in the lowering afternoon sun and the creeping chill in stony shadows, listening to rooks clammering in treetops and imagining a way of life long gone. There was even a grotesque head which could almost have been mistaken for a green man. Then a painful stroll up the short hill to Abbey House Hotel, designed by Edwin Lutyens and originally the home of Commander Craven, Chairman of Vickers, where I enjoyed a pint before my wife arrived to drive me home. I slept all the way back.

Afterword

SUDDENLY – buying and selling houses is like that – we left Cumbria on 30 July 2010 bound for my beloved Wiltshire. I'm delighted to be here: I miss the north far more, and far more vividly, than I thought I would, especially sitting here in my garden office writing about it. And there are places I still haven't been. But I've got to stop somewhere.

I may have followed Wordsworth all my life (dee-dum dee-dum dee-dum dee-dum) but in my wanderings around his landscape I often saw myself as more of a Coleridge: a southern boy here in the wake of another man's love of a landscape, exploring and seeking inspiration in the things that inspired someone whose writings I feel an empathy with, visiting the places which meant something to him to see what they might do to me.

Mountain Thirza.

The 'I' that is the focus of so many of Wordsworth's poems was, in reality, often a 'we', the most famous example of this being his most famous poem, *Daffodils*: "I wandered lonely as a cloud" was originally 'we', based as the poem is on an entry in his sister Dorothy's journal, while his wife Mary is supposed to have contributed the lines "they flash upon that inward eye/which is the bliss of solitude" (if you're interested, this is from the Fenwick Notes).

And so it is in this book, the 'I' often in reality having been myself and my wife Thirza; to whom, by way of apology for many of the things I dragged her across, through, around, over and, most usually, up, in our four years in Cumbria (and with apologies too to the ghost of Samuel Taylor Coleridge) I offer the following poem.

> The Rime of the Mountain Thirza
> *It is a mountain Thirza*
> *And she stoppeth at a cairn.*
> *"O tell me, husband, why can't I*
> *Keep up with yon wee bairn?*
>
> *"She barely looks six years of age*
> *And yet her climbing rate*
> *I'm finding difficult to gauge*
> *And hard to emulate."*
>
> *My Thirza, she did pant and moan,*
> *I led her up a cliff;*
> *"Tomorrow," she said, "I will be dead,*
> *"Or at least very stiff."*
>
> *At length the cliff top we did reach;*
> *A bog I did espy.*
> *My Thirza, then, she did beseech:*
> *"To cross that let's not try."*
>
> *"You wander on from peak to peak,*
> *It is a strange obsession;*
> *Some help for you I need to seek;*
> *It drives me to depression."*
>
> *I led my Thirza through the mire,*
> *Up to her waist she sank.*
> *Great gulps of air she did respire,*
> *Despite the mud, which stank.*

Amid the bog a barbed wire fence
Our pathless way did cross;
she sighed, and said to me, "from hence
You are my ALBATROSS."

My Thirza, bleeding, muddied, tired,
Through sundry streams I drag.
One had a ford: she did applaud;
I made her scale a crag.

It is a mountain Thirza
and she reacheth the summit cairn;
She looketh down with jealous frown
On a now-descending bairn.

Descending next a precipice
She got the collywobbles.
She turns, and asks "Must I do this?"
I nod, and on she hobbles.

"My husband thinks that this is bliss;
I'd rather in bed;
The nightmare DEATH-IN-LIFE is this;
It fills my soul with dread."

Shortly before the car we reach
Descend the fog and mist.
I say, "A lesson I must you teach,
Of navigation, I wist."

So, with no compass and no map,
I leave her far behind;
She wanders, fearing grave mishap;
Her teeth chatter and grind.

The rain did start, the wind picked up
And it grew wondrous cold;
"I fear," she said, "that before I sup
I shall grow grey and old."

I reach the car, remove my boots
And turn the heater on;

Souls of Lonely Places

> *Darkness gathers, an owl hoots;*
> *Still Thirza struggles on.*
>
> *She wandered here, she wandered there,*
> *She wandered round and round;*
> *She dreamed of hot chocolate,*
> *She pulled out her hair,*
> *She fell as if in a swound.*
>
> *The rain has stopped; the sky has cleared;*
> *The stars come rushing out.*
> *The voice, trembling, as if afear'd*
> *Of Thirza I hear shout.*
>
> *I find her cowering in a dell:*
> *The back wall she'd climbed down;*
> *She damnéd me and all to hell*
> *And used some other words as well*
> *swearing never again to leave town.*
>
> *Tired she was as ever in life*
> *since day that she was born:*
> *A battered, bruised and stiffer wife*
> *she rose the following morn.*

Thirza on Seat Sandal.

Bibliography

Adams, John, *Mines of the Lake District Fells* (Dalesman Books, 1988)

Bownass, Pam; Mutch, Penny; Trotter, Hartley and Wilson, John, *Cameos of Crosthwaite and Lyth: The Damson Valley* (Titus Wilson, 2002)

Charles Cox, *County Churches: Cumberland and Westmorland* (Unwin, 1913)

Clare, Tom, *Prehistoric Monuments of the Lake District* (Tempus, 2007)

Collingwood, W. G., and Rogers, J., 'Lost Churches in the Carlisle Diocese', Article XXVIII, Transactions of the Westmorland and Cumberland Antiquarian and Archaeological Society Old Series XV (1899), p. 294

Curwen, John F., *Kirkbie-Kendall: fragments collected relating to its ancient streets and yards, church and castle, houses and inns* (Titus Wilson, 1900)

Farrer, William, ed., Curwen, J. F., *Records relating to the barony of Kendale*, 3 vols (Cumberland and Westmorland Antiquarian and Archaeological Society Record or Chartulary Series, 4-6, 1923-6)

Forestry Commission, *Valuing Informal Recreation on the Forestry Commission Estate* (HMSO, 1992)

Hayes, Gareth, *Odd Corners around the Howgills* (Hayloft, 2004)

Jones, G. P., *A Short History of the Manor and Parish of Witherslack* (1850, Cumberland andWestmorland Antiquarian and Archaeological Society Tract Series, 18, 1971)

Lindop, Grevel, *A Literary Guide to the Lake District* (Sigma, 2005)

MacFarlane, Robert, *The Wild Places* (Granta, 2007)

Nicholls, Revd. William, *History and Traditions of Mallerstang Forest and Pendragon Castle* (1883)

Nicolson and Burn, *The history and antiquities of the counties of Westmorland and Cumberland* (1777)

O'Connor, Jack, *Memories of Old Kendal* (Westmorland Gazette, 1961)

Parrish, Constance (ed), *Isabella Lickbarrow: Collected Poems*, (Wordsworth Trust, 2004)

Parson, William, and White, William, *History, Directory, and Gazetteer, of the Counties of Cumberland and Westmorland with that part of the Lake District in Lancashire, forming the Lordships of Furness and Cartmel* (Edward Baines, 1829)

Pasqualetti, Martin; Gipe, Paul and Righter, Robert, *Wind power in view: energy landscapes in a crowded world* (Academic Press, 2002)

Richards, Mark, *Great Mountain Days in the Lake District* (Cicerone, 2009)

Robertson, Dawn and Koronka, Peter, *Secrets and Legends of Old Westmorland* (Hayloft/Cumbria County Council Library Service, 1992)

Rogan, Adrian, *1314* (Hayloft, 2007)

Symonds, H. H., *Afforestation in the Lake District* (Dent, 1936)

Thompson, B. L., *The Lake District and the National Trust* (Titus Wilson, 1946)

Thompson, Mary M., *Mallerstang: a Westmorland Dale* (J Whitehead, 1965)

Thompson, T. W., ed. Woof, Robert, *Wordsworth's Hawkshead* (OUP, 1970)

Tyler, Ian, *Lakes and Cumbria Mines Guide* (Blue Rock Publications, 2006)

Wainwright, Alfred, *A Pictorial Guide to the Lakeland Fells* (Westmorland Gazette): *Book 1: The Eastern Fells* (1955); *Book 2: The Far Eastern Fells* (1957); *Book 3: The Central Fells* (1958); *Book 4: The Southern Fells* (1960); *Book 5: The Northern Fells* (1962); *Book 6: The North Western Fells* (1964); Book 7: *The Western Fells* (1966)

Wainwright, Alfred, *The Outlying Fells of Lakeland* (Westmorland Gazette, 1974)

Wainwright, Alfred, *Walks in Limestone Country* (Westmorland Gazette, 1970)

Wainwright, Alfred, *Walks on the Howgill Fells* (Westmorland Gazette, 1972)

Wainwright, Alfred, *Westmorland Heritage* (Westmorland Gazette, 1975)

Wainwright's Coast to Coast Walk, Striding Edge Presentations DVD 2003, © BBC Worldwide 2007

Walker, Stephen, *Nine Standards: Ancient Cairns or Modern Folly?* (Hayloft, 2008)

Whellan, William, *The history and Topography of the Counties of Cumberland and Westmorland* (Whittaker, 1860)

Whitaker, Thomas Dunham, *The history and antiquities of the Deanery of Craven, in the county of York* (London, 1805)

William Farrer and John F. Curwen (eds), *Records Relating to the Barony of Kendale*, Cumberland and Westmorland Antiquarian and Archaeological Society Records series vol IV (1923)

Wordsworth, William, *The Prelude: 1799, 1805, 1850*, ed. Wordsworth, Abrams, M. H. and Gill, Stephen (Norton, 1979)

Wordsworth, William, *The Illustrated Wordsworth's Guide to the Lakes*, ed. Bicknell, Peter (New York, 1984)

About the Author

BROUGHT up in Wiltshire, James Deboo discovered Wordsworth's poetry at school. Following a degree in English and then a PhD on Wordsworth at Lancaster University, he moved to the Lake District, set up a business as a proofreader, editor and indexer, and at the same time set about exploring and writing about Cumbria. He and his family later moved back to Wiltshire: at the time of going to press, however, a return to the Fells, and to writing about Cumbria, looked imminent. This is his first book.

Souls of Lonely Places